CONSTRAINTS ON CONCEPTUAL DEVELOPMENT: A CASE STUDY OF THE ACQUISITION OF FOLKBIOLOGICAL AND FOLKSOCIOLOGICAL KNOWLEDGE IN MADAGASCAR

Rita Astuti
Gregg E. A. Solomon
Susan Carey

WITH COMMENTARY BY
Tim Ingold
Patricia H. Miller

Willis F. Overton
Series Editor

MONOGRAPHS OF THE SOCIETY FOR RESEARCH IN CHILD DEVELOPMENT

Serial No. 277, Vol. 69, No. 3, 2004

Boston, Massachusetts   Oxford, United Kingdom

CONSTRAINTS ON CONCEPTUAL DEVELOPMENT: A CASE STUDY OF THE ACQUISITION OF FOLKBIOLOGICAL AND FOLKSOCIOLOGICAL KNOWLEDGE IN MADAGASCAR

CONTENTS

ABSTRACT   vii

I. INTRODUCTION   1

II. STUDY 1. ADULTS: FAMILY RESEMBLANCE AND GROUP IDENTITY   25

III. STUDY 2. CHILDREN: FAMILY RESEMBLANCE AND GROUP IDENTITY   54

IV. STUDY 3. ADOLESCENTS: FAMILY RESEMBLANCE AND GROUP IDENTITY   75

V. STUDY 4. REASONING ABOUT ANIMALS AND SPECIES KIND   90

VI. GENERAL DISCUSSION   103

APPENDIX   119

REFERENCES   125

ACKNOWLEDGMENTS   134

COMMENTARIES

CONCEPTUAL DEVELOPMENT IN MADAGASCAR: A CRITICAL COMMENT
Tim Ingold   136

COGNITIVE DEVELOPMENT: HERE, THERE, AND EVERYWHERE
Patricia H. Miller   145

REPLY   153

CONTRIBUTORS   162

STATEMENT OF EDITORIAL POLICY   164

ABSTRACT

How different are the concepts held by children who grow up in a North American middle class neighborhood and by children who grow up in a rural Malagasy fishing village? By probing Malagasy children's and adults' conceptual representations of human and animal kind, biological inheritance, innate potential and family relations, the studies presented in this *Monograph* address current debates about the acquisition and the nature of concepts in the domains of folkbiology and folksociology. Cross-cultural and developmental studies of this kind bear on the hypothesis that conceptual development in these domains is supported and constrained by innate conceptual content. If so, one would expect cross-cultural universality in the relevant adult concepts and their early emergence in childhood regardless of widely different input conditions. We chose to conduct these studies among the Vezo of Madagascar because the ethnographic literature has attributed to them folkbiological and folksociological theories that are radically different, even incommensurable, with those of North American adults. Vezo therefore provide a challenging test for the innate conceptual constraints hypothesis.

Four studies probed aspects of biological and sociological reasoning of Vezo children, adolescents and adults through a number of adoption scenarios. Despite ethnographic reports to the contrary, we found cross-cultural convergence in adult concepts of *biological inheritance*, but the pattern of development of this concept differed greatly from that seen in North America. Moreover, in agreement with the ethnographic literature, we found that Vezo adults have constructed a distinctive theory of *social group identity*. However, we found that children's reasoning in this domain is under the influence of endogenous constraints that are overturned in the course of development. Finally, we found cross-cultural convergence in adults' concept of *species kind*, as well as evidence for the early emergence of this concept.

In light of these findings, we discuss the nature of the constraints on children's conceptual representations, the developmental process through which the adults' concepts are constructed, and relations between Vezo theories of folkbiology and folksociology.

I. INTRODUCTION

This *Monograph* reports the results of a collaboration between an anthropologist, who has conducted ethnographic research in a fishing village in Madagascar (R.A.), and two cognitive psychologists, who have studied conceptual development of urban North American children (G.S. and S.C.). Bringing together our unique expertise and distinctive methodologies, we have taken on the task of analyzing and comparing Malagasy adults' and Malagasy children's conceptual representations in the domains of folkbiology and folksociology. This *Monograph*, therefore, is a study of how conceptual development unfolds in a cultural, social, and educational environment radically different from the one that nurtures the North American and Western European children who are usually studied by developmental psychologists.

The value of studies of this kind has been underscored by developmental psychologists of different theoretical inclinations. For example, Diesendruck (2001) has recently advocated cross-cultural research, arguing that if psychologists wish to claim that a certain way of knowing the world (e.g., the essentialist construal of natural kinds) is a universal "habit of the mind", they must be able to show that the emergence of this habit does not depend on the specific cultural input received by middle-class North American children (see also Coley, 2000, and Walker, 1999, for a similar point). Conversely, the fact that biological knowledge emerges late in urban middle-class children in the U.S. (as argued by Carey, 1985) should not be taken as evidence of a universal pattern of cognitive development, because the delay may be caused by the peculiarly deprived exposure to the natural world experienced by this population (Medin & Atran, in press).

From the perspective of Vygotsky-inspired cultural psychology, every study of development must be culturally situated. This is because human development *is* a cultural process that can only be understood in light of the different cultural practices and circumstances of specific communities (Rogoff, 2003, pp. 3–4). Given the culturally specific goals of development and the varied ways in which children's apprenticeship (Rogoff, 1990) is

1

scaffolded by institutional contexts, technologies, and artifacts, different paths of development are to be expected. From this standpoint, documenting such diversity through cross-cultural research is the necessary first step, prior to theoretical interpretation of both variations and regularities in patterns of human development (Rogoff, 2003, p. 7).

The need for cross-cultural research is of course no news to anthropologists. However, they rarely pay close attention to the process of conceptual development. As often noted, mainstream anthropologists have tended to ignore children (e.g., Hirschfeld, 2002; La Fontaine; 1986; Toren, 1999; Montgomery, 2001). Arguably, this general lack of interest in children is rooted in what Boyer (1994, p. 22) calls the anthropological theory of "exhaustive cultural transmission," which assumes that the conceptual understanding of competent adults is entirely determined by the cultural representations on offer in the particular environment in which they grow up. According to this view, children are passive, and thus insignificant, receptors of ready-made culture, which they imbibe like sponges (see Strauss & Quinn's critique of the "fax model of internalization," 1997, p. 23).

On their part, those psychologists who have turned away from the Piagetian assumption that infants are endowed only with sensori-motor representations and who, instead, attribute to them rich innate conceptual representations (e.g., of number, Dehaene, 1997; Feigenson, Carey, & Hauser, 2002; Wynn, 1992; Xu & Spelke, 2000; of intentional agent, Csibra, Gergely, Biro, Koos, & Brookbank, 1999; Gergely, Nadasady, Gergely, & Biro, 1995; Gopnik & Meltzoff, 1997; Johnson, Slaughter, & Carey, 1998; Johnson, 2000; Woodward, 1998; of object, Carey & Xu, 1999; Leslie, 1994; Spelke, Phillips, & Woodward, 1995; Spelke, Breilinger, Macomber, & Jacobson, 1992) credit children with the creative capacity of producing—rather than just re-producing—adult culture. Because children bring their own knowledge and intuitions to the task of making sense of the world, they are capable of producing understandings that are independent, even at odds, with those of their parents, elders, and teachers. For example, Vosniadou (1994) has demonstrated how children's naïve theory of physics mediates their interpretation of the adult testimony regarding the shape of the earth. What children have known since they were at least 9 months old (Baillargeon, Kotovsky, & Needham, 1995; Spelke et al., 1995) about gravity (i.e., that unsupported objects fall downward) and about the properties of supporting surfaces (i.e., that the ground is flat) makes it hard for them to conceive of the earth as a spherical astronomical object. The mental models of the earth that they construct along the way—a flat disc, a dual earth, a hollow sphere—are far more than incorrect reproductions of adult culture. Rather, they are children's own culture (for another example, see the discussion of North American children's "cootie culture" in Hirschfeld, 2002).

2

Of course, whether rich innate knowledge potentiates and constrains children's conceptual representations in different domains of knowledge is a question that needs to be asked on a case-by-case basis. We are aware that the proposition that human infants come into their culturally and socially con- stituted world endowed with innately specified systems of knowledge and/or with highly constrained learning mechanisms is considered by most anthro- pologists as an obvious non-starter. The very concept of innate (pre-social) knowledge is deemed to be flawed because "[human] capacities are neither innately prespecified nor externally imposed, but arise within processes of development, as properties of dynamic self-organization of the total field of relationships in which a person's life unfolds" (Ingold, 2001, p. 131; see also Toren, 2001; for earlier formulations see Geertz, 1973). Cultural psycholo- gists, on their part, while not denying the existence of innate knowledge (see Shweder et al., 1998, pp. 919–922), submit that it is rarely a strong constraint. Their wager is that "relatively few components of the human mental equip- ment are so inherent, so hard wired, or fundamental that their developmental pathway is fixed in advance and cannot be transformed or altered through cultural participation" (Shweder et al., 1998, p. 867; see Cole, 1996, on how to relate phylogenetic and cultural constraints). Of course, this is recognized to be an empirical question, with profound theoretical implications.

We do not believe that there are a priori considerations against the hypothesis that innate constraints guide conceptual development. But granted this, the question still arises as to which domains of knowledge are so constrained. In this *Monograph*, we shall address this question through a cross-cultural examination of conceptual development in two related do- mains of knowledge: folkbiology and folksociology. Specifically, we will en- gage with Medin and Atran's (in press) proposal regarding the existence of a folkbiological module dedicated to acquiring and organizing knowledge of the organic world, and with a number of converging hypotheses regarding innate constraints on the representation of human kinds (Gil-White, 2001; Hirschfeld, 1996). Central to all these proposals is the same nexus of putative innate concepts, which include *biological inheritance*, *birth parentage*, *innate potential*, *animal species*, and *human kind*. As we shall see, from its earliest days anthropologists interested in the study of kinship have been concerned with this nexus of concepts. For this reason, the studies presented in this *Mon- ograph* meet one desideratum for successful inter-disciplinary collaboration: to seek data that have theoretical import for all disciplines involved.

INNATE CONSTRAINTS IN FOLKBIOLOGY AND FOLKSOCIOLOGY

In a series of papers, Atran, Medin, and their colleagues (Atran, 1998; Atran, Estin, Coley, & Medin, 1997; Lopez, Atran, Coley, Medin, & Smith,

1997; Medin & Atran, in press) have suggested that innate conceptual representations guide the construction of intuitive biological concepts. They have proposed the existence of a folkbiological module of the human mind, which "discriminates and categorizes parts of the flux of human experience as 'biological,' and develops complex abilities to infer and interpret this highly structured domain" (Medin & Atran, in press). While they themselves document the existence of significant cultural variations between different folkbiologies (e.g., Itza' Maya, Native American Menominee, urban Chicago, rural Michigan) caused by different histories and sets of available stimuli, they also contend that "these contingent factors of time and place interact with panhuman folkbiology module in every generation." This interaction between local peculiarities and universal mental endowment produces relative cultural stability and slow historical changes of folkbiologies, in addition to constraining their cross-cultural variability (Medin & Atran, in press).

The two hypothesized structural principles of folkbiology are *ranked taxonomy* and *teleological essentialism*. First, people in all cultures appear to organize living things into non-overlapping taxonomic structures, which vary little across cultures and that support systematic and graded inferences about the distribution of properties among species. Second, people across many different cultural contexts have been found to subscribe to the commonsense assumption that each species has an underlying internal essence, which is inherited from biological progenitors and that determines an individual's innate potential. In Medin and Atran's proposal, therefore, the folkbiology module has rich biological content, because the naturalization of species kind is said to implicate concepts of birth parentage, biological inheritance, and innate potential (Atran, 1998; Medin & Atran, in press).

Two types of data are offered to support the claim that this way of construing animals and plants is acquired under innate constraints. In addition to evidence of cross-cultural universality in adult conceptual representations (reviewed in Atran, 1990; see also Atran, 1998; Atran et al., 1997; Lopez et al., 1997), Medin and Atran (in press) review evidence that an essentialized and naturalized construal of species emerges early in development, under widely different conditions of cultural input. Developmental evidence shows that at least by age 4 or 5, most North American middle class children (Gelman & Wellman, 1991; Horobin, 1997; Johnson & Solomon, 1997), Menominee Indian (Medin & Atran, in press), Yukatek Maya (Atran et al., 2001), and Brazilian children (Sousa, Atran, & Medin 2002) understand that species kind is fixed at birth, even if an animal grows up with, is cared for, fed by, and is otherwise part of a "family" of animals of a different species (see also Gelman & Wellman, 1991, for a parallel finding regarding seeds). In these animal "adoption" studies, children predict that the adopted animal will have the same familiar kind of typical properties (e.g., will oink or will moo; will have a curly tail or a straight tail) as well as unfamiliar somatic properties (e.g., has a pink heart or a red heart) of its birth parents.

These developmental findings, together with those that suggest cross-cultural universality in the adult taxonomic system, have been taken to support the hypothesis that there are strong constraints—indeed, Medin and Atran argue for innate conceptual content in this domain—on how people organize their knowledge of biological kinds. Because these constraints are determined by pan-human mental capacities, it is predicted that they will produce convergent conceptual content even in the face of widely different inputs.

A similar hypothesis has been advanced by Hirschfeld regarding a different, but conceptually related, domain of knowledge. Hirschfeld argues for the existence of what he dubs the Human Kind Competence (Hirschfeld, 1996): a universal predisposition to reason about the social world in terms of distinct types or kinds of people. That is, Hirschfeld hypothesizes a universal ontological commitment to the existence of different kinds of people that is part of human nature. Further, he claims that humans are predisposed to reason about social kind identity with the implicit assumption that category members, despite superficial differences, share a fundamental and enduring essence, which causes them to develop and to retain the features that are characteristic of their kind. Consequently, despite accidental changes due to the process of maturation, aging, or death, the essential kind identity remains constant throughout one's life-span and beyond.

Hirschfeld (e.g., 1996, 1997, 1998) has been keen to emphasize that, although the Human Kind Competence (HKC) is a property of the mind that guides and constrains one's interpretation of the world, the specific ways in which the HKC gets deployed in different historical and cultural contexts are determined by the structure of that world (i.e., its socio-political organization and its system of inequalities and discriminations). Thus, "children spontaneously explore the social world around them in search of intrinsic human kinds or groups of individuals that are thought to bear some deep and enduring commonality. Different cultures inscribe the social environment with different human kinds" (Hirschfeld, 1997, p. 86). In one context, children will find racial kinds (human kinds predicated on common somatic features); in another they will find castes (human kinds predicated on common occupational destinies), and in yet another they will find genders (human kinds predicated on sexual differences). Critically, in *all* cases the HKC will ensure that somatic, occupational, sexual features, or whatever, are deployed so as to carve the social world into kinds that are *intrinsic* (such that what makes people of a kind is lodged deep inside them), *essentialized* (such that such kinds have a rich inductive potential), and *naturalized* (such that kind membership is biologically determined by inheritance from birth parents).

5

Gil-White (2001) has advanced a different, but related proposal. He argues that, because of the costs involved in interacting and marrying with people whose norms and behaviors were different from their own (see Rothbart & Taylor, 2001 for a criticism of this crucial assumption), our ancestors would have developed and enforced a system of normative endogamy (i.e., parents would have prevented their children from marrying outside their norm group). Endogamy is the key to Gil-White's argument: the fact that people married within the group meant that the properties acquired as a result of being *reared* in the midst of that group could be construed as if they were the result of having been *born* to parents of that group. When these groups, in addition, began "labelling and conspicuously marking themselves with cultural "phenotypes" to improve the accuracy of the interactional discriminations" (Gil-White, 2001, p. 532), the illusion that the difference between them was rooted in their different birth origins was complete. Thus, endogamous groups of people came to have all the diagnostic features of biological species and therefore came to prime the same module used to organize knowledge and make inferences about all other living kinds. As a result of this evolutionary history, ethnic groups are still represented by the human mind as animal species: as natural groups, whose members are what they are because of their innate potential.

This evolutionary story of how ethnic groups came to look like species motivates Gil-White's prediction: that the human brain will treat endogamous human groups (and those alone) in the same way in which it treats animal species. In this, Gil-White's proposal differs from the suggestion made by Atran (1990, 2001) that human kinds are naturalized by analogy to animal species. According to Atran's view, human groups come to be apprehended like animal species because of stable somatic differences associated with them, not because of stable clusters of norms.

Gil-White's proposal is far more specific than Hirschfeld's. Whereas Hirschfeld's HKC hypothesis does not specify *which* human kinds the human mind will apprehend in any one historical context, Gil-White's claim is that the human mind will naturalize and essentialize only those human groups that exhibit the strongly diagnostic features of biological species (i.e., endogamy and descent-based membership). There is another significant difference between these two positions: Gil-White argues that ethnic groups are naturalized and essentialized because the mind mistakes them for biological species, whereas Hirschfeld argues for the domain-specificity of the HKC and for the autonomy of folksociology from folkbiology (Hirschfeld, 1996; see also Gelman, 2003; Gelman & Hirschfeld, 1999).

Gil-White and Hirschfeld converge in claiming that the human mind is so designed as to exhibit a universal tendency to naturalize and essentialize some human kinds: to assume that "people-like-us" and "people-like-them" are different because each group shares a distinctive essence, which was inherited at birth, remains impervious to environmental influences, guides the unfolding of kind-typical properties, and realizes the innate potential of each group. Thus, the same nexus of concepts—*biological inheritance, innate potential, birth parentage*—that are claimed to be part of the folkbiology module is also crucially implicated in this other system of knowledge. This convergence is best demonstrated by the fact that Hirschfeld and Gil-White, just like Medin, Atran, and colleagues, have used the same adoption paradigm to test their hypotheses: all of them have asked participants to judge the properties and kind identity of people or animals born to one kind of parents and raised by another. It is because the very same concepts are at the core of each of these hypothesized systems of innately constrained knowledge that we address them together in a single *Monograph*.

The claims for innately constrained knowledge in the domains of folkbiology and folksociology have not gone unchallenged. In their own distinctive ways, both psychologists and anthropologists have raised (or could raise) objections to the proposals we have just reviewed. Psychologists' objections have focused on the critical issue of whether the concepts that are claimed to have innate content emerge early in development—evidence that they are indeed underdetermined by experience—or whether they are a later acquisition, the result of a protracted constructive process—evidence that they go beyond innately specified content. The objections that could be raised by anthropologists are instead grounded in their ethnographic experience, which directly challenges the claim that people universally construe certain phenomena as "biological," or that they universally construe human kinds as natural kinds. In the two sections that follow, we report these dissenting voices.

THE CHALLENGE FROM PSYCHOLOGY

In a series of writings going back to the 1980's, Carey has argued that there is no evidence for innate representations with biological content (Carey, 1985, 1995, 1999), for although infants clearly have a concept *animal* (Mandler, 2000; Waxman, 1999), they conceptualize animals as kinds of intentional agents rather than as kinds of living beings. Carey has thus proposed that North American children construct the biological concept *living thing* only at the end of the preschool years, and that this construction requires conceptual change (see also Inagaki & Hatano, 2002, for evidence that a vitalist biology is constructed only at the end of the preschool years). Data in support of this position derive from Piagetian clinical interviews concerning children's understanding of death, life, human bodily function, reproduction, and illness (Bernstein & Cowan, 1975; Bibace & Walsh, 1980; Crider, 1981; Koocher, 1973; Laurendeau & Pinard, 1962; Nagy, 1953; Perrin, Sayer, & Willett, 1991; Safier, 1964; Speece & Brent, 1985), from more focused and child-friendly studies designed to tap concepts in these domains (e.g., Au & Romo, 1996; Hergenrather & Rabinowitz, 1991; Inagaki & Hatano, 1993; Keil, 1989, 1992; Solomon & Cassimitis, 1999; Springer, 1996; Springer & Ruckel, 1992), from patterns of within-child consistency across different measures of relevant conceptual content (e.g., Jaakkola, 1997; Johnson & Carey, 1998; Slaughter, Jaakkola, & Carey, 1999; Solomon & Johnson, 2000), and from teaching studies (Au, Romo, & DeWitt, 1999; Slaughter and Lyons, 2003; Solomon & Johnson, 2000).

Most pertinent to the discussion at hand are a series of studies that suggest that the case that very young North American and European children have a biological understanding of family resemblance, and that they represent concepts such as biological inheritance, innate potential, or birth parentage, has been greatly overstated. Piagetian clinical interviews have shown that North American children do not come to understand human reproduction until late in the elementary school years (e.g., Bernstein & Cowan, 1975). Although it has been argued that these interviews underestimate preschool children's understanding (Atran, 1998; Hirschfeld, 1996; Solomon, Johnson, Zaitchik, & Carey, 1996; Springer & Keil, 1989; Wellman & Gelman, 1998), it is not clear that young children perform any better in switched-at-birth and adoption studies, which ask children to reason about the resemblance between offspring and their birth or adoptive parents and that do not require them to explicitly articulate their understanding of innate potential and of the role of birth parentage in the inheritance of properties (e.g., Arterberry, Barrett, & Hudspeth, 1999; Carey, 1995; Gimenez & Harris, 2002; Solomon, 2002; Solomon et al., 1996; Weissman & Kalish, 1999; Williams & Affleck, 1999). Indeed, the interpretation of these studies is under active debate.

On the one hand, as reviewed above, species adoption studies, in which a baby is born to one animal and raised by another of a different kind, reveal that in a wide variety of cultural contexts even preschool children expect that the baby will grow up to be the same species as its birth parent (Atran et al., 2001; Gelman & Wellman, 1991; Horobin, 1997; Johnson & Solomon, 1997; Sousa et al., 2002). This expectation appears to be universal and provides evidence for constrained conceptual development. On the other hand, there is evidence that young children do not yet construe the cause of the family resemblance in terms of biological inheritance. For example, Keil's (1989) transformation and discovery studies found that, even in the case of species fixation, middle-class North American children did not possess a robust understanding of the causal role of birth parentage until age 7–9: told that a raccoon gave birth to a certain animal and that this animal subsequently gave birth to more raccoons did not lead children to judge that the animal was a raccoon if it looked and acted like a skunk. This finding was replicated among rural and urban Yoruba children by Jeyifous (1992).

The possibility that children who know that like begets like may not understand why this must be so, raises the crucial issue of what kind of evidence can justify attributing to them an understanding of biological inheritance, a concept of innate potential and of birth parentage (see Sousa et al., 2002, for a detailed discussion of this point). We submit that it is possible for a child to predict reliably that babies are of the same species as their birth parents and that they have the properties characteristic of their species, without having an understanding of biological inheritance and innate potential. If a child essentializes species kind, s/he will assume that a tiger is a tiger during its whole existence, irrespective of outward transformations (e.g., shedding all its fur) or changed circumstances (e.g., growing up on a space station). It follows that all that is needed to judge that a baby born of a mother tiger is a tiger, even if it is raised by lions, is to realize that the baby already existed—and that therefore was already a tiger—before emerging from inside its first mother. Having established its kind, the child can derive all of the baby-tiger's properties: that it will have stripes and that it will be fierce because it is a tiger. By contrast, an understanding of biological inheritance requires an appreciation of the much deeper relation that exists between birth parents and their offspring—that birth parents pass on to their offspring a kind of "blueprint" that determines in the offspring the emergence of the same properties that are evident in the parents, causing them to be of the same species. From this vantage point, the reason why a baby tiger has stripes and will be fierce is that its mother has stripes and is fierce. In other words, the baby inherits from its mother the potential of *becoming* a tiger.

Which measure could establish whether children have this deeper understanding of biological inheritance? Consider that not all the properties of an individual are readily construed as kind-dependent: for example, the five fingers of the human hand are, but blond or dark hair is not. Moreover, many kinds of properties that are shared between parents and their offspring are not inherited: shared likes and dislikes for items of food, poetry, and leisure activities are not the result of an inherited blueprint, but are the result of eating, reading, and living together. Therefore, an adopted child will have blond hair like her birth parents, but she will resemble her adoptive parents in their likes and dislikes. Being able to differentiate between these two outcomes does seem to require a firm understanding of biological inheritance.

Many studies have demonstrated that this differentiation is not robust until age 6 or 7 in North American and European children. For example, in

Solomon et al.'s (1996) adoption study, children were told about a child born to one parent and raised by another, and were then asked which of the two parents the grown-up child would resemble on traits such as having curly hair or believing that skunks can see in the dark. It was only at age 7 that children reliably predicted similarity of bodily traits on the basis of biological inheritance, and similarity of beliefs on the basis of the child's learning environment (see Springer, 1996; Weissman & Kalish, 1999 for replications). Using a slightly different procedure, Springer and Keil (1989) also provided evidence that preschool children do not understand the role of biological inheritance in trait acquisition. They told children about a baby whose parents had an unusual trait (e.g., a pink rather than a red heart), and they asked whether the baby would also have this unusual trait. In one of the test items, the parents were said to have been born with the unusual trait, whereas in another they were said to have acquired the trait by accident. It was not until age 7 that children were swayed by whether the parents were born with the trait or not. Furthermore, Solomon and Johnson (2000) found within-child consistency in a sample of 6- and 7-year-olds on Springer and Keil's measure and on Solomon et al.'s (1996) measure of the understanding of biological inheritance, providing evidence that both tapped the same understanding. It is very likely that this is also what supports 7-year-olds' first success on Keil's discovery and transformation studies mentioned above.

These developmental findings indicate that, at least in North America and Europe, the nexus of biological concepts of *biological inheritance*, *birth parentage*, and *innate potential* emerges relatively late in the course of childhood. This suggests that rather than the output of a module of the human mind, these concepts are the result of a protracted process of cultural construction. Notwithstanding the significance of the developmental evidence reviewed so far, the claim that the acquisition of these concepts is innately constrained is undercut even more forcefully by developmental data from two cross-cultural studies. Using a version of Solomon et al.'s (1996) adoption task in a village in the interior of Madagascar, Bloch, Solomon, and Carey (2001) found that it was not until *adulthood* that a sample of Zafimaniry participants differentiated biological inheritance from learning mechanisms. And Mahalingham (1998), studying middle class Tamil children in India, found that it was not until *age 12* that they had made this differentiation.

In sum, the current state of the evidence for a cross-culturally universal early emergence of an understanding of biological inheritance is decidedly mixed. On the one hand, there is evidence that in a variety of cultural contexts very young children understand that babies are of the same species as their birth mother, and this leaves open the possibility that they also assume that human babies are of the same human kind as their birth parents. On the other hand, very young children's understanding of the fixation of species kind may not depend on biological concepts of inheritance and innate potential as claimed. When such concepts have been probed more stringently, as in Solomon et al.'s (1996) adoption study, North American and European children have failed to demonstrate a biological understanding of family resemblance until the age of 6 or 7, with the age increasing well into adulthood in a small sample of Zafimaniry participants.

The studies presented in this *Monograph* will add to these debates, by probing the understanding of the mechanisms through which an individual's properties are acquired (biological inheritance vs. learning/nurture) and the relations between this understanding and the participants' construal of human and animal kinds. The participants in question are children who live in a coastal village of Madagascar. They are virtually unschooled (see below), and they grow up in the kind of cultural environment that has led anthropologists to argue that many, if not all, non-western peoples do not "discriminate and categorize parts of the flux of human experience as 'biological'," as stipulated by Medin and Atran (in press), and that there are people who do not naturalize human kinds, as stipulated by Hirschfeld and Gil-White. It is to these arguments that we now turn.

THE CHALLENGE FROM ANTHROPOLOGY

Most anthropologists are likely to dismiss as nonsensical the claim that the acquisition and construction of concepts such as *biological inheritance*, *innate potential*, and *birth parentage* are innately constrained. This is because the theoretical advances made in the field of kinship studies in the past 30 years—most notably the realization that the representations of phenomena such as birth, filiation, and descent vary cross-culturally—appear to wholly contradict the claim that the construction of such representations is subject to *any* constraint. To appreciate the force of this argument, we need to briefly sketch the radical theoretical shifts that have characterized the anthropological study of kinship (see Bloch & Sperber, 2002; Sousa, 2003 for reviews).

The study of kinship organization has been central to anthropology from its earliest days. Starting with L. H. Morgan, who is credited with the discovery that human kinship is not natural but is pre-eminently cultural (Good, 1994; Trautmann, 1987), anthropologists realized that kinship relations were of crucial importance in organizing so-called primitive societies. This is what made the comparative study of kinship systems a worthwhile enterprise.

But comparison requires commensurability. The common denominator, which guaranteed the comparison across different kinship systems, was provided by what came to be known as "The Doctrine of the Genealogical Unity of Mankind": the confident assumption "that genealogical relations are the same in every culture" (Schneider, 1984, p. 174). Armed with the most powerful methodological tool devised for the study of kinship—W. H. R. Rivers's "genealogical method of anthropological enquiry" (Rivers, 1968)—anthropologists went around the world collecting their informants' pedigrees. This was followed by the comparative study of how natural pedigrees were culturally interpreted and manipulated to produce different terminological systems, different marriage patterns, different inheritance systems, and so on. Crucially, this method, and the "doctrine" built upon it, were predicated on the assumption that it was possible to identify the same basic genealogical units of father, mother, husband, wife, son, and daughter in every culture.

It was this assumption that was questioned in the 1950s and 1960s. Leach (1961) and Needham (1971b) echoed each other in arguing that anthropologists should abandon the futile attempt to find universal definitions for social phenomena such as marriage, filiation, incest, and, more generally, kinship itself. Thus, while Leach (1961, p. 27) proposed that if one approaches the ethnographic record without "prior assumptions," one is forced to realize that "English language patterns of thought [e.g., the categorical distinction between consanguinity and affinity] are not a necessary model for the whole of human society." Needham (1971b, p. 5) concluded that "there is no such thing as kinship, and [therefore] there can be no such thing as kinship theory." This debate was consciously framed in philosophical terms—kinship has no external reality; "kinship" is no more than a useful "odd-job word"—and anthropologists were asked to "school [themselves], by reflection and introspection, to a stance of systematic self-doubt", such that it could sustain "the quiet and patient undermining of categories over the whole field of anthropological thought" (Needham, 1971a, p. xviii).

But those who battled over the future of kinship theory also questioned the more specific and central claim made by its practitioners. Most notably, the critique of the study of kinship advanced by Schneider (1984) challenged the assumption that the reported diversity in kinship systems was due to *cultural variations* in the interpretation of *the same natural facts*—or, to use a metaphor that Schneider extensively criticized, the assumption that the anthropological study of kinship consisted in recording and comparing "the different ways of cutting the pie of experience" (Schneider 1965, p. 93). Noting that reality (the pie) cannot exist except by being invested with meaning, Schneider concluded that "the notion of a pure, pristine state of biological relationships 'out there in reality' which is the same for all

12

mankind is sheer nonsense" (1965, p. 97). He illustrated this point ethno-graphically, by arguing that for the Yap people of Micronesia, the relation between fathers and sons is not a biological relation invested with social meaning. Rather, the referent for this relation, as construed by the Yapese, is a link of dependence established through one's association with the land and through work, irrespective of filiation. The same applies to the relation between mothers and offspring, as demonstrated by the fact that this re-lation is not deemed permanent, as it would be if its referent were the relationship engendered by biological reproduction (i.e., if the mother di-vorces her husband, she ceases to be mother to her children).

Many details of Schneider's Yapese ethnographic material and inter-pretation have been questioned and criticized (e.g., Lingenfelter, 1985; Kuper, 1999; Scheffler, 1991). Schneider's theoretical influence on the an-thropological study of kinship, however, has been enormous. Following in Schneider's footsteps, many anthropologists have argued that the people they study do not define human relatedness by reference to birth and fil-iation (e.g., Nuttall, 2000; Marshall, 1977; Witherspoon, 1975) and that, crucially, they do not recognize the ontological distinction between rela-tionships engendered by biological reproduction and relationships engen-dered by social interactions such as sharing food and locality (e.g., see Carsten, 2000, pp. 25–27; Ingold, 1991, p. 362 for a particularly clear for-mulation of this point). For example, Carsten (1995, 1997) has argued that the distinction between "facts of biology" and "facts of sociality" is mean-ingless for the Malay people she studied on the island of Langkawi. In her detailed ethnographic analysis, she argues that Malay people attribute greater significance to post-natal influences than to procreative ones. While they recognize the role of semen and blood in the making of children, they emphasize that food also makes a person's blood. This means that sharing food is, just like sharing blood, a vehicle for the creation of relatedness—to the extent that fostered children who eat the food cooked on their adoptive parents' hearth are said to take on character traits and physical attributes of those who raise them (Carsten, 1991, p. 431; 1995, p. 229). Carsten thus concludes:

> Ideas about relatedness in Langkawi show how culturally specific is the separation of the "social" from the "biological" and the reduction of the latter to sexual reproduction. In Langkawi relatedness is derived both from acts of procreation and from living and eating together. It makes little sense in indigenous terms to label some of these activities as social and others as biological. I certainly never heard Langkawi people do so. It is clear that the important relationships of kinship involve what we would regard as both. If blood, which is the stuff of kinship and to some extent of personhood, is acquired during gestation in the uterus and, after birth, in the house

through feeding with others as people in Langkawi assert, is it, then, biological or social? The impossibility of answering this question merely underlines the unsatisfactory nature of this distinction (1995, pp. 236–237; 1997, pp. 291).

Carsten's conclusion is a particularly fine example of a well-established constructivist position in anthropology, which cuts across the studies of kinship, gender (e.g., Yanagisako & Collier, 1987), personhood (e.g., Marriot, 1976; Strathern, 1988), emotion (e.g., Lutz, 1988), self (e.g., Scheper-Hughes & Lock, 1987), and much more (but see e.g., Astuti, 1998; Bloch, 1977; Bloch & Sperber, 2002; Lambek, 1998; Middleton, 2000; Ortner, 1996; Spiro, 1993, for dissenting positions). Its implications for the proposal that the representation of biological processes is innately constrained are clear: *if* populations outside the western world do not distinguish between biological and social processes, the claim that the human mind is designed to discriminate and categorize parts of the flux of human experience as "biological" (Medin & Atran, in press) becomes untenable. It follows that concepts such as *biological inheritance*, *birth parentage*, and *innate potential* are not innately constrained. Rather, conceptual content is culturally constructed, and is thus likely to exhibit cross-cultural variability and incommensurability as amply demonstrated by ethnographic reports.

The anthropological challenge extends to the hypothesized universal propensity to naturalize human kinds. In the same way in which human relatedness need not be rooted in the biological relations engendered by sexual reproduction, human group identities need not be ascribed and fixed at birth. Rather, group identities can be molded and can be gradually acquired by inhabiting a particular environment, by practicing certain activities, or by adopting distinctive ways of doing and being (e.g., Linnekin & Poyer, 1990 for a review of this performative view of social identities). As we shall see, this is precisely how Astuti (1995a, 1995b) has described the way in which the people studied in this *Monograph* define and experience their group identity.

COMPETING HYPOTHESES AND THEIR PREDICTIONS

Our study of conceptual development in Madagascar will engage with the diverging and apparently irreconcilable positions we have just reviewed. For the sake of clarity, we shall now name the different hypotheses we will be testing.

We shall use the label "Unconstrained Learning" hypothesis to refer to the position adhered to by most mainstream anthropologists that concepts can vary widely across different cultural environments, because their construction and acquisition are in no way constrained by the phylogenetic properties of the human mind (see Sperber & Hirschfeld, 1999 for a review). According to this view, the outcome of conceptual development is open-ended. Because language, artifacts, and sociocultural practices are the input into the process of knowledge acquisition in childhood, different courses of conceptual development are predicted, leading to radical incommensurability in the adult end-states across cultures.

We will contrast this position with the "Innate Conceptual Content" hypothesis, which posits instead that rich conceptual knowledge potentiates and constrains conceptual development. According to this view, innate constraints on conceptual development are expected to lead to cross-cultural universality in adult conceptual representations.

The case study we present in this *Monograph* will give support to the Innate Conceptual Content hypothesis if, as posited by Medin and Atran, Hirschfeld and Gil-White, we find that concepts of *biological inheritance, innate potential, birth parentage*, and *natural human kinds* are in evidence among rural Malagasy adults as they are among their urban North American counterparts. The Unconstrained Learning hypothesis will instead receive support if we find that Malagasy adults have constructed radically different concepts, as suggested by the ethnographic reports reviewed below. Note, however, that neither outcome by itself is enough to validate one or the other hypothesis. In the case of the Innate Conceptual Content hypothesis, cross-cultural universality in the adult end-state could also result from unconstrained learning, if the outside world provides massive data in favor of certain conceptual representations. What is needed therefore, in addition to cross-cultural convergence in the adult conceptual repertoire, is evidence that the relevant concepts emerge early in development irrespective of widely different input conditions. In the case of the Unconstrained Learning hypothesis, cross-cultural divergence in the adult end-state could result from the culturally orchestrated overturn of innately supported conceptual representations that emerged spontaneously early in development despite contradictory input from the adult world. What is needed therefore, in addition to cross-cultural divergence in the adult conceptual repertoire, is evidence that the relevant concepts have been constructed steadily and incrementally as the unmediated result of the input that children derive from adult culture. In short, both hypotheses need the validation of supporting developmental evidence.

Finally, we shall consider a third hypothesis, which we label the "Constrained Conceptual Construction" hypothesis. This is a weaker version of the Innate Conceptual Content hypothesis in that it proposes that each child must construct anew the concepts in question (hence "constructivist"). Nonetheless, this construction is not open-ended as claimed by the Unconstrained Learning hypothesis, but is enabled and constrained by powerful innate domain-general learning mechanisms, such as causal analysis (Gopnik et al., 2004) or teleological (Keleman, 1999) and essentialist modes of construal (Gelman, 2003). The Constrained Conceptual Construction hypothesis does not make strong predictions regarding cross-cultural universality, because the outcome of development depends on the interaction between the input the child receives from the cultural environment and the hypothesized learning mechanisms that the child brings to the task of interpreting that input. Whenever cross-cultural universality is observed, however, the Constrained Conceptual Construction hypothesis makes different predictions from the Innate Conceptual Content hypothesis. Whereas the latter predicts the spontaneous emergence of innately supported concepts, the former expects to find traces of the constructive process, for example some evidence of within child consistency in the understanding of theoretically related concepts.

CONCEPT DIAGNOSIS: THE FUNDAMENTAL PROBLEM

The empirical questions we shall be pursuing in this *Monograph*—do Malagasy adults have concepts that are commensurable with those of North Americans, and do Malagasy children have the same concepts as their parents—raise a serious analytical challenge: How do we know whether two individuals have the same concepts of x or y? This is a challenge faced by all scholars—anthropologists, developmental psychologists, and historians of science alike—engaged in theoretical debates about incommensurable conceptual systems, for they cannot begin to address the question of whether Malagasy adults have a concept of biological inheritance that is the same as that of American college students, whether the child's concept of living thing is the same as the adult's, or whether Priestley's concept of element is the same as Lavoisier's without specifying what these questions mean and what is to count as evidence that bears on answering them (see Carey, 1988; Kitcher, 1988; Kuhn, 1983; Nersessian, 1992; Thagard, 1992 for extended discussions of this issue).

We take concepts to be structured mental representations. The content of a concept is determined by its extension (the entities, properties, processes it refers to) and by its inferential role. To ask, then, whether a concept is shared across social groups, or across historical or developmental time, is to ask whether there is sufficient overlap of content determining inferential role and reference fixation. To address this question in the present context, we need to probe Malagasy concepts of biological inheritance, of learning and practice, of birth and reproduction, of adoptive and biological parentage, of bodily and mental traits, of species, and of human kinds. To do so, we asked our informants to reason about an adoption scenario similar to that used by Solomon et al. (1996) in North America, by Bloch et al. (2001) in Madagascar, and by Mahalingham (1998) in Tamil Nadu. Participants were told about a baby born to one set of parents, who subsequently died. The baby was safely discovered and raised by another set of parents. Birth and adoptive parents were then attributed contrastive individual properties, and participants were asked to predict which parent the child would resemble with respect to these. Crucially, the properties were of different kinds: bodily traits, such as shape of the nose or ears; beliefs about the world, such as how many teeth a chameleon has; and skills such as carpentry or making ropes. The adoption task was designed to probe whether participants hold conceptual representations of two different mechanisms for the transmission of properties: one mediated by biological inheritance from birth parents and one mediated by socially mediated learning. That a given participant represented these two different mechanisms could be revealed both in the pattern of judgments and in the explicit justifications given for these judgments. These data—judgment patterns and justifications—provide evidence of the underlying representations and their conceptual role.

It is important to interpret these data correctly and avoid the trap of over-interpreting them. If Malagasy and North American participants systematically judge that the adopted child will have the bodily properties of the birth parent, but the beliefs and skills of the adoptive parent, then surely both of these participants have differentiated between two causal mechanisms (one having to do with generating children, the other one having to do with nurturing them) for the transmission of two distinct kinds of properties (bodily and mental/experiential traits). One can thus infer that both Malagasy and North American participants make the same ontological cut. However, one must then ask whether the concepts of biological inheritance and socially mediated learning of a Malagasy adult are identical to those of a North American adult, in the same way in which one must ask whether the concept of biological inheritance of an embryologist or geneticist is identical to that of an North American undergraduate or of a Tamil adolescent. Most likely, the answer to these questions will be negative. Nonetheless, the content of the concepts that underlie the ontological distinctions made by our Malagasy and North American participants is the same in that it picks out the same processes and kinds in the world and shares a relevant content determining inferential role. As we shall see, the comments provided by participants to justify their resemblance judgments in the adoption task can throw some light on both differences and overlap in content (see Study 1).

But the anthropological literature reviewed above claims that in at least some cultural contexts there will be no cut at all: that people will draw no principled distinction between biological and adoptive family, between biological inheritance and socially mediated learning. As we shall see shortly, the group of Malagasy people we are investigating in this *Monograph*—the Vezo of western Madagascar—could be construed as one such case. However, if we were to show that Vezo participants predict that adopted children resemble birth parents in their bodily properties and adoptive parents in their beliefs and skills, we will be able to claim that their conceptual representations, like those of North American undergraduates, of embryologists, of geneticists, of Tamil adolescents, play the same inferential role of distinguishing between a biological and a social mechanism for the transmission and acquisition of an individual's properties. And this would be a significant finding.

It could of course be argued that the adoption task imposes on the participants the ontological categories of the researcher—the dualism of sociality and biology, of organism and person, of mental and bodily properties of the person. But although the task is undoubtedly *constructed* around these distinctions, it does *not* force them on the participants. The task is a diagnostic task: if participants do not distinguish between social and biological parenthood, between birth and nurture, between bodily and mental traits, they will sail through the task blissfully unaware of the distinctions being probed.

THE CASE STUDY: THE VEZO OF MADAGASCAR

The studies presented in this *Monograph* have been conducted in a fishing village on the western coast of Madagascar, where Astuti has conducted extensive periods of anthropological fieldwork (1987–1989, 1994, 1998). The village of Betania has a population of about 800 adults. It lies a few miles south of Morondava, the main town in the area, which hosts governmental offices, a market, a hospital, a post office, and an airport. The livelihood of the village depends on a variety of fishing activities, and on the trading of fish at the Morondava market. Typically, men go out fishing daily with their dugout outrigger canoes and, daily, women sell the catch. With what they earn, women buy rice, the staple food, and other essential foodstuff (as well as luxury items such as foam mattresses and shiny synthetic dresses). The development of tourism in recent years has made Morondava a much busier place than it was in the 1980s. This has created a new outlet for the fish caught by Betania fishermen, in addition to generating employment opportunities for some of the villagers. Nonetheless, most villagers still regard fishing as their most profitable, if erratic, source of livelihood (see Astuti, 1995a, for further details). From an early age, children contribute to fishing, trading, child rearing, and to a variety of domestic chores (e.g., fetching water, collecting firewood), although the extent of the contribution they are asked to make varies greatly depending on the structure of their domestic unit. To an outsider, the most remarkable aspect of Vezo children's lives is the virtual absence of schooling. The village has a school building and two designated teachers. However, due to the deterioration of public administration in Madagascar, the building and the teachers are hardly ever occupied. Whenever children are in the building, and if the teacher has not run out of chalk, the teaching largely consists in copying letters, numbers, and short sentences from the blackboard onto the child's own A5 size blackboard. Understandably, the many children who do not own a blackboard are allowed to play in the burning heat outside (see Bloch, 1998, and Freeman, 2001, for more detailed analyses of similar pedagogical practices in other areas of Madagascar).

Like other people who live on the coast and who "struggle with the sea," the inhabitants of Betania call themselves Vezo. We have chosen them as the focus of our enquiry because they provide an ideal context for testing the proposals (and counter-proposals) we have reviewed so far. This is so for two reasons. First, ethnographic descriptions of how Vezo adults describe the process through which an individual's traits are acquired appear to contradict flatly the claim that the understanding of biological inheritance is innately constrained. Second, Vezo adults hold an elaborate and explicit theory about group identity, which is at odds with the claim that the human mind is predisposed to naturalize human kinds. We shall briefly review the ethnographic data on Vezo adults' conceptualization of trait and group identity acquisition, thereby introducing the reader to the ethnographic backdrop of our studies.

Babies' Looks and Biological Inheritance

Madagascar has been recognized by anthropologists as one of those places where traditional procreational models of kinship do not work because people emphasize the importance of post-natal processes in determining kinship and personhood over the facts of procreation. Southall (1986, p. 417) identifies the root of the problem in the fact that "what seems to be distinctive about all Malagasy kinship systems is [. . .] their emphasis on kinship and descent status as something achieved gradually and progressively throughout life, and even after death, rather than ascribed and fixed definitely at birth." Bloch (1993) has similarly contrasted birth-based kinship systems such as those typically found on the African continent, to those found in Madagascar, in which birth is not the mechanism that determines who people are and the extent of their kinship relations. Vezo views of relatedness fit nicely in this pan-Malagasy pattern (but see Middleton, 1999, for qualifications), in so far as affiliation to the kind of unilineal descent groups described for sub-Saharan Africa is not fixed at birth but is realized only at the moment of burial (Astuti, 1995a, 2000a).

Consistent with the cultural emphasis on the processes through which human relatedness evolves during a person's lifetime rather than on its instantaneous fixation at birth, we find across Madagascar a series of beliefs about the transmission of properties from parents to children, which systematically downplay the role of birth and procreation. In the case of the Vezo, when adults explain how babies turn out to look the way they do (e.g., big eyes, light skin color, bent nose, etc.), they invoke mechanisms other than procreation, and the contribution of people other than the baby's birth parents.

For example, Vezo assert that if a pregnant woman takes a strong dislike to someone, whether related to her or not, the baby will come to resemble the disliked person. By contrast, spending considerable time with, or even just thinking a lot about someone during pregnancy, will cause the child to look like the frequented person. More seriously: why was that baby born with a club-foot? Because when his mother was a child she used to tease one of her friends who had a club-foot, the result of a badly administered quinine injection. When she gave birth, she was shocked to see that her baby had a defect identical to the one she used to make fun of. While still in the uterus, if not before, the baby's appearances are thus shaped by the social relations in which it is already fully—if only vicariously—immersed. Such immersion will intensify after birth, resulting in the further molding of the baby's physiognomy. During the first few weeks after birth, mother and baby are literally fused into one another as they lie together wrapped up in layers and layers of blankets; at this time, it is the mother's responsibility to protect and guard the baby from the many wandering spirits that, if they find the baby alone, will take hold of it and change its physiognomy—erasing, in so doing, the traces left by previous human relationships. Such spirits have an easy job because of babies' purported phenomenal plasticity—they are wobbly, bendable, boneless.

Taken together, this evidence suggests that the Vezo, just like the Malays studied by Carsten, blur a number of distinctions, including that between the baby as a biological organism and the baby as a social person. It is indeed difficult to see where one begins and the other one ends, given that social causes—such as teasing or spending time together—are said to shape its organic makeup. By implication, the distinction between birth (as a biological process) and nurture (as a social process) is also blurred, insofar as biological parenthood is socialized (as evidenced by the many people the baby will resemble) and nurturing relations are somatized (because of the effect that nurture has on the baby's bodily makeup).

20

This ethnographic context provides us with an ideal setting for pitting the Innate Conceptual Content hypothesis and its claim that the conceptual representations of *biological inheritance*, *birth parentage*, and *innate potential* are innately constrained against the Unconstrained Learning hypothesis and its claim that the Malays, the Yap, the Vezo, and, some anthropologists would argue, most non-western peoples hold radically different representations of these phenomena, elaborated over an incommensurable, non-dualistic ontology. It is likely that most anthropologists will not see the point for this empirical exercise, for they *know* that the people they study do not share the conceptual representations that are allegedly innately constrained. We do not doubt the accuracy of the ethnographic descriptions produced by anthropologists (one of whom is an author of this *Monograph*). That is, we believe that informants do state that food makes blood or that babies do not resemble their birth parents. However, our investigation will explore whether the kind of evidence traditionally used by anthropologists—reflective statements, codified beliefs, narratives that expound conventional wisdom, etc.—is adequate for revealing the conceptual knowledge and the ontological commitments of the people they study.

The investigation conducted by Bloch in a Zafimaniry village in Madagascar suggests that it is not. Zafimaniry adults, like their Vezo counterparts, routinely explain the bodily properties of their children by reference to social processes of companionship, friendship, spiritual intervention, and so on. Yet, as reported in Bloch et al. (2001), half of the seven adults who participated in a version of Solomon et al.'s (1996) adoption task provided patterns of judgments and justifications indistinguishable from those given by North American adults on the same task. That is, they judged that the child would resemble the adoptive parents in their beliefs, preferences, and skills, and the birth parents in bodily traits. Although these are preliminary results, given the small size of the sample and the fact that almost half of the participants did not provide a differentiated pattern of responses, they point to a striking discrepancy between the biological knowledge people use in their inferential reasoning and the culturally endorsed statements they produce about their babies' physiognomy.

If we were to discover that, despite what they say, Vezo adults have embedded their understanding of the acquisition of an individual's properties within a biological framework, which specifies the causal role of procreation, differentiated from the causal role of other mechanisms of social transmission such as learning and imitation, this discovery would give support to the contention that such an understanding is cross-culturally universal. Would this outcome decide in favor of the Innate Conceptual Content hypothesis? As mentioned above, cross-cultural universality per se is not sufficient evidence that a conceptual representation is innately constrained. For the Innate Conceptual Content hypothesis to be supported, evidence of the early emergence of the understanding of the mechanism of biological inheritance is also needed. And this is why, apart from delineating Vezo adults folkbiological knowledge, we also seek developmental evidence from Vezo children and adolescents.

Group Identity: A State of Being or a Way of Doing?

Astuti (1995a, 1995b) reports that her Vezo informants claim that "the Vezo are not a kind of people". The term translated as kind can be applied to any entity: for example, sandals are a kind of shoes, mackerel are a kind of fish, rice is a kind of food, and so on. When used to refer to kinds of people, the term becomes indistinguishable from the term that refers to the ancestors, the dead people one was generated from. Therefore, the statement that the Vezo are not a kind of people means that, unlike mackerels, Vezo are not what they are because of their birth and ancestral origins. But if it is not ancestry, what is it? The answer that Vezo adults give to this question is that what makes people Vezo is living on the coast and "struggling with the sea" (i.e., fishing, sailing, paddling, swimming, etc.). This captures how Vezo adults classify themselves and other people into different groups: by where they live and what they do.

This way of categorizing the social world, which we will refer to as the Vezo performative theory of group identity, is typically articulated by Vezo adults in a variety of informal contexts that portray the contrast between themselves and their immediate neighbors, the Masikoro. Adults constantly and consistently invoke the principle that being Vezo is to live on the coast and do Vezo things such as fishing, sailing, and eating fish, whereas being Masikoro is to live inland, and do Masikoro things, such as cultivating, raising cattle, and—so Vezo say—eating grass. Of course, this definition of what it means to be Vezo or Masikoro not only implies that one does not need to be born Vezo or Masikoro to be one but also that people who are Vezo can become Masikoro and vice versa (which they do) by way of learning and adopting Vezo or Masikoro ways of doing. Importantly, Vezo adults also say that being born of Vezo parents does not, by itself, make a person Vezo. Consequently, children are said not to be Vezo, as they are not yet competent at "struggling with the sea" (see Astuti, 1995a, p. 16).

Vezo and Masikoro group identities, then, do not appear to be construed around the essentialist presumption that to be of a kind is to share an essence, that ensures the maintenance of one's identity through time and space, and which engenders innate predispositions. In other words, Vezo and Masikoro are not *kinds* of people, at least not in the sense implied by Hirschfeld's HKC. It is important to point out, however, that Vezo and Masikoro are nonetheless extremely rich inferential categories. To know that someone is Vezo or Masikoro is to know an almost infinite number of his or her properties, ranging from the most obvious ones (e.g., occupation, preferred foodstuff) to others such as the way people wear their sarong, the way they speak (fast and loud or slow and softly), the way they scold their children, the way their children respond to the scolding, they way they walk, the way they save or squander money, the way they organize funerals and marriages, the way women braid their hair, etc. The fact that Vezo and Masikoro are such inferentially rich categories means that they pick out the kind of human groupings that could be targeted by the HKC, and it is therefore of some consequence that they do not seem to be.

Nonetheless, we accept that the discontinuity between Vezo and Masikoro may be a poor candidate for testing the alleged universality of the HKC. One might argue that the reason the difference between Vezo and Masikoro is construed performatively, in terms of their different ways of doing, is simply that both groups of people are assumed to be part of the same, essentialized, and ancestrally defined super-ordinate group (this was the prevalent interpretation in the ethnographic literature reviewed in Astuti, 1995a). Moreover, we recognize that the finding that Vezo and Masikoro group identities are not naturalized is tangential to Gil-White's claim that endogamous groups trigger the construal of ethnic groups as animal species, because Vezo and Masikoro intermarry.

What we need, then, is a stronger test for the ethnographically based claim that Vezo have a performative theory of group identity. Crucially, we need to establish whether Vezo informants would extend their way of reasoning about the Masikoro to a group of people of unquestionably separate ancestral origins, and with whom they do not intermarry. The group of people we have chosen to explore this question are the Karany. The Karany are the descendants of Indo-Pakistani immigrants. They are town-dwellers; they are wealthy and well educated; and they are shopkeepers and money lenders. They are predominantly Muslim and, although fluent in Malagasy, they speak their own language among themselves. Unlike the Masikoro who, at birth, are indistinguishable from the Vezo, the Karany are somatically different in that their skin is light and their hair straight. Vezo villagers have regular interactions with the Karany: they buy goods from their shops (e.g., fishing tools, clothes, soap), they sell fish to them, and occasionally they entertain large Karany families who take Sunday walks and have picnics on the village beach, by offering them fresh coconuts. However, Vezo and Karany do *not* intermarry.

On the face of it, the Karany appear to be a perfect candidate for the deployment of the HKC, and for triggering the analogy to animal species. Thus, if Vezo informants were to extend to the Karany their way of reasoning about the Masikoro—in other words, if they were shown to construe the Karany in terms of what they do rather than in terms of what they essentially are—this would pose a significant challenge to both Hirschfeld's

23

and Gil-White's claims and would thus question the validity of the Innate Conceptual Content hypothesis in this domain. If not, Astuti's claim about the Vezo performative theory of group identity would have to be modified.

Whatever the outcome of our investigation with Vezo adults, once again we shall also seek developmental data. Even if Vezo adults were to reason in a manner that supports Astuti's ethnographic analysis and not Hirschfeld's and Gil-White's predictions, it is possible that children have different intuitions. If children were to naturalize and essentialize group differences that adults construe in performative terms, thereby trumping the cultural input they receive, they would provide evidence that the conceptual development in this domain is under some kind of endogenous constraint—either of the kind posited by the Innate Conceptual Content hypothesis or by the Constrained Conceptual Construction hypothesis.

PLAN OF THE *MONOGRAPH*

We shall start our investigation (Chapter II) by exploring Vezo adults' understanding of the process of biological inheritance and their theory of group of identity, using the adoption scenario adapted from Solomon et al. (1996). Given that adult conceptual systems are the output of developmental processes, whether the adult end-state is cross-culturally universal or not directly bears on the question of how constrained the developmental process is. Our data on adult representations are thus essential to the task of evaluating competing developmental hypotheses.

We then turn to studies of children (ages 6–13; Chapter III) and adolescents (ages 14–20; Chapter IV). At issue is whether the findings of Mahalingham (1998) and Bloch et al. (2001) concerning the late emergence of the understanding of biological inheritance are replicated in this context. Also, these studies explore the development of children's reasoning about group identity, and their grasp of the adult's performative theory of group identity. Finally, in Chapter V, we probe children's and adult's understanding of the determination of animal kind. In order to engage with the hypothesis that human kinds are naturalized and essentialized by analogy to animal species, we need to establish what Vezo know about the process by which ducks have baby ducks and chickens have baby chickens.

The pattern of cross-cultural variation and similarity between North American and Vezo adults on these tasks, as well as the patterns of later and earlier emergence of the target concepts across the two cultures, will set the stage for a discussion of the existence and of the nature of constraints on knowledge acquisition in the domains of folkbiology and folksociology.

II. STUDY 1. ADULTS:
FAMILY RESEMBLANCE AND GROUP IDENTITY

Study 1 tests the competing predictions of the Innate Conceptual Content hypothesis and of the Unconstrained Learning hypothesis regarding the cross-cultural universality of adult representations in the domain of folkbiology and folksociology. At issue is whether Vezo and North American adults share commensurable concepts of biological inheritance and of human kinds, or whether, as suggested by ethnographic reports, Vezo adults have created culturally specific representations of the mechanisms that endow people with their properties, including their group identity.

To address these competing claims, we explore whether Vezo adults differentiate between the biological and social processes implicated in the transmission of an individual's properties by using three different adoption scenarios. The preliminary data from a similar study by Bloch et al. (2001) among the Zafimaniry suggest that, in spite of ethnographic reports to the contrary, Vezo adults' understanding of biological inheritance might be convergent, rather than incommensurable, with that found among North American adults. Such a result would be consistent with the Innate Conceptual Content hypothesis.

If Vezo adults were to differentiate biological inheritance from learning, practice and habituation, they could recruit their differentiated understanding to reason about the transmission of group identity in two contrasting ways. As predicted by Hirschfeld's and Gil-White's proposals, Vezo adults might naturalize group identity, construing it as a property of the person that is passed on through descent, and is thereby impervious to one's upbringing. By contrast, as predicted by Astuti's (1995a, 1995b) ethnographic analysis, Vezo adults might reason that ancestry is irrelevant to the determination of a person's identity, as this is acquired by way of learning and performing the practices typical of the group. Two of our adoption scenarios are designed to address these different predictions, and to explore the relation between participants' understanding of the transmission of an individual's properties and their construal of group identity.

25

METHOD

Overall Design

Each participant heard two adoption scenarios. In one, both sets of parents were Vezo (the Vezo–Vezo scenario) and in the other, one set was Vezo and the other Masikoro or Karany (the across-group scenario). For roughly half of the participants the contrast in the latter scenario was Vezo–Masikoro and for the other half it was Vezo–Karany. The order of presentation of the Vezo–Vezo scenario and the across-group scenario was counterbalanced across participants. Adult participants took part in both versions of the task during the same session, and for this reason only a summary of the second story was presented, with the salient new features highlighted (e.g., the fact that the group identity of the birth and adoptive parents was different).

Participants

Participants were 31 adults (mean age = 42 years, range 22–90-years). Of these, 8 men and 7 women took part in the Vezo–Masikoro version of the task and 9 men and 7 women took part in the Vezo–Karany version. Preliminary analyses showed no significant effect of sex in this or any of the other studies; therefore, we have collapsed across sex in all analyses reported in this *Monograph*.

All participants in this and subsequent studies were from the Vezo village of Betania on the western coast of Madagascar. The interviews were all conducted in Malagasy by one of the researchers (R.A.) who has been working in this village over the past 10 years and is well known to the villagers. In return for their work, participants were offered a small sum of money.

Vezo–Vezo Procedure

In the Vezo–Vezo variation on the Solomon et al. (1996) adoption task, participants were told a story of a baby who is born to one set of parents, but is raised by another (see Appendix A, Vezo–Vezo Adoption Scenario; all of the adoption scenarios, in English and in Malagasy, are available on-line at http://www.wjh.harvard.edu/~lds/pdfs/vezo.pdf, Astuti, Solomon, & Carey, 2003). One set was said to be from a village to the north and the other from a village to the south (no cultural significance is attached by Vezo to the north/south contrast). The birth parents (described in Malagasy as "the parents who generated the child") were said to have died at the hands of a group of bandits roaming in the forest, and the people who subsequently found the baby and adopted it (described as "the parents who raised the child") had no knowledge of what had happened to the birth parents. In view of the fact that Vezo adoption normally occurs among closely related people, so that the adopted child maintains close contacts with his/her birth parents if they are still alive, our stories introduced the death of the birth parents as a way of preventing the conflation of the birth/nurture contrast targeted by the task.

The death of the birth parent was also introduced to distinguish the story presented in the task from other culturally salient stories about babies abandoned in dangerous locations in the forest because they were born on inauspicious days (according to local divination systems). If such abandoned children are found alive, their inauspiciousness is thought to have no effect on their adoptive parents. When Vezo informants report such instances, they point out that once the child is grown-up and ready to be of help, the birth parents will claim the child back (and the child typically refuses to follow them). The story used in the task was devised to reduce the likelihood that participants would consider the birth parent as having any lingering claim over the child.

After hearing the story, participants were asked a series of 12 resemblance questions in a two-alternative forced-choice paradigm. The birth parent was described as having one of a pair of features, the adoptive parent as having the other, and the participants were asked what they thought the little boy would be like when he grew up. For example, "The father who generated the boy, the one from the northern village who died, he had shortish and wide feet; the father who raised the boy, the one from the southern village, he had longish and narrow feet. In your opinion, when the child is all grown up, will he have shortish and wide feet like the father who generated him, or longish and narrow feet like the father who raised him?" Participants were not specifically asked for explanations of their judgments, although they often spontaneously offered them. Justifications were recorded by hand, in Malagasy, and later translated into English for coding.

The 12 feature pairs comprised 3 types of traits (see Appendix B, Table B1): 4 *Bodily traits* (e.g., longish, narrow nose/broad, flat nose); 4 *Beliefs* (e.g., believes that cows have stronger teeth than horses/believes that horses have stronger teeth than cows); and 4 *Skills* (e.g., knows how to be a mechanic but not a carpenter/knows how to be a carpenter but not a mechanic). The feature pairs of each trait type were presented in blocks to make the task easier. In each scenario, half of the participants heard the physical properties first, followed by the beliefs and then the skills, whereas the other half heard the beliefs first, followed by the bodily traits and then the skills.

Vezo–Masikoro Procedure

The Vezo–Masikoro version of the adoption task was identical to the Vezo–Vezo version in all but a few important ways. As in the Vezo–Vezo version, participants were told a story of a baby who is born to one set of parents who die in the forest, and is found and raised by another. The critical feature of this version is that one set of parents is Vezo and the other is Masikoro, making the adoption occur across different groups. Crucially, after completing the property resemblance questions, participants were asked whether the child would be Vezo or Masikoro (e.g., "Finally, in your opinion when the child is all grown up, is he going to be Masikoro like the father who generated him or Vezo like the father who raised him?"), and in this case they were asked to justify their answer.

The across-group adoption scenarios probed two types of traits: Group-Neutral Traits and Group-Typical Traits. The 8 Group-Neutral feature pairs comprised 3 types of traits (see Appendix B, Table B2): 4 pairs of *Group-Neutral Bodily traits* (e.g., pointed ears/roundish ears); 2 *Group-Neutral Beliefs* (e.g., believes that chameleons have 20 teeth/believes that chameleons have 30 teeth); and 2 *Group-Neutral Skills* (e.g., knows how to roll cigarettes but doesn't know how to make ropes/knows how to make ropes but doesn't know how to roll cigarettes). These traits allow for an internal replication of the patterns of judgments and justifications on the individual properties probed in the Vezo–Vezo scenario.

Participants were also tested for their judgments on Group-Typical features, features that are not neutral with regard to group identity. One value of each of the 6 group-typical feature pairs was typical of the Vezo and the other was typical of the Masikoro. They comprised 2 *Group-Typical Bodily traits* (e.g., has scarred fingers from the fishing line (typical of the Vezo)/has hard calluses on his palms from hoeing (typical of the Masikoro), 2 *Group-Typical Beliefs* (e.g., believes that an offering of rum is enough to complete the marriage ritual (Vezo)/believes that the marriage ritual cannot be completed unless one head of cattle is sacrificed (Masikoro)), and 2 *Group-Typical Skills* (e.g., knows how to fish (Vezo)/knows how to cultivate rice (Masikoro)). The Group-Typical traits followed the Group-Neutral Traits of the same type, such that traits of each type (bodily traits, beliefs, skills) remained blocked.

If Astuti's ethnographic description of how Vezo construe the difference between themselves and the Masikoro is accurate, adults should reason that all of these group-typical traits are acquired by learning and doing, and therefore that the child will resemble the adoptive parent both in the group-typical traits and in the group identity that is conferred upon him by those traits. Consistency in these judgments will become an issue when we turn to the children's data in Study 2. If, by contrast, Vezo were to judge that group identity is fixed at birth, they could derive their predictions about group-typical properties from essentialized kind. This possibility is particularly important in the Vezo–Karany adoption scenario, to which we now turn.

Vezo–Karany Procedure

The Vezo–Karany scenario was identical to the Vezo–Masikoro scenario in all ways except that the contrast of note was between the Vezo and the

Karany rather than the Vezo and the Masikoro. The details of the story were changed slightly in order to make it plausible that a Vezo or a Karany baby might end up with adults of the other group. As in the Vezo–Masikoro scenario, participants were asked to make judgments about Group-Neutral Bodily traits, Beliefs, and Skills, as well as Group-Typical Bodily traits, Beliefs, and Skills (see Appendix B, Table B3). All group-typical feature pairs were changed such that one was typical of the Karany (e.g., "believes that one should fast each year" or "knows how to drive") rather than of the Masikoro. We also included one additional trait type, *Group-Typical Inborn Bodily traits* (i.e., black vs. light skin, curly vs. straight hair). Given that we expect the patterns of judgments on group-neutral traits to reflect a differentiated understanding of the mechanisms of birth and social learning, we expect adults to judge that the child will resemble his birth father on these two inborn features. We included them for two reasons: first, we did not want to restrict our probing to learned group-typical traits, for we did not want to bias participants to judge the child's group identity in accordance with the performative theory of group identity. Second, these somatic differences, often commented upon by Vezo informants, might drive group identity judgments in the opposite direction (e.g., participants might reason that if the boy has light skin and straight hair, he is Karany; if he has black skin and curly hair, he is Vezo).

The Vezo–Vezo, Vezo–Masikoro, and Vezo–Karany scenarios were each balanced across participants according to a Latin-Square design in order to control for the following potential confounding factors: whether the bodily traits were presented before or after the beliefs (skills were always introduced last); which value of a pair of features was attributed to the birth parent; whether the Vezo–Vezo task was administered first or second, and, in the cases of the Vezo–Masikoro and Vezo–Karany versions, whether the birth parent was Vezo. Preliminary analyses conducted on these factors revealed no significant effects, and hence all subsequent analyses collapse over these variables. Moreover, analysis revealed there to be no difference in the Vezo–Vezo judgments between those participants who had also taken part in the Vezo–Masikoro task and those who had also taken part in the Vezo–Karany task. Preliminary analyses showed this also to be true for Studies 2 and 3. Thus, in this and in Studies 2 and 3, the data from all participants in each age group will be pooled when discussing the Vezo–Vezo results.

RESULTS

The results will be presented in three sections. We first provide a qualitative sense of the adults' reactions to this task, followed by analyses of their patterns of judgments and justifications concerning the resemblance of the child to his parents on group-neutral traits. Finally, we turn to the judgments about the child's social group identity and about his group-typical traits in the across-group adoption scenarios.

Adults' Reactions to the Task

We give a brief sense of Vezo adults' overall response to our protocol as a way of addressing the issue of its cross-cultural feasibility. As previously mentioned, the researcher who administered the task was known to all adult participants as a result of her previous extended periods of anthropological fieldwork in the village. Villagers were used to the fact that she asked several questions, and were generally very cooperative in providing the necessary answers. However, the adoption task was markedly different from the informal questioning the researcher had used previously, and adult participants were initially rather doubtful about the seriousness of the exercise (during the piloting stage, the researcher became aware that the rumor that she was wasting people's time by asking silly questions was going around the village). We suspect that most of the frustration was generated by the fact that people assumed that the researcher actually knew the "right" answer to the questions she was posing, thereby making their own contribution redundant and pointless. Aware of this problem, the researcher introduced the task by explaining that some of the questions she was about to ask could be answered in more than one way and that she was interested in the different opinions that people might have about them. Also, she pointed out that she had been sent to do this job by her elders and teachers, and she asked her interlocutors to be supportive of her efforts to advance her studies, as they had so generously done in the past. This appeal almost always managed to well-dispose adult participants. Nonetheless, at the outset participants were visibly puzzled by the procedure, and it was only when they were well into the task—when they had realized that some of the questions were about the adopted boy's physical appearance while others were about his mind or character—that they became more engaged. Although not quantifiable, there were at this point clear signs of recognition (e.g., "Now I can see what this is all about!") as participants saw the point of what had seemed until then a pointless conversation.

Anticipating the results analyzed below, in Table 1 we present one full protocol, which gives a feel for the kind of response we elicited with the adoption task. Despite the unusual format of the questions, Vezo adults were clearly able and willing to engage our task, as revealed by the thoughtful justifications provided by this participant (other protocols are available on-line, Astuti et al., 2003). This is further revealed by the analysis of their patterns of judgments, to which we now turn.

TABLE 1

A Typical Study 1 Adult Protocol of the Vezo–Vezo Scenario and Vezo–Masikoro Scenario; Participant was a 49-Year-Old Female

Traits (Birth Father vs. Adoptive Father)	Responses
Vezo–Vezo scenario	
Shortish/wide feet versus longish/narrow feet	Like the father who generated him
Broad/flat nose versus longish/narrow nose	Like the father who generated him
Longish kidneys versus roundish kidneys	Like the father who generated him
Straight eyes versus cross-eyed	Like the father who generated him
Believed that horses have stronger teeth than cows versus believed that cows have stronger teeth than horses	Like the father who raised him
Believed that pineapple is healthier than papaya versus believed that papaya is healthier than pineapple	Like the father who raised him
Believed that there are kinds of lemurs that do not see at night versus believed that there are kinds of dogs that do not see at night	Like the father who raised him
Believed that frogs have green hearts versus believed that frogs have black hearts	Like the father who raised him
Knew how to be a carpenter but not a mechanic versus knew how to be a mechanic but not a carpenter	Like the father who raised him
Didn't know how to whistle versus knew how to whistle	Knowing how to whistle is not like work, but is a talent. Whistling is like singing, these are not things that one learns and they are not inherited, but are individual gifts
Knew how to fish with nets versus knew how to fish with the line	He will know both because he is Vezo
Didn't know how to fell trees for canoe making versus knew how to fell tree for canoe making	He will know like the father who raised him
Vezo–Masikoro scenario (Vezo birth vs. Masikoro adoptive)	
Roundish ears versus pointed ears	Like the father who generated him
Flat appendix versus roundish appendix	He will look like the father who generated him. In his body he will be like the one who generated him
Short/wide hands versus long/slender hands	Like the father who generated him
Big lower lip versus small lips	Like the father who generated him
Had scarred fingers from the fishing line versus had hard calluses on his palm from hoeing	He will be like the father who raised him because this has to do with work
Had a callus on top of his foot from sitting on the canoe versus had hard calluses on his toes from walking on hard soil	Like the father who raised him

Table 1. (Contd.)

Traits (Birth Father vs. Adoptive Father)	Responses
Believed that chameleons have 30 teeth versus believed that chameleons have 20 teeth	Like the father who raised him because this is about his character and not about his body, and he will believe the same as the father who brought him up because he hears his words
Believed that chicken liver is harder than duck liver versus believed that duck liver is harder than chicken liver	Like the father who raised him
Believed that corpses should not be kept for long at the village before burial versus believed that corpses should be kept long at the village before burial	Like the father who raised him
Believed that an offering of rum is enough to complete the marriage ritual versus believed that the marriage ritual cannot be completed unless a head of cattle is sacrificed	Like the father who raised him
Knew how to make ropes but did not know how to roll cigarettes versus knew how to roll cigarettes but did not know how to makes ropes	Like the father who raised him
Didn't know how to cut hair versus knew how to cut hair	Like the father who raised him
Knew how to sail versus knew how to ride a cart	Like the father who raised him
Knew how to fish versus knew how to cultivate rice	Like the father who raised him
Finally, in your opinion when the child is all grown up, is he going to be Vezo like the father who generated him or Masikoro like the father who raised him?	Masikoro, of course!

Folkbiology: Resemblance Judgments for Group-Neutral Traits

Vezo–Vezo Scenario

In order to capture how Vezo adults reasoned about the inheritance of properties, and whether they drew the distinction between two chains of causal mechanisms (one associated with procreation and the other with learning), participants were first characterized according to their individual judgment patterns, as in Solomon et al. (1996). Each individual could, in principle, adopt three different, equally coherent reasoning strategies: the first one, most consistent with the ethnographic data discussed in the Introduction, would be an adoptive bias, according to which the child is judged to resemble his adoptive parents on all traits. The second one, least consistent with the ethnographic data, would be a birth bias, according to which the child is judged to resemble his birth parents on all traits. The third one, which we take as evidence that the participant has a concept of biological inheritance, would be a differentiated pattern in which the child is judged to resemble his birth parents on bodily traits and his adoptive parents on beliefs.

In the Vezo–Vezo task, participants were said to have shown a *Differentiated Pattern* if they judged the boy to resemble the birth father on at least three of the four Bodily traits and on none of the four Beliefs, or on all four Bodily traits and on not more than one of the four Beliefs. This criterion was chosen in order to allow for some reasonable deviation from a perfect categorical pattern. The probability that such a pattern would emerge as a result of chance responding is .04, as determined by the binomial theorem; thus, we can be confident that participants who show a Differentiated pattern of judgments distinguish between bodily traits and beliefs with respect to the causal processes through which they are transmitted from parents to offspring. Note that judgments on skills were not considered in determining the Differentiated pattern, because there is no reason that skills as a broad category should be considered a priori to be biologically inherited or not (consider, for example, the case of musical talent).

The other two systematic patterns of judgments were defined as follows. Participants were considered to have shown a *Birth Parent Bias* if they judged the boy to resemble the birth father on at least 10 of the 12 features, and to have shown an *Adoptive Parent Bias* if they judged the boy to resemble the adoptive father on at least 10 of the 12 features. Each of these patterns has a .02 probability of arising from a given participant's chance responding. Finally, those participants who did not show any of the above patterns were considered to have shown a *Mixed Pattern*.

We will also report parametric analyses of participants' judgments. However, on their own such group analyses can obscure the performance of individuals. For example, if a minority of participants were more likely to judge the adopted boy to resemble his birth father on bodily traits than on beliefs, while the rest of the participants judged at chance, an overall t-test would still be significant. Hence, we give priority to our pattern analysis.

The data from the pattern analysis are consistent with the hypothesis that the understanding of biological inheritance develops under innate constraints. In spite of the vastly different cultural context of development, most Vezo adults, like their North American counterparts, understand that bodily features are determined by a chain of causal mechanisms associated with birth, whereas beliefs are determined by upbringing. As can be seen in Table 2, 77% of adults showed a Differentiated pattern of judgment. The remaining adults showed a variety of non-differentiated patterns: 6%

showed a Birth Parent Bias, 3% showed an Adoptive Parent Bias, and 13% showed a Mixed pattern. A second-order application of the binomial theorem, based on a probability of .04 that a participant would show a Differentiated pattern by chance, indicates that the 24 adults who showed this pattern is vastly more prevalent than would be expected by chance ($p < .001$).

Another indication that Vezo adults understand the mechanism of biological inheritance is that they were virtually categorical in judging that the boy would resemble his birth father on bodily characteristics. Adults, including those who showed non-differentiated patterns, did so in spite of the statements reported in the ethnographic literature about the unformed, water-like state of newborns, and the influence of experiential factors on all traits of an individual. As can be seen in Table 3, adults overall distinguished between bodily traits and beliefs in their resemblance judgments (95% of bodily traits and 19% of beliefs were judged to be like those of the birth father). Vezo adults, like Zafimaniry (Bloch et al., 2001) and North American adults (Solomon et al., 1996), also tended to make resemblance judgments about skills much as they did about beliefs (24% favored the birth father).

TABLE 2

PERCENTAGE OF ADULTS IN STUDY 1 SHOWING EACH RESEMBLANCE JUDGMENT PATTERN, BY SCENARIO (GROUP-NEUTRAL TRAITS)

	Study 1 Scenario		
Pattern	Vezo–Vezo	Vezo–Masikoro	Vezo–Karany
Differentiated	77	80	69
Birth bias	6	7	13
Adoptive bias	3	0	0
Mixed	13	13	19

TABLE 3

MEAN PERCENTAGE OF ADULTS' BIRTH PARENT RESEMBLANCE JUDGMENTS FOR EACH TYPE OF GROUP-NEUTRAL TRAIT, BY STUDY 1 SCENARIO

	Study 1 Scenario		
Trait type	Vezo–Vezo	Vezo–Masikoro	Vezo–Karany
Bodily	95	98	92
Belief	19	20	22
Skill	24	20	34

As reported in the Introduction, Astuti's ethnographic observations provided many examples in which children's bodily traits (e.g., a club foot, a large nose) were attributed to the actions, likes, and dislikes of the parents or of other socially significant people, rather than biological factors. Such reports suggest that Vezo adults might have reasoned that the protracted nurturing relations with his adoptive parents would shape the adopted boy's physical characteristics. Instead, only one out of the 31 adult participants showed an Adoptive Parent bias pattern (see Astuti et al., 2003 for this participant's full protocol).

Vezo–Masikoro and Vezo–Karany Scenarios

Before turning to an analysis of participants' justifications, we present the data for the group-neutral traits from the two across-group adoption scenarios. This analysis provides a strong test of the conclusion that Vezo adults have differentiated social and biological mechanisms of transmission, for these scenarios introduce the complication of adoption across different social groups.

In the Vezo–Masikoro and Vezo–Karany scenarios, as in the Vezo–Vezo scenario, participants' responses were characterized according to their individual judgment patterns on the group-neutral traits: Differentiated Pattern, Birth Parent Bias, Adoptive Parent Bias, and Mixed Pattern. Because there were fewer group-neutral beliefs included in the across-group adoption scenarios, slightly different criteria were adopted. Participants were said to have shown a *Differentiated Pattern* if they gave birth father judgments on at least three of the four group-neutral bodily traits and on neither of the group-neutral beliefs ($p < .08$, binomial theorem); they were said to have shown a *Birth Parent Bias* if they gave birth father judgments on at least 7 of the 8 Group-Neutral features ($p < .04$); and they were said to have shown an *Adoptive Parent Bias* if they gave adoptive father judgments on at least 7 of the 8 features ($p < .04$).

Overall, the adults made inheritance judgments on the Vezo–Masikoro and Vezo–Karany tasks much as they did on the Vezo–Vezo task: the majority showed a Differentiated pattern (see Table 2). As in the Vezo–Vezo scenario, they were also categorically more likely to judge that the child would resemble his birth father in bodily traits and his adoptive father in beliefs, and, again, judgments on the group-neutral skills patterned with beliefs (Table 3).

A $2 \times 2 \times 3$ repeated-measures analysis of variance (ANOVA) examined the effects of across-group scenario (Vezo–Masikoro vs. Vezo–Karany), adoption type (across-groups vs. within-group), and trait type (bodily traits vs. beliefs vs. skills) on the percentage of birth parent resemblance

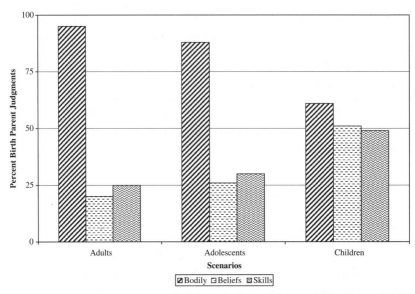

FIGURE 1.—Mean percentage of adults in Study 1, adolescents in Study 3, and children in Study 2 making birth parent resemblance judgments for each type of group-neutral trait (collapsed across the Vezo–Vezo, Vezo–Masikoro, and Vezo–Karany scenarios), by age.

judgments. There was a significant main effect for trait type, $F(2, 58) =$ 98.38, $p < .001$. Averaged across all scenarios, adults judged that the child would resemble his birth father on physical traits 95% of the time, on beliefs 20% of the time, and on skills 25% of the time (see Figure 1). Post hoc analyses indicate that, as was expected, adults were significantly more likely to judge the bodily traits to be inherited than they were the beliefs or the skills, which did not differ significantly from one another. There were no other significant effects or interactions, indicating that Vezo adults did not alter their judgments according to whether the adoption contrasted Vezo with Vezo, Vezo with Masikoro, or Vezo with Karany.

Justifications: All Scenarios

Adult participants were not asked to justify their resemblance judgments, but in several cases they spontaneously did so. Because the task was very repetitive, quite reasonably the participants gave justifications only for a selection of their judgments (17%), which they considered worthy of comment (see protocol in Table 1, and those in Astuti et al., 2003). Justifications were coded according to the criteria shown in Table 4.

Origins justifications were those that mentioned a mechanism that invoked the boy's birth origins in some manner, such as an explicit reference

36

TABLE 4

CRITERIA FOR CODING JUSTIFICATIONS (GROUP-NEUTRAL AND GROUP-TYPICAL TRAITS)

Code	Criteria
Origins	Invoke child's birth origins through reference to sex, filiation, or ancestral origins ("because it comes from one's line of descent;" "because that's where the child gets his template from")
Nurture	Invoke a psychological or intentional mechanism such as teaching, seeing, and getting used to ("because the father who raised him is his school;" "because the words of the father who generated him are lost")
Like Adoptive Parent	Simple restatement of the participant's judgment ("because he is like the father who raised him")
Like Birth Parent	Simple restatement of the participant's judgment ("because he is like the father who generated him")
Raised	Simple restatement of the Malagasy term for adoptive parent ("because he raised him")
Generated	Simple restatement of the Malagasy term for birth parent ("because he generated him")
Group	Refer to boy's group identity as a sufficient explanation for the acquisition of traits ("he'll know how to fish with nets because he is Vezo")
Truth/Desirability	Invoke the truth or desirability of a property ("he will believe that rum is enough [to complete the marriage ritual] because that's true")
Individual Intrinsic	Deny that the property is acquired through either inheritance or learning, but is the result of random individual variations ("whistling is a kind of gift from God which has nothing to do with one's father")
Spiritual Connection	Invoke the dead parent's spiritual influence or the intervention of a metaphysical entity ("the beliefs of the father who generated him will sound true to him;" "God will tell him what the father who generated him used to believe")
Other	All other justifications

to reproduction, or the boy's ancestral origins. *Nurture* justifications were those responses that mentioned a mechanism such as teaching, seeing, becoming used to, growing up with, hearing the words of, following, and so on. Both of these types of justifications give evidence of causal reasoning. By contrast, *Generated* and *Raised* justifications were simple restatements of the Malagasy term for the birth or the adoptive father used by the experimenter, and *Like Birth Father* and *Like Adoptive Father* were simple restatements of the participant's own judgment. These latter types of justifications were not considered references to a causal mechanism, and for this reason they were conservatively coded as distinct from Origins or Nurture justifications. *Group* justifications were those that referred to the boy's group identity. These explanations suggested that group identity itself sufficed as an explanation, or at least was central to any explanation and was a basis for understanding the transmission of traits. Justifications were coded as

Individual Intrinsic if they denied that the property under consideration is acquired through either inheritance or learning, but is the result of random individual variations. Justifications were coded as *Spiritual Connection* if they invoked the dead parent's spiritual influence over the child or the intervention of metaphysical entities such as spirits or God. Finally, *Truth/Desirability* justifications were those that invoked the truth or desirability of a property. All other justifications were coded as *Other*. Two experimenters coded the English translation of the justifications with 92% reliability; the first author resolved disagreements by consulting the original Malagasy version.

Vezo adults gave a total of 108 justifications, with 29 of the 31 (94%) adults producing at least one. Thus, the mean number of justifications per participant was 3.5. Nurture justifications were the most common, accounting for 43% of all justifications, followed by Origins justifications, accounting for 15% of the total. Adults also gave Spiritual Connection justifications 8% of the time and Individual Intrinsic justifications 9% of the time. The less informative Generated and Like Birth Parent justifications accounted for 13% of the total, Raised and Like Adoptive Parent accounted for 4%, Truth/Desirability and Group for 2% each, and the remaining 3% were coded as Other. This means that 76% of adults' justifications spelt out a clear causal mechanism for the transmission of an individual's properties (i.e., Nurture, Origins, Spiritual Connection, or Individual Intrinsic). Ninety percent of adults who ever gave a justification produced at least one that spelt out a causal mechanism.

Across the three scenarios, adults always gave justifications that were consistent with the reasoning implicit in their judgment (i.e., they only gave Origins justifications for birth judgments and Nurture justifications for adoptive judgments). Adults were also vastly more likely to offer a justification whenever their judgment deviated from the canonical Differentiated pattern than when it conformed to it. Of the 236 times participants judged a bodily trait to be like that of the birth father, justifications were offered only 7% of the time. By contrast, of the 12 times participants judged bodily traits to be like those of the adoptive father, justifications were offered 67% of the time. The difference is significant ($\chi^2(1) = 46.85$, $p < .001$). Similarly, of the 150 times participants judged beliefs to be like those of the adoptive father, they offered justifications only 15% of the time, whereas of the 36 times they judged beliefs to be like those of the birth father, they offered justifications 42% of the time. This difference is also significant ($\chi^2(1) = 12.38$, $p < .001$). This distribution indicates that participants' decisions as to whether a particular judgment was worthy of explanation is significantly associated to whether the judgment departed from the understanding that birth parentage determines bodily traits and that nurture shapes beliefs. This suggests that whenever participants gave judgments that departed from the

Differentiated pattern, they were aware of the violation implied by their judgments and therefore made the effort of commenting on it.

A detailed reading of the justifications reveals the coherence of the theories held by adults, as well as their ability to articulate the theoretical and ontological presuppositions underlying their judgments. As we shall see, Vezo adults drew a number of distinctions: between the body, and the mind, character or spirit of the person; between skills that are passed on through one's line of ancestry and skills that are acquired by listening and looking; between believing that one's adoptive father is one's birth father and finding out that he is not.

Let us start with the distinction that motivated the performance of the overwhelming majority of adults: As exemplified by the full protocol presented above (see also the protocols available on-line in Astuti et al., 2003), adult reasoning was guided by the distinction between "body" on the one hand, and "character," " mind," or "spirit" on the other, and between the causal mechanisms that affect each of these. Overall, adults who judged that the adopted boy would resemble his birth father in bodily traits and his adoptive father in beliefs and skills were more articulate in describing the causal mechanism involved in the transmission of beliefs and skills than in describing the causal mechanism involved in the transmission of bodily traits. For the former, they invoked learning, teaching, looking, hearing the words of the father who raised him, following him, living with him, being used to him, working with him, as ways by which the adopted boy will come to acquire the beliefs and skills of his adoptive father; in negative terms, they talked about the fact that the child was not around to catch the words of his birth father, that the father is not around to teach the boy what to believe or what to do, or that there is no way for the father who generated him to be close to him.

By contrast, informants rarely expanded on the causal mechanism by which the boy would come to have the same bodily properties as his birth father. Two older women jokingly referred to sex, reminding the researcher that the man she had described as "the father who generated the boy" was the *husband* of the boy's mother, and that supposedly he was the one who had made the child—or wasn't he? (see Protocols 5 and 6 in Astuti, et al., 2003). One other informant referred to the mediation of blood, and yet another explained that the child resembles his birth father because he got his "template" from him (see Protocols 2 and 3 in Astuti, et al., 2003). Otherwise, despite the overwhelming percentage of birth judgments on bodily traits (95% in the Vezo–Vezo task, 98% in the Vezo–Masikoro task, and 92% in the Vezo–Karany task), adults' explanations of the specific mechanism that causes the resemblance were hard to come by.

The fact that Vezo adults were more prone to discuss the mechanism of nurture than the mechanism of birth is perhaps not surprising, given that

39

the former is arguably more transparent than the latter, especially for people who do not have access to scientific descriptions of the process of human reproduction (notably, none of the participants resorted to "western" accounts of biological inheritance). Nonetheless, because Vezo adults' folk theories about procreation include the view that men contribute semen to the making of the child (see Astuti, 1993), one could have expected adults to be more fluent in their explanations of the transmission of bodily traits from birth parents to offspring. That adults did not articulate these processes is consistent with the ethnographic observation that nurture (learning, becoming, being used to) is a much more prominent feature of Vezo adults' discourse than birth (see Introduction). However, it is important to emphasize that the lack of verbal fluency is not a good predictor of participants' inferential reasoning—in other words, even if it is the case that their cultural preferences make Vezo adults less likely to produce explanations for their birth judgments on bodily traits, this did not make them any less likely to judge that birth parentage *is* part of the causal process that determines such traits.

Not all Vezo adults showed the canonical Differentiated pattern. However, it is our contention that most of the adults who showed a Non-Differentiated pattern did so as a result of a conscious and motivated violation of what they consider the usual processes that determine mental and bodily properties, that is, in the light of this distinction rather than as a consequence of an ontological monism that collapses it. Several details of participants' justifications substantiate this claim (see samples of non-differentiated protocols in Astuti et al., 2003).

First, like the rest of our sample, adults who did not show a Differentiated pattern were nonetheless more likely to offer a justification for judgments that deviated from the canonical pattern than for judgments that conformed with it ($\chi^2(1) = 8.02$, $p < .005$). That is, they gave justifications 43% of the time they made adoptive judgments on bodily traits or birth judgments on beliefs, as compared to only 17% of the time they made birth judgments on bodily traits or adoptive judgments on beliefs. We have suggested earlier that this distribution indicates that participants chose to comment on those judgments that violated the understanding that birth parentage determines bodily traits and that nurture shapes beliefs. Of course, for this to be the case, they would have to have held a representation of the distinctions that underlie the violation.

Second, the justifications given by adults for non-canonical judgments about bodily traits (i.e., that the child would resemble the adoptive father) were entirely consistent with their having a differentiated understanding. For example, the adults who did not show a Differentiated pattern and made such non-canonical judgments explained that the shape of the kidneys or the shape of the appendix is determined by what one eats, or that the shape of one's hands is determined by one's occupation. In all of these cases, the justifications were clearly intended to rectify what the participant regarded as our incorrect choice of trait (i.e., in their view, we had chosen an acquired rather than an inborn trait), and they thus reveal that the participants who made these non-canonical judgments were reasoning within a coherent theory of biological inheritance.

Similarly, justifications given by adults for non-canonical judgments regarding beliefs (i.e., that they will resemble those of the birth father) reveal a differentiated understanding. These justifications are particularly interesting for they point to a type of mechanism not found in studies of North American adults. Most of these justifications (9 out of 15) were of the Spiritual Connection type (see Protocols 4–6 in Astuti et al., 2003). They invoked a variety of supernatural or psychological interventions through which the adopted child would come to share the beliefs of his birth father who, crucially, died when the child was just a baby. Some participants invoked God as either the messenger between the father and the child or as the originator of the child's thoughts, who forges the child's mind to be like that of the birth father. Other participants concentrated instead on the state of mind of the child, and suggested that the child will intuitively doubt what his adoptive father says to him. This intuition is believed to occur especially when/if the true identity of the boy's adoptive parents is disclosed to the child (i.e., when he discovers that those he thought were his parents had not, in fact, generated him); at this point, the character and dispositions of the parents who generated him would inevitably begin to "work" on him.

These comments suggest that most Vezo adults probably construe procreation as engendering a strong emotional and mental bond between birth parents and their children (certainly far stronger than is captured in Astuti's, 1995a, ethnographic description). Notably, the overwhelming majority of Vezo adults who participated in our task did not recruit this idea to argue that this bond would continue to influence children once they were separated from their parents, and judged instead that the parental influence over children would die out if it were not nourished through everyday interactions. Nonetheless, those few adults who gave birth judgments on beliefs and produced Spiritual Connection justifications reasoned that parental influence is never extinguished, even in the face of death. Spiritual Connection justifications give us a sense of the extraordinary ways (by comparison with listening, hearing, looking, being raised, etc.) in which participants stipulated that a *dead* birth father continues to inform his child's beliefs.

While we do not wish to deny that these Spiritual Connection justifications genuinely depart from reasoning likely to be found among North American adults, we also wish to point out that these participants were probably aware that by invoking God, spirits, and the child's own

41

psychological intuitions, they were violating their own understanding of the mundane ways in which beliefs are transmitted from parents to children. We suggest that their "spiritual" justifications served them to bridge the knowledge of how beliefs are normally transmitted, with the knowledge that children are (ought to be) powerfully connected to their birth parents.

In sum, we suggest that even the very few adults who did not show a Differentiated Pattern of judgments were sensitive to the distinction between birth and nurture as two separate causal mechanisms for the transmission of different kinds of properties. Of theoretical significance is the fact that these non-canonical judgments were given by participants who differentiated between the biological mechanism responsible for the transmission of bodily properties, and a variety of *non-biological* interventions (a message from God, a psychological intuition, etc.) responsible for the transmission of beliefs (but see Protocol 4 in Astuti et al., 2003, for an exception).

To conclude the present analysis, we must briefly turn to the justifications provided for the judgments about the transmission of skills. When reasoning about skills, adults made some fine discriminations. Although informants disagreed on points of detail, there was convergence on the following distinctions: there are skills that are easily learnt just by looking, and by participating in the relevant activities (e.g., rolling cigarettes, making ropes); there are skills that are acquired as a result of living in a certain environment where one has to provide for one's livelihood (e.g., fishing with nets, fishing with the line); there are skills that are passed on from generation to generation, and are acquired by each new generation without effort—almost by instinct (e.g., carpentry); and finally, there are talents that are individual gifts from God, intrinsic to the person (e.g., singing and dancing).

The motivation for exploring how Vezo participants reason about the transmission of a variety of different skills was the ethnographic observation that skills play a central role in defining what it means and what it takes to be Vezo. As we shall see in the section on resemblance judgments for group-typical properties, Vezo participants are categorical in judging that the adopted boy will acquire the group-typical skills of his adoptive father. However, their responses about group-neutral skills reveal that the apparently simple notion that people are Vezo because they know how to fish, and that they know how to fish because of the environment in which they live, emerges against a far more complex theoretical background in which some skills are learnt (just like fishing), while others are inherited from one's line of ancestors, and others still are given as gifts by God or by one's personal destiny.

A final point to be derived from the overall analysis of the justifications offered by our Vezo informants is that the theoretically motivated differentiation between biological inheritance and learning allows adults to elaborate nuanced and idiosyncratic theories about the transmission and acquisition of different types of skills, as well as to entertain the existence of extraordinary mechanisms that ensure that birth parents never cease to work on their children's minds. Despite the vastly different social, cultural, and educational contexts in which Vezo adults come to elaborate these views, the fundamental questions they grapple with are arguably no different from those that engage North American adults as they debate about the origin of such properties as intelligence or artistic genius (see Gelman, 2003, pp. 287–288 for a North American example).

Conclusions

In striking contrast to what Vezo informants state when they comment on the physiognomy of their babies—statements that anthropologists may be tempted to use as evidence of incommensurable ontological commitments—the present results show that Vezo adults clearly differentiate between the effects of the biological process of procreation (resemblance in bodily traits) and the effects of social processes of nurturing, teaching, and learning (resemblance in beliefs and skills). Even those Vezo adults whose individual pattern of judgments deviated from the canonical Differentiated Pattern nonetheless gave justifications that revealed ideas formulated in terms of this principled differentiation. Some adults evinced beliefs in supernatural causal factors, but these beliefs did not vitiate their differentiation of biological inheritance from socially mediated learning mechanisms revealed by their overall performance in this task.

These results extend in a more rigorously controlled manner those of Bloch et al. (2001) regarding the Zafimaniry and, taken together with converging results from Tamil and North American adults, they bolster the claim made by the Innate Conceptual Content hypothesis that the understanding of biological inheritance may be an adult universal.

Folksociology: Group Identity Judgments and Resemblance Judgments for Group-Typical Traits

We are now in a position to ask how Vezo adults reason about the acquisition of group identity. Participants were asked, at the end of the Vezo–Masikoro and Vezo–Karany adoption tasks, to judge what the adopted boy's group identity would be. On the basis of ethnographic data, Astuti (1995a, 1995b) argued that Vezo informants classify social groups on the basis of activity criteria, rather than in terms of common origins and shared descent. Given the reiteration in everyday discourse of the point that being Vezo or Masikoro depends on what people do, we predicted the following outcome: that Vezo participants would judge that a boy raised by Vezo parents, in a coastal village, would acquire the properties typical of Vezo people and would become Vezo as a result, no matter who his father was. Similarly, we predicted that they would judge that a boy raised by Masikoro parents, in a village in the interior, would acquire the properties typical of Masikoro people and would consequently become Masikoro.

Of greater theoretical significance is the outcome of the Vezo–Karany task. In contrast to the Vezo–Masikoro scenario, in this case the adoption takes place between people of clearly separate ancestral origins, who are somatically different, do not intermarry, are of diverging economic status, and practice a different religion. The question of whether a boy born of Vezo parents and adopted by Karany parents is Vezo or Karany (or vice versa) is the real test case for the ethnographic claim that Vezo classify social groups in terms of their activities. If Astuti's analysis is an accurate description of Vezo reasoning about group identity, then birth origins should not be a determining factor in participants' reasoning even in the case of the Vezo–Karany adoption. Alternatively, according to Gil-White's analysis, the nature of the contrast between Vezo and Karany should trigger the hypothesized naturalization of ethnic kind, and it might also trigger Hirschfeld's universal Human Kind Competence. If so, the adopted boy's group identity will be naturalized, in the sense of being judged to be inherited from his birth parents, and essentialized, in the sense of driving the attribution of group-typical traits.

Group Identity Judgments

As predicted, the overwhelming majority of adults (87%) who participated in the Vezo–Masikoro scenario gave judgments that were consistent with Astuti's ethnographic description: they judged that a boy born to one set of parents but raised by another would grow up to be of the same group as his adoptive parents. More importantly, the majority of adults (78%) in the Vezo–Karany version of the task also judged that the boy would be of the same group as his adoptive parents. He would be Vezo if born to Karany and raised by Vezo parents, or Karany if born to Vezo and raised by Karany parents. Of the remaining 22% of adult participants, three gave straightforward birth judgments, and the remaining adults judged the boy to be "metisse," a term normally used to refer to people whose birth parents belong to different "racial" groups, most commonly to children of Malagasy and European parents. Participants were not significantly more likely to make adoptive group judgments in the Vezo–Masikoro task than they were in the Vezo–Karany task.

Despite the striking similarity between judgments in the two scenarios, participants' reaction to the question about the adopted boy's group identity was markedly different in the two cases. In the Vezo–Masikoro task, adults took no time to come up with the answer—the response was automatic, given without much reflection. This is consistent with the observation that the labeling of people as "Vezo" or "Masikoro" on the basis of their abilities to perform Vezo or Masikoro activities (e.g., fishing as opposed to planting) permeates everyday conversations, and that the transition between being Vezo and becoming Masikoro (or vice versa) is not an unknown occurrence. By contrast, participants in the Vezo–Karany task often hesitated before answering the question about the boy's group identity. They sometimes stated that they were unsure, that they needed a bit more time to think about the issue; they often commented that this was a difficult question. For sure, the Vezo–Karany scenario presented them with a novel situation they had never contemplated in their conversation nor had they ever encountered in real life, because no Vezo has ever become Karany, nor has a Karany ever become Vezo. Yet, having thought long and hard about it, the overwhelming majority of participants recruited the way of reasoning they normally apply to the familiar Vezo–Masikoro scenario (that group identity is determined by what people do), and they productively extended it to this novel social context.

Resemblance Judgments for Group-Typical Traits

In both Vezo–Masikoro and Vezo–Karany versions of the adoption tasks, participants were asked to judge whether the adoptive boy would resemble the birth or the adoptive father on a number of properties that Vezo informants regard as typical of Vezo, Masikoro, and Karany people. In both Vezo–Masikoro and Vezo–Karany scenarios, we tested three types of properties: bodily traits that result from one's occupation; occupational skills; customary practices and religious beliefs. Because there are no inborn somatic differences between Vezo and Masikoro, we were able to test these traits (skin color and hair type) only in the Vezo–Karany scenario.

In the case of the Vezo–Masikoro version of the task, adults gave adoptive parent judgments for 100% of the group-typical traits. For example, they judged that a child raised by Masikoro parents will grow up to believe that the marriage ritual cannot be completed unless the family of the groom offers one head of cattle to the family of the bride (Masikoro-typical custom), and that he will know how to ride an oxen-driven cart (Masikoro-typical activity). Note that in the same scenarios, the very same participants gave birth parent judgments 20% of the time on group-neutral beliefs and 20% of the time on skills. However, when they considered group-typical properties, they became categorical in judging that nurture, learning, and habituation are the only causal mechanisms responsible for the transmission of such properties. In the case of the Vezo–Karany scenario, participants'

45

judgments were similarly categorical. Only 6% of the time participants gave birth parent judgments on group-typical beliefs and acquired bodily properties, and only 2% of the time on skills (in the Vezo–Karany scenario, these very participants gave 22% birth judgments on group-neutral beliefs and 34% on group-neutral skills).

When, in the Vezo–Karany task, participants were asked about the skin color and hair type of the adopted boy, they overwhelmingly responded that the boy would resemble his birth father on these traits (88% of birth judgments for skin color, and 94% for hair type). These results confirm that Vezo adults understand that qualitatively different causal mechanisms lead to the transmission of inherited and non-inherited traits, and show that these mechanisms are held to operate whether or not the traits could potentially be construed as markers of group identity.

Although these results are not surprising in the light of the data presented above on resemblance judgments concerning group-neutral traits, it is nonetheless worth pointing out that participants could have construed the group-typical properties differently from the way they did. For example, they could have reasoned, as some adults did in the case of neutral beliefs, that one's religious beliefs are implanted in one's mind or spirit through one's spiritual connection with one's birth parents; or they could have reasoned, as some adults did in the case of neutral skills, that one's occupational dispositions are transmitted through one's line of descent (this is precisely the view that informs the Indian caste system). Instead, the small but consistent margin of deviation from the canonical Differentiated Pattern that we observed when participants answered questions about neutral properties entirely disappears when they were asked to reason about group-typical properties (compare Figures 1 and 2; adult participants).

Justifications

We present participants' justifications for group identity judgments together with their justifications for resemblance judgments on group-typical properties. The reason for this is that these judgments are closely linked in people's reasoning about group identity. There are two ways in which participants could have established this link: (a) by essentializing group identity, and deriving a person's group-typical properties from it (e.g., the person is Vezo and therefore she has Vezo group-typical properties) or (b) by appealing to the acquisition of group-typical traits to derive the person's group identity (e.g., the person has acquired Vezo-typical properties and therefore she is Vezo). Consistently, our adult participants adopted the second strategy.

In both the Vezo–Masikoro and Vezo–Karany scenarios, participants offered justifications for their judgments on the resemblance on

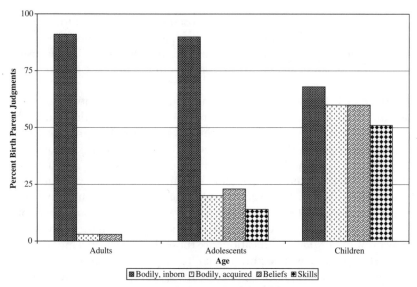

FIGURE 2.—Mean percentage of adults in Study 1, adolescents in Study 3, and children in Study 2 making birth parent resemblance judgments for each type of group-typical trait (collapsed across Vezo–Masikoro and Vezo–Karany scenarios), by age.

non-inherited group-typical properties roughly 1/5 of the time (18% in the Vezo–Masikoro task, 22% in the Vezo–Karany task). Twenty-three of the 31 adults provided a total of 37 justifications, an average of 1.6 per participant offering any justification at all. The same coding criteria used for the justifications given for group-neutral properties were used for the justifications given for group-typical properties (see Table 4).

In both tasks, the overwhelming majority of justifications given in support of adoptive judgments were coded as Nurture justifications (75% in the Vezo–Masikoro scenario, 90% in the Vezo–Karany scenario). This means that participants made explicit reference to mechanisms of transmission such as learning, teaching, seeing, and being used to the adoptive father's ways. By contrast, only 19% of the justifications for adoptive judgments in the Vezo–Masikoro scenario, and none in the Vezo–Karany scenario, were Group justifications, which invoked the boy's group identity (i.e., he has property × because he is Vezo or Masikoro or Karany) as a sufficient explanation for why the boy has a certain group-typical property.

Justifications given for resemblance judgments on inborn group-typical bodily traits (skin color and hair type) similarly reflected direct reasoning about the transmission of the trait, not inference from group categorization, regardless of whether they were given to explain the boy's resemblance to his birth parent or adoptive parent (e.g. the boy's skin will be black like his birth father's because skin color cannot change, or it will be black like that of

47

his adoptive father because it will get exposed to sea water and to the sun). Two of the three justifications given for birth parent judgments were coded as Origins and one was coded as Generated and two of the three justifications given for adoptive parent judgments were coded as Nurture and one as Other.

Participants were explicitly asked to provide a justification for their judgment on group identity. Justifications were given 73% of the time in the Vezo–Masikoro task, and 94% of the time in the Vezo–Karany task (recall that each participant only made one such identity judgment). In order to capture more precisely the nature of participants' reasoning about group identity, we have broken the broader Nurture justification type into four subtypes (see Table 5): *Upbringing* justifications are those that refer to the fact that the boy was brought up by Vezo, Masikoro, or Karany people; *Environment* justifications are those that specifically mention the place where the boy grew up; *Customs* justifications are those that specifically mention the customs that the boy will acquire (or fail to acquire) as a result of his upbringing; and *Occupation* justifications are those that specifically mention the boy's occupation.

TABLE 5

CRITERIA FOR CODING JUSTIFICATIONS (GROUP IDENTITY)

Code	Criteria
Origins	Invoke child's birth origins through reference to sex, filiation, or ancestral origins ("he'll be Karany because this is his ancestry")
Occupation	Invoke the child's occupation ("he is Masikoro because he can grow rice")
Upbringing	Invoke the fact that the child was brought up by Vezo, Masikoro or Karany people ("he is Masikoro because the people who brought him up were Masikoro")
Environment	Invoke the place where the child grew up ("he is Vezo because he grew up on the coast")
Customs	Invoke the customs that the child will follow ("what makes him a Karany is that he follows Karany customs from the time he was a tiny baby"; "he'll be Vezo because he doesn't know what would make him a Karany, but he knows Vezo customs and Vezo livelihood, as he did not receive Karany customs")
Like Adoptive Parent	Simple restatement of the participant's judgment ("because he is like the father who raised him")
Like Birth Parent	Simple restatement of the participant's judgment ("because he is like the father who generated him")
Raised	Simple restatement of the Malagasy term for adoptive parent ("because he raised him")
Generated	Simple restatement of the Malagasy term for birth parent ("because he generated him")
Other	All other justifications

48

The results reveal an interesting qualitative difference between the justifications offered by adults on the two tasks. The majority of the justifications given by participants in the Vezo–Karany task made explicit reference to the fact that the child would follow the customs of the adoptive family (54% of all the justifications given for adoptive judgments were coded as Customs, 15% as Environment, 15% as Upbringing, and 15% as Other). By contrast, participants in the Vezo–Masikoro task were usually content to mention that the child was being brought up by Vezo or Masikoro parents, or that he was being raised in a Vezo or Masikoro village (56% of the justifications for adoptive judgments were coded as Upbringing, 33% as Environment, and only 11% as Customs).

Thus, the adults who participated in the Vezo–Karany task were more likely than were those in the Vezo–Masikoro task to invoke customs than environment or upbringing in their justifications ($\chi^2(1) = 5.69, p < .02$). This result suggests that, having never thought about a Vezo–Karany adoption scenario before, participants had to reconstruct in their minds the entire causal sequence step by step: Which "ways of doing" is the child going to acquire? What kind of person will he be, given that he has got used to follow these "ways of doing?" Note that participants could have pursued the reverse strategy; they could have assigned the adopted boy to a group (e.g., he is Karany), and they could have stipulated that because he is Karany, he will grow up to believe Karany beliefs and follow Karany customs. Instead, the direction of participants' causal reasoning was reversed: it is because the boy has a certain group-typical property, that he has a certain group identity.

Arguably, determining that a Vezo baby adopted by Karany parents is going to be Karany requires significantly more novel reasoning than does determining that a Karany baby adopted by Vezo parents is going to be Vezo. The latter scenario can be easily accommodated by the explicitly held theory that Vezo identity is a matter of performing Vezo activities. According to this view, anybody can become Vezo, as long as one learns to act in Vezo fashion (and indeed this judgment was extended to the foreign anthropologist, once she familiarized herself with Vezo life style). However, the scenario where a Vezo baby is adopted by Karany people requires a much more radical extension of Vezo identity theory, because it requires attributing to the Karany the notion that being Karany is a matter of performing Karany activities. Given that there is very little evidence in the social world to support this view, Vezo participants might well have thought that the Karany would not accept a Vezo child into their ranks. But the results show that adults were not, in fact, more likely to judge the boy to have the group identity of his birth father when the adoptive parent was Karany (25%) than when the adoptive parent was Vezo (19%).

In both tasks, about a quarter of the participants reasoned that the adopted boy would grow up to be Vezo, Masikoro, or Karany like his *birth* father, and offered justifications that referred to the boy's birth origins and ancestry. There are two important points that should be stressed here: first, despite their birth judgments on group identity, participants reasoned that the adopted boy would have the group-typical properties of the social group that raised him, as is consistent with a differentiated understanding of biological inheritance and social learning. Second, by mobilizing such differentiated understanding, these adults were able to redefine Vezo, Masikoro, and Karany group identities as a feature of the person that is fixed at birth and cannot change as a result of upbringing. Although this view goes against the cultural consensus, it does so by resorting to the same theoretically motivated ontological distinctions.

DISCUSSION

We have begun this SRCD monograph on conceptual development with a study of adults for two reasons. Obviously, adult knowledge is a major source of input into the developmental process, and we cannot take adult conceptualization of any given domain of knowledge for granted. This is especially true in a cross-cultural study such as this one. But equally significantly, we must interrogate the adult end-state to establish whether the developmental process yields representations that are cross-culturally universal (as predicted by the Innate Conceptual Content hypothesis) or cross-culturally variable (as predicted by the Unconstrained Learning hypothesis), as a way of deciding between competing views of the nature of conceptual development.

Study 1 failed to support the widespread anthropological claim about cross-cultural variability in the ontological commitments that underpin the conceptual representations of processes of biological and social transmission of a person's individual properties. Ethnographic descriptions of Vezo cultural statements and beliefs about babies' physiognomy motivated the hypothesis that Vezo adults might not differentiate bodily from mental properties of the person, biological from social family, nor the mechanisms of transmission that depend on biological inheritance from those that depend upon learning. Patterns of family resemblance judgments as well as the justifications for those judgments showed this hypothesis to be false. Every single Vezo adult whom we interviewed judged that a child born to one set of parents and raised by another would resemble his birth father on bodily traits, and differentiated these resemblance judgments from those on beliefs and skills. Most Vezo adults did so categorically, just as North American adults do.

The extent to which these results contrast with much of current anthropological literature may be difficult for psychologists to fully appreciate.

To illustrate, consider the comment made by an anthropologist discussant on a panel at the American Anthropological Association conference in which Astuti presented some of these data: "I'm suspicious of the discovery of our own cultural categories in the non-verbal subterranean recesses of other people's minds" (McKinnon, 2002). It is certainly right to be deeply suspicious, but in the end, it is an empirical question whether and when non-western peoples have different cultural categories from our own. As we have already noted, our adoption scenarios may have elicited a differentiated understanding that is not normally evident in Vezo discourse, but such an understanding had to be available to Vezo participants in order to be elicited. Furthermore, the explicit justifications our informants produced showed these categories not to be in the subterranean *recesses* of their minds.

One might reply that we are over-interpreting our data. Perhaps participants judged that the child would resemble his birth parent on bodily traits not because of their understanding of biological inheritance as distinct from social learning mechanisms as we claim, but because they reasoned that prenatal *social* influences determine these traits. Several considerations militate against this possibility. First, not a single participant ever made this argument in a justification for the judgment that the child would resemble his birth father. Second, Astuti, Solomon, and Carey (in preparation) carried out an additional study designed to elicit precisely such reasoning, if available. In this study, the adoption scenario involved two classificatory sisters, and the child was a girl instead of a boy. The fact that the targeted parents were closely related women meant that the new scenario drew particular attention to the prenatal period, when the fetus is said to be particularly susceptible to the molding influence of its mother's actions and social interactions (e.g., whether she keeps to her taboos, whether she has lovers, the people she befriends, the people she accepts food from), as well as to the nurturing contribution of the adoptive mother, who was described as having breast-fed the baby-girl. This adoption scenario could thus have encouraged participants to give more adoptive resemblance judgments on bodily traits and qualitatively different justifications. Instead, both the patterns of resemblance judgments and the justifications were identical to those of the present study in every respect.

In sum, these data are consistent with the hypothesis that conceptual representations of biological inheritance develop under innate constraints, leading to cross-cultural convergence of, rather than to incommensurability between, adult representations in this aspect of the domain of folkbiology. But although cross-cultural universality in the adult end-state is a prediction of the Innate Conceptual Content hypothesis, it does not provide knock-down evidence for it. After all, even the Unconstrained Learning hypothesis can accommodate the fact that, if the world provides massive data in favor of some conceptual representations, those could emerge cross-culturally in the absence of innate constraints on learning. Thus, as noted in the Introduction, the Innate Conceptual Content hypothesis needs validation through developmental data. Study 2 will therefore turn to Vezo children to test the specific prediction made by the Innate Conceptual Content hypothesis: that irrespective of significant cross-cultural variations in input conditions, the conceptual representations in question emerge early in development in all cultural contexts.

Turning now to the domain of folksociology and to the naturalization of human kinds, adult judgments and justifications confirmed that Vezo consider group identity to be determined by what people do, by the customs they follow, and by the beliefs they hold. Most importantly, Vezo adults extended this theory of group identity from the contrast between Vezo and Masikoro, a contrast that is the object of much cultural elaboration and is the subject of everyday conversations, to a novel contrast, that between Vezo and Karany. This finding not only demonstrates that Vezo theory is productive, allowing for generalization to novel instances, but also that it applies to distinctions that would be construed in racial terms in western folksociology. Despite the fact that Karany people are explicitly represented by Vezo informants as somatically, linguistically, religiously, and economically different from themselves, and despite the fact that Vezo and Karany do not intermarry, the majority of adult participants extended to them a system of social classification that is activity based, that does not essentialize their identity, and does not naturalize their difference (i.e., Vezo adults do not appeal to birth origins and biological inheritance to explain it). This finding challenges both Hirschfeld's claim about the universal deployment of the Human Kind Competence and Gil-White's claim about the universal construal of ethnic kinds as animal species. Our data on folksociology, therefore, provide supportive evidence for the claim that adult representations in this domain of knowledge are not cross-culturally universal. In Study 2, we shall turn to developmental data to explore two contrasting predictions arising from this finding: the first one, motivated by the Unconstrained Learning hypothesis, is that the construction of the adult theory is a steady and incremental process of internalization, the unmediated result of the input that children derive from the adult culture; the second one, motivated by the Innate Conceptual Content hypothesis, is that the construction of the adult theory requires children to overturn their initial intuitions, which run counter to the adult culture and that are not generated from it.

Finally, the results of Study 1 allow us to explore the relations between a differentiated understanding of the transmission of individual traits and the Vezo performative theory of group identity. Resemblance judgments on group-typical traits were categorically differentiated. All adults in the Vezo–Karany task judged that the child would have the somatic traits (skin color and hair type) of his birth father, but judged that the child would have the group-typical skills, customs, and beliefs of the adoptive father. In accord with the claim that group identity is not essentialized, participants' judgments about group-typical properties were not derived from their judgments about group identity. On the one hand, the former were not justified by invoking the latter; rather, participants' group identity judgments were justified in terms of the occupation, beliefs, and customs acquired by the adopted boy as a result of his upbringing and place of residence. On the other hand, the substantial minority of participants (about 20%) who judged that the adopted child's group identity would be that of his birth father did not reason any differently from the rest about the adopted boy's group-typical properties (i.e., the boy was judged to resemble the adoptive father on all of these).

These data suggest that the Vezo performative theory of group identity depends upon the differentiation of biological inheritance from social learning. In the face of such a differentiated understanding, some Vezo adults naturalized group identity, taking it to be fixed by a person's ancestral origins. Nonetheless, in this study there was no evidence that group identity was also essentialized, for these participants' reasoning about group-typical properties was not driven by their group identity judgments. Study 2 will enable us to further explore the relation between a differentiated understanding of the mechanisms of trait transmission and the performative theory of group identity, by asking whether young children have such a differentiated understanding and, if not, whether in its absence they understand their parents' theory.

III. STUDY 2. CHILDREN: FAMILY RESEMBLANCE AND GROUP IDENTITY

The finding that Vezo adults have an understanding of biological inheritance that is commensurable with that of their North American counterparts gives support to the hypothesis that folkbiological concepts develop under some form of innate constraints. In this chapter, we shall test the prediction of the Innate Conceptual Content hypothesis that concepts with innately specified biological content ought to be in evidence in early childhood. Specifically, the data presented in this chapter address the claim that young children have a biological understanding of family resemblance (Atran et al., 2001; Gelman & Wellman, 1991; Hirschfeld, 1996; Springer & Keil, 1989, 1991). A number of studies have already reported data that challenge this claim. For example, Solomon et al. (1996) found that it is not until 6 or 7 years of age that the majority of North American children can be credited with this understanding (see also Gimenez & Harris, 2002; Springer, 1996; Weissman & Kalish, 1999; Williams & Affleck, 1999 for converging results). Mahalingam (1998) found that the majority of urban Tamil children in India did not show this understanding before the age of 12 years. Finally, Bloch et al.'s (2001) preliminary data suggest that among rural Zafimaniry in Madagascar, an understanding of biological inheritance is only attained in adulthood. Studies 2 and 3 seek to verify Bloch et al.'s findings with a larger sample of Malagasy children (Study 2) and adolescents (Study 3) in a more systematic fashion, using better controlled and counterbalanced materials.

With respect to folksociological concepts of human groups, the adult data presented in Study 1 failed to support the hypothesis that all humans, irrespective of the socio-political environment in which they live, will conceptualize human groups as if they were natural kinds, that is by naturalizing and essentializing them (i.e., believing that membership in them is inherited from birth parents, and that a person's properties can be predicted from membership). Nonetheless, the performative theory of group identity we have documented among Vezo adults could be the result of two

54

very different developmental processes: it could result from a gradual and incremental process of internalization entirely shaped by culturally specific input, as posited by the Unconstrained Learning hypothesis; or it could be the result of a historically contingent process of cultural construction, which overturns the earlier predisposition both to naturalize and to essentialize human kinds that is hypothesized by Hirschfeld (1996) (Gil-White's, 2001 proposal has unclear developmental implications, because it is unlikely that young children are aware of the social rule of endogamy, which is said to trigger the naturalization of ethnic groups). The developmental data presented in this chapter bear on this critical issue.

Finally, Study 2 explores the relationship between understanding biological inheritance and reasoning about group identity. If the reasoning about group identity shown by Vezo adults in Study 1 depends upon the differentiation of biological and social mechanisms for the transmission of bodily and mental/experiential properties of the person, then the question of whether children show a similar differentiated understanding is of added theoretical importance. It is to be empirically demonstrated whether Vezo children have mastered this differentiation, and, furthermore, whether they must have such conceptual resources in order to understand their parents' performative theory of identity. Study 2 allows us to explore these possibilities.

METHOD

Participants

The participants were 40 children (mean age = 9 years, range 6–13 years) from the same Vezo village of Betania as the adults. Twenty children, 12 girls and 8 boys, took part in the Vezo–Masikoro version of the task (mean age = 9 years, range = 6–13 years) and 20 children, 10 girls and 10 boys, took part in the Vezo–Karany version (mean age = 10 years, range = 7–13 years).

The age of 13 years was defined, a priori, as separating childhood proper (Study 2) from adolescence (Study 3). The distinction between children and adolescents roughly corresponds to the local distinction between sexually inactive children and sexually active but still unmarried boys and girls, a transition marked by the fact that at around the age of 13 boys and girls are no longer allowed to sleep in their parents' house. Adolescents may have children of their own, but they are not normally responsible for them if they are not formally married. The age at which the adolescent and adult groups are divided roughly corresponds to the age at which boys and girls begin to have families of their own, which involves having a stable partner, children, a separate house, and an independent source of livelihood.

55

The age ranges in these groups are large. For every analysis we present in these chapters, preliminary analyses were first conducted that compared the performance of the younger half of the sample to the older half. That is, we compared the 6–9-year-olds to the 10–13-year olds, and we compared the 14–16-year-olds to the 17–19-year-olds. In no case was the result significant. No doubt, with larger samples, differences within these age ranges would emerge, but for a first pass these age ranges allow us to sketch the broad strokes of the course of conceptual development in the related domains of folkbiology and folksociology.

With few exceptions, children came to the researcher's house as, according to local customs, they are expected to do when a grown-up needs them. In return for their participation, they were offered a small sum of money. Although permission to work with the children was formally granted at the village assembly, Vezo parents expressed the view that their consent was both superfluous and ineffective because their "hard-headed" children would be free to decide whether they wanted to work with the researcher or not. They warned the researcher that their children did not know anything and that she would be wasting her time trying to get any sense out of them.

Procedure

The procedures for this study were like those of Study 1 with a few minor changes. As the story was recited, children were shown pictures of Vezo or Masikoro villages or of a Karany compound (not recognizable as any actual village or compound) in order to make the story and the questions easier to follow. None of the traits probed in the task was represented in the pictures. Before proceeding with the testing, the experimenter questioned the participants to make sure that they understood the story. Participants were asked: "Who was the father who generated the boy? Was he the man from this village [pointing to one picture] or the man from this village [pointing to the other picture]?" and "Who was the father who raised the boy? The man from this village or the man from this village? [pointing to the pictures] Where was the child raised? Here or there? [pointing to the pictures]." Participants who failed the comprehension probes were told the story a second time. One child did not pass the probes after two tellings of the story and was dropped from the study. Children participated in the two tasks (within-group and across-groups tasks) on different days, and the second story was narrated to them in full. Unlike Study 1, at the end of the across-groups task, children were also asked to rate whether each of the group-typical beliefs attributed to the birth parent were in fact typical of the parent's group (e.g., "Do you remember, I told you that the Vezo father from this village on the coast [pointing to the picture] believed that an

56

offering of rum is enough to complete the marriage ritual? In your opinion, is it just him who believes this, or is it the majority of Vezo people who believe that way?"). The final difference is that children were explicitly asked to justify their resemblance judgments for individual properties as well as for their group identity judgments (adults were only asked to justify the latter). Children were asked to justify at least one judgment for each of the sets of bodily traits, beliefs, and skills. If no justification was forthcoming, the experimenter asked them to justify the following judgment of the same type. Counterbalancing was conducted as in Study 1.

RESULTS

Children's Reactions to the Task

As mentioned earlier, Vezo parents regarded their children as free agents who could decide whether they wanted to participate in the task or not. As it turned out, children were eager to do so, probably because they enjoyed being at the center of attention, and because they knew they would get a small gift at the end. The children referred to the adoption task as a tapasiry, the local term for fictional tales (as opposed to ancestral narratives) that are traditionally recounted as an evening pastime. Numerous children gathered each day around the researcher's house. Korsia, the researcher's Vezo "sister," helped each day to recruit the children of the right age and sex, and chased the rest away.

Children came into the researcher's house for the administration of the task; most of the children had been there before to play with the researcher's son, and having him around made her house a far less intimidating place than it would have been otherwise. In most cases, children took time to observe their surroundings (e.g., the researcher's belongings), and when their curiosity was satisfied they were introduced to the task. Children were then told that they were going to hear a story and be asked some questions about it. The researcher stressed that she wanted to know what they thought about it, and that it was not a case of giving right or wrong answers because different people, even grown-ups, have different opinions on these things. They were asked to listen carefully and to think hard about the questions. They all nodded contentedly and set out to listen.

During the piloting stage, it became obvious that children younger than 6 or 7 would not be able to participate in the task. Vezo adults were adamant that all children lack wisdom and hence are unable to answer questions sensibly. In fact, it is likely that these younger children were simply too shy and too intimidated by the testing situation. Vezo children are not used to having genuine questions put to them (i.e., questions to which they are expected to have independently formed answers), and the youngest children responded with total passivity. It should be added that the main problem did not seem to be the researcher's foreignness, because the children seemed far less intimidated by her than by her Vezo "sister," who would quickly lose her temper and, in typical adult fashion, would tell them to stop wasting our time by sitting with their mouths shut! Even the 6–13-year-old children who were able to cope with the formal structure of the procedure were generally shy. Many chose to answer the questions by pointing to the picture associated with the trait or parent of their choice. As reported below, most children gave at least one justification for their judgments, but this often required repeated probing.

Folkbiology: Resemblance Judgments for Group-Neutral Traits

Vezo–Vezo scenario

As in Study 1, participants' responses were characterized according to their individual pattern of judgment for group-neutral traits. The same criteria as in Study 1 were used to classify children's judgment patterns as *Differentiated* (i.e., judged the boy to resemble his birth father on bodily traits and his adoptive father on beliefs), *Birth Parent Bias* (i.e., tended to judge the boy to resemble his birth father on most all traits), *Adoptive Parent Bias* (i.e., tended to judge the boy to resemble his adoptive father on most traits), and *Mixed*. Table 6 shows the distribution of patterns.

Unlike the majority of adults in Study 1, only 13% of children showed a Differentiated understanding of the inter-generational transmission of properties. As a group, children did not differentiate between bodily traits and beliefs or skills in their resemblance judgments. On average, they judged the adopted boy to resemble his birth parent 58% of the time on bodily traits, 49% of the time on beliefs, and 50% of the time on skills (see Table 7). Moreover, regardless of whether they were able to differentiate their judgments by property types, children showed no evidence of

TABLE 6

PERCENTAGE OF CHILDREN IN STUDY 2 SHOWING EACH RESEMBLANCE JUDGMENT PATTERN, BY SCENARIO (GROUP-NEUTRAL TRAITS)

	Study 2 Scenario		
Pattern	Vezo–Vezo	Vezo–Masikoro	Vezo–Karany
Differentiated	13	0	15
Birth bias	30	40	20
Adoptive bias	18	10	25
Mixed	40	50	40

TABLE 7

MEAN PERCENTAGE OF CHILDREN BIRTH PARENT RESEMBLANCE JUDGMENTS FOR EACH TYPE
OF GROUP-NEUTRAL TRAIT, BY STUDY 2 SCENARIO

	Study 2 Scenario		
Trait Type	Vezo–Vezo	Vezo–Masikoro	Vezo–Karany
Bodily	58	66	61
Belief	49	60	45
Skill	50	58	38

understanding that an individual's bodily traits are inherited from the birth parents: even those children who were first asked to make resemblance judgments on bodily traits, and therefore could not have been confused or influenced by the other questions about beliefs, judged that the boy would resemble his birth father on bodily traits only 53% of the time.

The lack of differentiation shown by children as a group does not indicate that children individually were necessarily responding randomly in their resemblance judgments. Although the 40% of children who showed a Mixed pattern may have been doing so, the 13% who showed a Differentiated pattern should be credited with a biological understanding of family resemblance. A second-order application of the binomial theorem, based on a probability of .04 that a participant would show a Differentiated pattern by chance, indicates that the 5 children who showed this pattern is significantly more than would be expected by chance ($p < .05$). Furthermore, it is clear that the 30% of children who showed a Birth Parent Bias, and the 18% who showed an Adoptive Parent Bias were not responding randomly. What is less clear is just why the children with biased patterns responded as they did. It might be that they were reasoning causally about birth (in the case of those showing a Birth Parent Bias) or nurture (in the case of those showing an Adoptive Parent Bias) as the mediating mechanism for the transmission of *all* properties, bodily as well as behavioral and mental. However, as noted by Solomon et al. (1996), it is also possible that the children who showed Birth or Adoptive Parent Bias patterns were drawing instead on the simple non-causal knowledge that offspring tend to resemble parents, as well as on an idiosyncratic sense that one of the two parents in the story (whether birth or adoptive) was the boy's "real" father. We will return to this possibility in the discussion of the children's justifications.

Vezo–Masikoro and Vezo–Karany Scenarios

Participants' responses on the Vezo–Masikoro and Vezo–Karany tasks were characterized according to the same criteria for Differentiated pattern,

59

Birth Parent Bias, Adoptive Parent Bias, and Mixed pattern that had been used in Study 1. As on the Vezo–Vezo task, few children showed an adult-like Differentiated pattern, none of those in the Vezo–Masikoro task and only 15% of those in the Vezo–Karany task. A glance at the overall distribution of children across the various judgment patterns (see Table 6) and at the mean percentages of birth parent resemblance judgments (see Table 7) indicates that the children performed on the Vezo–Masikoro and Vezo–Karany tasks roughly as they had on the Vezo–Vezo task. The Birth Parent Bias pattern was shown by 40% of the children in the Vezo–Masikoro task and by 20% in the Vezo–Karany task; the Adoptive Parent Bias pattern was shown by 10% of the children in the Vezo–Masikoro task and by 25% of those in the Vezo–Karany task; and the Mixed pattern was shown by 50% of the children in the Vezo–Masikoro task and by 40% of those in the Vezo–Karany task.

The similarity of children's performance across the three scenarios (Vezo–Vezo, Vezo–Masikoro, and Vezo–Karany) is also borne out by a 2 × 2 × 3 repeated-measures ANOVA examining the effects of adoption type (within-group vs. across-groups), across-group scenario (Vezo–Masikoro vs. Vezo–Karany), and trait type (bodily traits vs. beliefs vs. skills) on the percentage of birth parent resemblance judgments. As with the adults, there were no main effects or interactions involving scenario, indicating that Vezo children did not alter their judgments according to whether the adoption contrasted Vezo with Vezo, Vezo with Masikoro, or Vezo with Karany. This is reflected in the similarity of the mean percentage of birth parent judgments made by children overall across the tasks, as shown in Table 7. Moreover, unlike the adults, there was no significant main effect for trait, $F(2, 76) = 2.96$, $p < .10$, $\eta = .26$. That the effect size is small (Hair, Anderson, Tatham, & Black, 1998) is consistent with there being a minority of the children differentiating among traits. Over all children, the proportion of judgments that the boy would resemble his birth father on any given trait-type (bodily traits, beliefs, skills) did not differ significantly from the chance level of 50% (see Figure 1).

Justifications

Despite the fact that children were explicitly asked to justify their resemblance judgments, they gave fewer justifications than did the adult participants. Whereas the pool of 31 adults produced a total of 108 justifications of judgments on group-neutral properties, the 40 children only produced 58, for an average of a little over 1 justification per child. Moreover, only 60% of children gave any justifications at all, whereas 94% of adults spontaneously offered at least one justification.

The justifications were coded according to the same criteria used in Study 1 (see Table 4). Two experimenters coded the English translation of the justifications with 89% reliability; as in Study 1, the first author resolved disagreements by consulting the Malagasy original. *Nurture* justifications accounted for 27% of all justifications, *Origins* accounted for 2%, and *Spiritual Connection* accounted for 3%. The *Generated*, *Like Birth Parent*, *Raised*, and *Like Adoptive Parent* justifications, arguably no more than restatements of the resemblance judgment, accounted for fully 49% of the total, appeals to *Truth/Desirability* accounted for 16%, and the uninterpretable *Other* accounted for the remaining 3% of justifications. This means that only 32% of children's justifications spelt out a clear causal mechanism for the transmission of an individual's properties (i.e., Nurture, Origins, Spiritual Connection, or Individual Intrinsic). Only 29% of children who ever gave a justification produced at least one that spelt out a causal mechanism, as compared to 90% of adults. This result suggests that the majority of Vezo children may not have reasoned causally about the resemblance between the child and his parent.

Nonetheless, children did give justifications in a manner that is consistent with the reasoning implicit in their resemblance judgment. That is, all of the Origins, Generated, and Like Birth Father justifications were offered only to explain judgments that the boy would resemble his birth father on the property under consideration. Similarly, 97% of the Nurture, Raised, and Like Adoptive Father justifications were offered to explain judgments that the boy would resemble his adoptive father on that property. This basic finding suggests that children had engaged the task and were not simply overwhelmed by the procedure. Their undifferentiated answers cannot be passed off as the result of the demand characteristics of the task. Rather, children's answers are diagnostic of their lack of understanding of the difference between the biological process of inheritance and social processes of transmission such as learning and imitation.

Children's Nurture justifications are of particular theoretical interest because they invoke at least one of the causal mechanisms targeted by the adoption task (there were virtually no Origins justifications). Although children produced Nurture justifications almost categorically to explain resemblance to the adoptive father, it is notable that only the children who had shown a Differentiated pattern restricted their use of Nurture justifications to support a judgment about beliefs or skills. Other children, by contrast, extended Nurture justifications to explain their judgments about bodily traits. For example, one 10-year-old girl explained that the boy would have longish and narrow feet like his adoptive father "because the boy lives with him, with the one who raises him," and a 12-year-old boy argued that the boy would have pointed ears like the adoptive father "because he will follow his father's way of thinking." It would appear that these children have yet to distinguish properties of the person that are affected by living, eating, and thinking together from those that are not.

We suggest that those children who lack a causal understanding of the mechanisms of nurture and biological inheritance are likely to be swayed by the implicit emotional dimension of seemingly simple questions about the resemblance of children to parents. Just how it is that they are swayed and how it is that they interpret the story is likely to depend more on their personal circumstances than on causal reasoning about either the mechanism of birth or nurture. For example, one girl, aged 13, showed a Birth-Parent Bias in both the Vezo–Vezo and Vezo–Masikoro scenarios. She gave birth judgments on every property of the adopted child, and she asserted that even if the birth father had died when the baby was very small, the boy would nonetheless be like him in all ways. A few weeks later, the researcher discovered an explanation for this girl's staunch Birth Parent Bias when, during the funeral of one of the girl's paternal uncles, it became apparent that the girl's own father had died the previous year and that she had been adopted by her father's youngest brother. As the girl approached the cemetery for the first time after she had gone to bury her father, she burst out crying. As the researcher witnessed her intense pain and tried to console her, she realized that perhaps the reason the girl had refused to give in to the idea that nurture is more powerful than procreation in shaping people's beliefs, skills, and livelihood had a lot to do with her own predicament and loss, and her intense desire to be like the father she had lost.

Conclusions

The present finding that most 6–13-year-old Vezo children do not yet understand that the biological process of reproduction is implicated in the transmission of bodily properties from parents to their offspring runs counter to the prediction of the Innate Conceptual Content hypothesis that an understanding of biological inheritance ought to be in evidence in early childhood, irrespective of widely different input conditions.

Our results confirm those of Bloch et al. (2001) with the Zafiminary. Nonetheless, our findings on Vezo children diverge from those on Zafimaniry children in one notable regard. The Adoptive Parent Bias pattern was the modal judgment pattern among Zafimaniry children (shown by 57% of 6- to 10-year-olds and by 45% of 11–15-year-olds), whereas only between 10% and 25% of Vezo children across the three scenarios (Vezo–Vezo, Vezo–Masikoro, Vezo–Karany) produced Adoptive Parent Bias patterns. Indeed, Birth Parent Bias patterns were more frequent (between 20% and 40% across the three scenarios). It is conceivable that subtle differences in the cultural milieu in which Zafimaniry and Vezo children grow up make the adoptive family more salient among the Zafimaniry. However, due to the small sample size in the Zafimaniry study, and the fact that the materials in that study were not counterbalanced, this aspect of the Zafimaniry results may not be robust.

Despite the overall convergence of our data with those from studies with Zafimaniry children (Bloch et al., 2001), Tamil children (Mahalingham, 1998), and European and North American children (e.g., Gimenez & Harris, 2002; Solomon et al., 1996; Springer, 1996; Springer & Keil, 1989; Williams & Affleck, 1999) in showing that an understanding of biological inheritance takes time to develop, there is considerable divergence in the age at which Vezo, Zafimaniry, Tamil, European, and North American children succeed in exhibiting a differentiated pattern of reasoning. Most strikingly, whereas European and North American children succeed by the age of 6 or 7, it takes Vezo children another 6 or 7 years to do so (see Study 3). We explore below some reasons as to why this might be the case, but first we turn to the children's group identity judgments on the Vezo–Masikoro and Vezo–Karany adoption scenarios and to their reasoning about group-typical properties.

Folksociology: Group Identity Judgments and Resemblance Judgments for Group-Typical Traits

Group Identity Judgments

Most of the children in the Vezo–Masikoro task judged that the adopted boy would have the same group identity as his adoptive parent, and the proportion of children who did so (65%) was not significantly less than that of the adults (87%). Most Vezo children, therefore, made judgments about the acquisition of group identity that are in accord with the explicit statements that they hear about how Vezo and Masikoro identities are acquired. A boy born to Masikoro parents, but raised by Vezo parents, will grow up to be Vezo, and vice versa.

However, children performed differently when they were asked to reason about the adoption between Vezo and Karany, a scenario they are unlikely to have ever heard discussed explicitly. A majority (73%) judged that the boy would have the group identity of his *birth* parents. The children who took part in the Vezo–Karany task were significantly more likely to make such a birth parent judgment about group identity than were those who took part in the Vezo–Masikoro task, $\chi^2(1) = 5.66$, $p < .02$. Furthermore, the number of children in the Vezo–Karany task who made birth parent group identity judgments is significantly more than that of adults, $\chi^2(1) = 9.11$, $p < .005$, who did not differ significantly in their judgments on group identity in the two tasks (see Figure 3, p. 94). When presented with an adoption scenario for which they had no ready-made answers, children, unlike adults, would appear to have been unable to extend the causal reasoning that is implicit in what they know about Vezo and Masikoro group identities to their reasoning about Vezo and Karany identities. This finding calls into question just how deeply children in the Vezo–Masikoro task had understood the causal principles underlying their adult-like judgments. It may be that instead of deploying the notion that people's group identity is determined by and is contingent on what they do, children used an alternative mode of reasoning, judging that Vezo and Karany people are born what they are, and that their identity is impervious to change. This possibility would undermine the Unconstrained Learning hypothesis, while it would be compatible with the suggestion that the later construction of the adult performative theory of identity requires the overturning of children's early predisposition to naturalize human kinds.

An analysis of the relation between group identity judgments on the one hand, and patterns of resemblance judgments on group-neutral traits on the other, confirms that children in the Vezo–Karany task reasoned about group identity quite differently from the children in the Vezo–Masikoro task. Interestingly, this difference was not dependent on how children reasoned about the transmission of other properties of the person, as shown by the fact that children in the Vezo–Karany task were not more likely to show Birth Parent Biases and children in the Vezo–Masikoro task were not more likely to show Adoptive Parent Biases (see Table 6). One might have expected the group identity judgments of those children who showed either bias to be driven by their overall preference for either adoptive or birth parent. This, however, is true only for the minority of children who, in the Vezo–Karany task, judged that the adoptive boy would have the same group identity as his adoptive father (80% of these children showed a congruent Adoptive Parent bias), and for the minority of children who, in the Vezo–Masikoro task, judged that the adoptive boy would have the same group identity as his birth father (71% of these children showed a congruent Birth Parent Bias). By contrast, as many as 71% of the children who gave a *birth* judgment on group identity in the Vezo–Karany task had *not* shown a congruent Birth Parent bias, and as many as 85% of the children who gave an *adoptive* judgment on group identity in the Vezo–Masikoro task had not shown a congruent Adoptive Parent Bias. This finding suggests that the reasoning of these children was guided by specific knowledge and intuitions about the nature of group identity, rather than reflecting a generic Birth or Adoptive Parent Bias. Thus, as a group, children took Vezo identity (relative to Masikoro) to be determined by where one grows up, but Vezo identity (relative to Karany) to be determined by one's birth origins. An examination of children's justifications as well as their judgments concerning group-typical traits will provide evidence concerning how deeply the children understand these two alternative ways of acquiring group identity.

Resemblance Judgments for Group-Typical Traits

As in Study 1, participants were asked to judge whether the adoptive boy would resemble the birth or the adoptive father on a number of properties that Vezo adults regard as typical of Vezo, Masikoro, or Karany people. Of course, whether Vezo children regard such properties as typical of a certain group is an open question. Astuti's ethnographic experience indicated that children knew that certain skills (and the traces that such skills leave on the body, such as scars from the fishing line) are typical of Vezo, Masikoro, and Karany people. Furthermore, in explicit testing, we found that most children did know that certain practices, customs, and beliefs were typical of each targeted group (78% of the children correctly judged the typicality of the Vezo, Karany, or Masikoro funerary practices, 65% recognized the typicality of the Vezo or Masikoro marriage practices, and 75% recognized the typicality of the Vezo or Karany beliefs about fasting).

Unlike adults, who were categorical in judging that, except for the inborn group-typical traits (skin color and hair type), the adopted boy would resemble his adoptive father on all group-typical properties, children's judgments on all of these properties were not different from chance (see Figure 2). Collapsing across the two across-group tasks, children on average judged that the boy would resemble his birth father 60% of the time on group-typical acquired bodily traits, 60% of the time on group-typical beliefs, and 51% of the time on group-typical skills. In the Vezo–Karany task, children gave birth parent judgments on inborn group-typical traits 68% of the time. The fact that the mean percentage for inborn group-typical traits is also not different from chance is particularly important, in view of Hirschfeld's specific claim that children, even 3- and 4-year-olds, understand that racial traits are fixed at birth (Hirschfeld, 1996; but see Solomon, 2002), which he interprets as lending support to the "contention that the understanding of the role of birth in inheritance is part of young children's naïve biology" (Hirschfeld, 1996, p. 109). Our data do not support that claim.

Nonetheless, the children (14 out of 20) in the Vezo–Karany task who judged the adopted boy to have the group identity of his birth father also judged 86% of the time that he would have the same *inborn* group-typical traits (i.e., skin color and hair type) as his birth father, significantly more often than one would expect by chance, $t(13) = 3.68$, $p < .002$. This suggests that those children who reasoned that Vezo and Karany identities are "natural"—that is, that they are acquired as a consequence of one's birth

65

origins were also inclined to naturalize the somatic markers that distinguish Vezo from Karany people.

Across all the children, there was no significant difference between those who participated in the Vezo–Masikoro task and those who participated in the Vezo–Karany task in their judgments of *acquired* group-typical properties. A 2×3 repeated-measures ANOVA, with the between-subjects factor of task (Vezo–Masikoro vs. Vezo–Karany) and the within-subjects factor of group-typical trait type (acquired bodily traits, beliefs, and skills) showed no significant main effects or interactions. Moreover, all etas were less than. 20, indicating that the effect sizes, in and of themselves, were too small to warrant further testing with a larger sample (Hair et al., 1998). Recall that the majority of children in the Vezo–Masikoro task, when asked about the adopted boy's group identity, gave adoptive parent judgments, whereas the majority of children in the Vezo–Karany task gave birth parent judgments. It is surprising that the two groups of children did not differ in their attributions of group-typical properties to the adopted child.

The above result raises the question of how much Vezo children, even those who gave correct adult-like answers to the question about group identity, understand of the adult testimony about the performative nature of group identity. According to the adult theory, it is *because* one has acquired properties that are typical of a group that one can be said to be of that group; none of the adults in Study 1 who judged that the adopted boy would belong to the group of his adoptive father ever judged that he would resemble his birth father in any of the group-typical properties. By contrast, only 2 (15%) of the 13 children who gave adoptive judgments on the boy's group identity gave adoptive judgments on all group-typical properties (and of these, 1 showed an overall Adoptive Parent Bias pattern). Strikingly, the other 11 children who gave adoptive parent judgments on group identity gave *birth* parent resemblance judgments for group-typical traits 61% of the time.

This lack of fit between children's adoptive judgments on group identity and their judgments on group-typical properties should not be taken as an indication that they do not know which traits are typical of Vezo and Masikoro people. Apart from the typicality ratings mentioned above, we can report one anecdotal piece of evidence. During Astuti's fieldwork, a group of children gathered around her son's colored felt pens and started to draw pictures. As is often the case when children have a chance to draw (e.g., by tracing pictures in the sand), they drew outrigger canoes, fish, palm trees, and sea turtles. When Astuti asked them why they were drawing these things, they replied: "because we are Vezo;" and when she asked what they thought Masikoro children would draw, they answered: "cattle, spades, and corn fields." This much they clearly know. They also can recite that people are Vezo *because* they have (and draw) outrigger canoes, eat fish, and hunt sea turtles, while people are Masikoro *because* they have (and draw) cattle, they carry spades, and grow corn. This way of reasoning is made available to—one could perhaps even say that it is inculcated in—Vezo children in a number of ways. For example, children often hear adult conversations about some people whose customs really prove that they are Vezo or Masikoro (for example, during funerals), or whose exceptional skills at sea have shown them to be "very Vezo." They also hear discussions about the transformation of specific individuals into Vezo or Masikoro. But above all, there are numerous occasions when children are directly told that *they* are Vezo or Masikoro because of what they do or fail to do. Thus, if children are taken out on a canoe journey and they are sick, they are teased and humiliated by being told that they are Masikoro; if instead they successfully catch fish or manage to sell their catch at the market, they are praised that they are becoming Vezo or, even, that they are "very Vezo" (see Astuti, 1995a, for more details).

It seems likely that the reason children performed inconsistently in our Vezo–Masikoro task is not that they do not know how to use group membership to predict group-relevant properties (X is Vezo and *therefore* X knows how to sail), but that they failed to reason causally about the specific mechanism (nurture) that transmits such group-typical properties. Note that participants were asked to stipulate whether the adopted child would be Vezo or Masikoro only at the end of the task. As a result, for each resemblance question on group-typical traits, they had to identify the causal mechanism responsible for the transmission of such traits, rather than automatically relying on group membership to guide their judgments. And children failed to reason that group-typical properties are transmitted through learning, practice, and habituation, unlike adults, who did so categorically.

Justifications

Vezo–Masikoro task. Ninety percent of the children in the Vezo–Masikoro task justified their group identity judgments. Of the 13 children who judged that the adopted boy would be Vezo or Masikoro like his adoptive father, 12 gave justifications that were consistent with their adoptive judgment (one child remained silent): 42% were coded as Environment justifications, 42% were coded as Raised or Like Adoptive Father justifications, 8% as Occupation justifications, and the remaining 8% were coded as Other (see Table 5 for coding criteria).

At first glance, the finding that 92% of these children's justifications for group identity judgments invoke processes that are at least consistent with the Vezo adult performative theory (i.e., Environment, Raised, Like

67

Adoptive Father, and Occupation) might be taken as evidence that a majority of the children in our sample have in fact mastered that adult theory. However, the striking discrepancy between children's adult-like justifications for their group identity judgments and their judgments about group-typical properties weighs against our drawing such a conclusion. By way of illustration, consider the case of a child who judged that the adopted boy would be Vezo like his adoptive father because the boy grew up in a Vezo village on the coast, but who at the same time judged that the boy would know how to cultivate rice and ride ox-driven carts like his Masikoro birth father.

Despite such incoherent answers, there is no doubt that the children who gave adoptive group identity judgments have learnt something specific about the nature of Vezo and Masikoro identities. Most likely, what children learn first is the simple association between living on the coast and being Vezo, and between living in the interior and being Masikoro. Thus, when answering our group identity questions, children were able to use the boy's place of residence as a clue to his group identity, and to produce adult-like Environment justifications. Nonetheless, their inconsistent judgments on group-typical properties reveal that they were still far from understanding the chain of causal mechanisms that underlies the adult theory: that the place where one lives determines the activities that one performs, the beliefs and customs that one adopts, the skills that one masters, and that these activities, beliefs, customs, and skills determine the kind of person that one is; or, in reverse order, that one is the kind of person that one is because of one's activities, beliefs, customs, and skills, which are determined by the place where one lives. In the absence of such causal understanding, the children who participated in our task were clearly untroubled by, or unaware of, the inconsistencies in their answers.

We now turn to the 35% of children who judged that the adopted boy would be Vezo or Masikoro like his birth father. Of these 7 children, 6 (86%) offered a justification for their group identity judgments: 2 (33%) gave Like Birth Father or Origins justifications and the other 4 (67%) gave Occupation justifications (e.g., the boy is Vezo like his *birth* father because he knows how to sail). Although small in number, these latter justifications are still quite telling because of their inconsistency: they invoke a property that is acquired through learning and practice to justify a group identity that is attributed to birth origins. We speculate that the reason for such unusual performance is that these children first judged that the boy would be Vezo or Masikoro like his birth father and that, when asked to justify their judgment, they automatically fell back on the standard stock explanation, which they have heard so many times, that people are Vezo or Masikoro because of what they do and where they live—the kind of explanation that is "in the air." In other words, they were repeating what they hear, without fully understanding what they say.

The important but speculative conclusion to be drawn from our reading of the justifications is that the children who participated in the Vezo–Masikoro task had learned to mimic key aspects of the adult performative theory of identity. On the one hand, most of the children were able to answer correctly the question about the group identity of someone who is raised on the coast or in the interior, and they could produce appropriate justifications. A minority of children, on the other hand, had yet to learn to produce the correct answers, but had begun to accommodate to the way in which adults justify their way of classifying people into groups. The result is a curious mismatch between (birth) judgments and (nurture) justifications. Thus, although in the Vezo–Masikoro task the percentage of children's adoptive judgments about the adopted boy's group identity was not significantly different from that of adults, children's grasp of the adult theory about people's group identity would appear to be very shallow indeed.

Vezo–Karany task. In our analysis so far, we have suggested that the adoptive judgments on group identity given by the majority of participants in the Vezo–Masikoro task resulted from the testimony that children receive from their parents and elders, and that the inconsistency characteristic of children's performance is due to their limited understanding of that testimony. The prediction that follows from this suggestion is that Vezo children might reason differently, and perhaps more coherently, in the absence of any direct adult guidance. The prediction is borne out by the results of the Vezo–Karany task in which a majority of children judged that the adopted boy would be Vezo or Karany like his *birth* father. As mentioned in the Introduction, Vezo villagers are familiar with the Karany as they buy goods from their shops, sell them fish at the market, and occasionally see whole Karany families taking leisurely walks on the village beach in their best clothes and expensive jewelry. Children have plenty of occasions to observe all of these interactions. However, the possibility that a Karany might become Vezo or that a Vezo might become Karany is never discussed. This means that children in the Vezo–Karany task had to figure out the answer to our group identity question on their own accord.

Of the 14 children in the Vezo–Karany task who judged that the boy would have the group identity of this birth father, 12 gave justifications: Origins justifications accounted for 42% of these, Like Birth Father accounted for 25%, and Occupation accounted for the remaining 33%. Most remarkable was that the children who offered Origins justifications were unusually explicit and resourceful in their attempts to describe the mechanism they considered responsible for the fixation of the boy's group identity. For example, a 10-year-old girl explained that the boy was going to be Karany "because he is Karany on his father's side, he came from the tummy of his [father's] wife, he is white, and he is Karany," while a 13-year-old boy asserted that the boy would be Vezo "because he carries the line of descent of the father who generated him". Two girls (9- and 13-years-old) found an alternative way to express the nature of the connection between the adopted boy and his birth father by stating that the boy will be Karany like his birth father because his *mother* is Karany. These children seem to be guided by the strong intuition that if a child is born to Karany or Vezo parents he will be Karany or Vezo no matter where he is raised, and they were able to link their intuition to the mechanics of birth and procreation.

As in the Vezo–Masikoro task, some of the children who judged the adopted boy to have the group identity of his birth father gave justifications that implied that the adopted boy would learn the occupational skills of his dead birth father. The inconsistency of such justifications suggests that in searching for an explanation for their birth judgments on group identity these children, like the ones in the Vezo–Masikoro task, fell back on the standard explanatory mode they hear applied to Vezo and Masikoro people.

Only 5 children in the Vezo–Karany task reasoned that the adopted boy would have the same group identity as his adoptive father (one child judged that the boy would be both Vezo and Karany) and only 3 of them justified their judgments: one was coded as Upbringing and two were coded as Like Adoptive Father. As noted earlier, all but one of the children who made an adoptive parent group identity judgment also showed an Adoptive Parent Bias on group-neutral traits. There is thus no evidence that their judgments on the child's group identity were the result of a dedicated theory about social categorization, because they judged the boy to resemble his adoptive father on all properties, including somatic traits such as skin color and nose shape.

DISCUSSION

Study 2 had three goals. First, we sought evidence concerning Vezo children's understanding of biological inheritance, as this bears on the prediction made by the Innate Conceptual Content hypothesis that such an understanding emerges early in development. Second, we sought evidence that bears on Hirschfeld's hypothesized Human Kind Competence. We asked: How do Vezo children approach the task of learning and reproducing the adult performative theory of identity? Might they not, as suggested by Hirschfeld, naturalize human group identity, believing it to be inherited from birth parents? And might they not essentialize it, deriving from it predictions about a person's properties? Third, we explored the relation between children's understanding of the mechanisms for the transmission of an individual's traits (both biological inheritance and learning/socializat-ion) and their construal of group identity.

The first finding of Study 2 is that Vezo children between the age of 6 and 13 years do not understand the biological mechanism through which an individual's bodily traits (as opposed to other traits, such as beliefs) are transmitted from parents to offspring. Our results replicate the findings of Bloch et al. (2001) and of Mahalingham (1998) regarding Zafimaniry and Tamil children, respectively. Taken together, these studies demonstrate that in a variety of different cultural contexts, children have yet to construct a concept of biological inheritance even by the age of 13 years. This finding undermines the claim that universally children as young as 4 or 5 years of age have a biological understanding of family resemblance, and is a challenge to the hypothesis that innate conceptual representations guide the constructions of intuitive concepts of birth parentage and biological inheritance.

An obvious question raised by these cross-cultural data is why, by com-parison with children in urban India and in rural Madagascar, children in North America and Europe come to an understanding of biological inher-itance many years earlier (by age 6 or 7 years, see Gimenez & Harris, 2002; Solomon & Johnson, 2000; Solomon et al., 1996; Springer, 1996; Springer & Keil, 1989; Williams & Affleck, 1999). Here, we can only address the differences between North American and Vezo children.

There are a number of possible reasons why it takes Vezo children longer than it takes urban middle-class North American children to develop the concept of biological inheritance. One is that the testimony they receive from their parents and elders explicitly conflates the distinction between the biological mechanism of reproduction and the social mechanism of nurture, as when Vezo adults assert that a baby's physical features depend on what kind of people (e.g., light skinned, short, plump) her mother befriended or disliked when she was pregnant (see Introduction). Contrast this with the testimony received by North American children, whose parents routinely comment on the fact that such and such a baby got her big eyes from her father and her blond hair from her mother. True, this testimony alone does not provide North American children with the understanding of biological inheritance, but it is at least consistent with it, contrary to the testimony received by Vezo children. Another likely reason is that Vezo children are virtually unschooled and that, unlike North American (middle-class) chil-dren, they are not encouraged by either teachers or parents to engage in the kind of explicit, analytic reasoning that is needed to engage in theory

71

building (see Cole & Scribner, 1974, for a classic illustration of the effects of schooling on conceptual development). As reported earlier (see also Astuti, 2000b), Vezo adults are adamant that their children "don't know anything at all," that they "understand nothing," and that they "lack wisdom." For this reason, adults nurture and love their children, but they do not engage them in reasoning, while actively discouraging them from asking inquisitive questions (because adults consider asking children's question as pointless as asking for their opinions, as we did with our tasks). This way of apprehending children's cognitive capacities came to the fore as a result of Astuti's son's presence in the village. Confronted with a radically new way of life, Sean, aged 4 and a half years, was "naturally" inclined to ask his mother a million questions a day about why women carried buckets of water on their head and men did not, why small children were allowed to use dangerous implements such as machetes and knives and he was not, why people allowed pigs to soil the village sand instead of keeping them inside their pens, and so on and so forth. On hearing him ask "why?" so many times a day, people were quick to nickname him "Perchè?" (Italian for "why?"). When Astuti explained what her son's new name meant, adults marveled at the fact that such a small child could ask so many questions, and they concluded that the reason he was so clever was that he was so inquisitive. Astuti pointed out that the reason "Perchè?" asked "perchè?" so often was that he got an answer from his mother every time he did so. But none of her interlocutors seemed willing to pick up on her hint (see Levine et al., 1994, for similar findings among the Gusii of Kenya).

If these considerations go some way towards explaining the difference in the age at which North American and Vezo children succeed at our task, one might use such considerations to argue that our task simply defeated Vezo children *because* they are unschooled and *because* they are not used to being engaged in analytic reasoning. After all, one might argue, their responses to our resemblance questions were mostly random. We disagree. We do not believe that it was the form of the task itself that defeated the children, but the content of the questions. Despite the unusual setting, the children were engaged in the task, passed memory probes for the story, and justified their judgments relatively consistently (although usually quite emptily). Moreover, although the group means for each trait did not differ from chance, *individual* children's judgment patterns were decidedly non-random. The Differentiated pattern, Adoptive Parent, and Birth Parent Bias patterns all occurred more than would be expected by chance. Most importantly, children's judgments on Vezo, Masikoro, and Karany group identity were systematically non-random, despite the fact that these questions came at the end of the task—in other words, the children were still with us. Finally, we report below children's success on a species version of the same adoption task in which they faced the same task demands (Study 4).

We conclude that children's incoherent responses in Study 2 reflect the lack of an integrated understanding of the mechanisms through which an individual's traits are transmitted, an understanding that, against cultural odds, gets constructed by adulthood (see Study 1). Given that children have not constructed this understanding, and adults have, adolescence must be the transitional age. Study 3 provides a detailed analysis of the intermediate steps that children take to construct a fully differentiated understanding of biological inheritance and socially mediated learning.

Study 2 also addressed the question of how Vezo children come to understand and reproduce their parents' performative theory of group identity. The study yielded two important results, which directly bear on Hirschfeld's Human Kind Competence hypothesis. First, Vezo children did not naturalize all human kind distinctions—they did not judge that Vezo and Masikoro group identities are fixed at birth. This is not entirely surprising, given that Vezo adults do not naturalize Vezo and Masikoro group identities either, and that they provide children with a vast amount of very explicit testimony to this effect. Indeed, in view of how much input children get, what is surprising is that their responses in the Vezo–Masikoro task were not *more* robust and coherent. This is consistent with Hirschfeld's hypothesis that the human mind is predisposed to naturalize human kinds, for this would make the Vezo performative theory of identity somewhat "unnatural" and hard to grasp. At any rate, another striking finding emerged from the Vezo–Masikoro task: despite their adult-like answers about group identity, children did not understand *why* living on the coast makes one Vezo, or *why* living inland makes one Masikoro, as shown by the incoherence of their judgments on group-typical traits and by some of their justifications. This is an indication that the constructive process children go through in mastering the adult performative theory of identity is not remotely complete by age 13.

The second and most important result concerning the development of intuitive concepts of human kinds emerged from the Vezo–Karany task. Unlike the majority of adults, who extended the performative theory of group identity to their reasoning about the Karany, the majority of children reasoned that people are Vezo or Karany because of their birth origins. These data are important for two reasons. First, they confirm that children have an immature and superficial understanding of the adult theory; what they do know—that Vezo people live on the coast; that Masikoro people live in the interior; that Karany people live in towns—is not enough to grasp the general principle that people's identity is determined by what they do, by the beliefs they hold, by the customs they practice, and to extend it to the novel case of the Karany. Second, they suggest that children may have access to an alternative, coherent theory: that people are born the kind of people that they are. These data are consistent with Hirschfeld's Human Kind

73

Competence hypothesis, and they suggest the possibility that some understanding of innate potential—with respect to human kinds as opposed to individual traits—may develop early, even when it is not scaffolded by adult cultural beliefs and practices.

Our data are also interpretable in terms of Atran's hypothesis that human kinds get construed by analogy to species kinds. As Atran (1990) suggests, the analogy to species kind might be triggered by the kind of striking somatic differences that exist between Vezo and Karany people. Consistent with this is the finding that those children who judged that the adopted child would have the group identity of his birth father also judged that the child would have the same skin color and hair type as the birth father— the only children other than the few who showed a Differentiated pattern on group-neutral traits not to be at chance on these judgments. We will return to these competing hypotheses in Study 4, which explores Vezo children's reasoning about species kind, and in the General Discussion. What seems clear at this stage is that the Unconstrained Learning hypothesis, which predicts that children acquire adult knowledge through a steady and incremental process of internalization, cannot account for how Vezo children come to understand who they are.

Finally, our results indicate that a differentiated understanding of the mechanisms of biological inheritance and cultural transmission may not be necessary for naturalizing group identity. However, this lack of differentiation may be implicated in children's failure to understand the adult performative theory of group identity. We explore this possibility in Study 3 by examining the transitional age between childhood and adulthood: adolescence.

IV. STUDY 3. ADOLESCENTS: FAMILY RESEMBLANCE AND GROUP IDENTITY

Study 1 showed that Vezo adults differentiate between two distinct causal processes of trait acquisition: a process of biological inheritance from birth parents, and a process of socially mediated learning. Study 2 showed that up until the age of 13, the majority of Vezo children have not yet constructed this differentiated understanding. Study 3 examines Vezo adolescents. Logically, the target concepts that support the adult understanding must emerge during the years between 13 (when they are largely absent) and 21 (when they are universally present). Study 3 will allow us to explore some of the details of the constructive process—which aspects of the adult conceptual system emerge first, and how the various components are interrelated in development.

Studies 1 and 2 further showed that the Vezo performative theory of group identity may also be the result of a constructive process, which by age 13 has not been mastered. Again, the relevant concepts must emerge during adolescence. Study 3 will allow us to establish whether the intuitions that may have led a majority of Vezo children to naturalize group identity in the context of the Vezo–Karany adoption task are still demonstrated in adolescence. It also allows us to test the hypothesis that the construction of the adult performative theory of group identity depends on the conceptual differentiation of the mechanism of biological inheritance from that of social learning, and on the differentiation of the different kinds of properties that are acquired through those mechanisms.

Finally, with this study we will have completed the presentation of our data regarding the domain of folkbiology (the biological inheritance of individual properties) and folksociology (the determination of group identity) from three different age groups: children, adolescents, and adults. Implicit in our discussion have been claims of massive developmental differences between children and adults. In this chapter, we present the statistical analyses across all three age groups that establish these claims.

METHOD

Participants

Participants were 38 adolescents (mean age = 17 years, range = 14–20 years), from the same Vezo village of Betania as the adults and the children. Of these adolescents, 9 young men and 9 young women took part in the Vezo–Masikoro version (mean age = 17 years, range = 14–20 years), and 9 young men and 11 young women took part in the Vezo–Karany version (mean age = 17 years, range = 14–20 years). Adolescents, like the adults, were approached in their houses, and in return for their participation they were offered a small sum of money.

Procedure

The procedure in Study 3 was the same as that of Study 2, except that adolescents, like adults, participated in both tasks on the same day.

RESULTS

Adolescents' Reactions to the Task

As a group, the adolescents who participated in the task were generally less cooperative than the adults, but less shy than the children. Most of them were less familiar with the researcher (R.A.) than were the adults, because they were still children at the time of her longest period of fieldwork in the village ten years earlier. They were motivated to participate in the study by curiosity, the monetary reward, and their parents' pressure to be helpful towards their "sister" (i.e., the researcher). Unlike children, who are not expected to understand the obligations inherent in kinship or quasi-kinship relations, adolescents are considered to be fully responsible social actors whose cooperation with the researcher was expected from their parents (who would have felt ashamed had they failed to comply). Even if at times visibly bored, the young men and women who took part in the study were nonetheless more forthcoming than the children, expressing their judgments more readily and needing less probing in order to provide justifications.

Folkbiology: Resemblance Judgments for Group-Neutral Traits

Vezo–Vezo Scenario

The judgments of Vezo adolescents suggest that it is at this age that most have begun to resemble adults in their reasoning about biological inheritance. The majority of adolescents, 58%, showed the Differentiated pattern

TABLE 8

PERCENTAGE OF ADOLESCENTS IN STUDY 3 SHOWING EACH RESEMBLANCE JUDGMENT
PATTERN, BY SCENARIO (GROUP-NEUTRAL TRAITS)

| Pattern | Study 3 Scenario | | |
	Vezo–Vezo	Vezo–Masikoro	Vezo–Karany
Differentiated	58	61	65
Birth bias	8	6	10
Adoptive bias	0	0	0
Mixed	34	33	25

typical of adults (see Table 8). A second-order application of the binomial
theorem, based on a probability of .04 that a participant would show a
Differentiated pattern by chance, indicates that the 22 out of 38 participants
who showed this pattern is significantly more than would be expected by
chance ($p < .001$). Another 8% of the adolescents showed a Birth Parent Bias
pattern and 34% showed a Mixed pattern. Unlike children, no adolescent
showed an Adoptive Parent Bias pattern.

As can be seen in Table 9, adolescents on average differentiated between
trait types in their resemblance judgments in a manner much like that shown
by adults, if less sharply. Adolescents overall judged the adopted boy to resemble his birth parent on 88% of bodily traits, 30% of beliefs, and 25% of skills.

Vezo–Masikoro and Vezo–Karany Scenarios

As with children and adults, adolescents overall made judgments about
the group-neutral traits on the Vezo–Masikoro and the Vezo–Karany tasks
much as they had on the Vezo–Vezo task. The distribution of patterns was
very similar across the three scenarios (see Table 8). In each, a majority of
adolescents showed a Differentiated pattern (58% in the Vezo–Vezo scenario, 61% in the Vezo–Masikoro scenario, and 65% in the Vezo–Karany

TABLE 9

MEAN PERCENTAGE OF ADOLESCENTS' BIRTH PARENT RESEMBLANCE JUDGMENTS FOR EACH
TYPE OF GROUP-NEUTRAL TRAIT, BY STUDY 3 SCENARIO

| Trait Type | Study 3 Scenario | | |
	Vezo–Vezo	Vezo–Masikoro	Vezo–Karany
Bodily	88	89	84
Belief	30	19	25
Skill	25	25	45

scenario), and most of the rest showed Mixed patterns, with a few others showing Birth Parent Bias patterns. No adolescent showed an Adoptive Parent Bias pattern on either task.

Table 9 further shows that the distributions of birth judgments made by adolescents in the three scenarios were very similar. Overall, adolescents judged that the boy would have the bodily properties of his birth father (ranging from 84% to 89% across the scenarios) and the beliefs and skills of his adoptive father (ranging from 19% to 30% on beliefs and from 25% to 45% on skills). As in Studies 1 and 2, a $2 \times 2 \times 3$ repeated-measures ANOVA examined the effects of adoption type (within-group vs. across-groups), across-group scenario (Vezo–Masikoro vs. Vezo–Karany), and trait type (bodily traits vs. beliefs vs. skills) on the percentage of birth parent resemblance judgments. The results show that Vezo adolescents, like Vezo adults and children, did not alter their judgments according to whether the adoption contrasted Vezo with Vezo, Vezo with Masikoro, or Vezo with Karany, as was indicated by the lack of significant main effects or interactions involving scenario. As can be seen in Figure 1, adolescents overall differentiated among trait types, showing a significant main effect for trait across the three scenarios, $F(2, 72) = 75.25, p < .001$.

Adults, Adolescents and Children Compared

We are now in a position to compare the children, adolescents, and adults directly on their resemblance judgments for group-neutral traits in the three scenarios. In a $3 \times 2 \times 2 \times 3$ repeated-measures ANOVA, the 3 levels of the between-subjects factor of age was crossed with the 2 levels of the within-subjects factor of whether the adoption was Vezo–Vezo or across-groups (Vezo–Vezo scenario vs. Vezo–Masikoro or Vezo–Karany scenario), the 2 levels of the between-subjects factor of across-groups scenario (Vezo–Masikoro vs. Vezo–Karany), and the 3 levels of the within-subjects factor of trait type (bodily traits, beliefs, and skills). The dependent measure was the percentage of birth parent resemblance judgments.

Not surprisingly, given the distributions of judgments across traits types shown in Figure 1, adolescents overall are not significantly different from adults, and both adults and adolescents are significantly different from children. There was a main effect of trait type ($F(2, 206) = 142.30, p < .001$) and an interaction of age by trait type ($F(4, 206) = 22.78, p < .001$). Post hoc analyses reveal that this interaction derives from the greater tendency of adults and adolescents, relative to children, to differentiate between bodily traits, on the one hand, and beliefs and skills, on the other. No other main effects or interactions were significant. At no age was there a significant effect of scenario. That is, adolescents' judgments of resemblance on group-neutral traits was unaffected by whether the birth and adoptive father were Vezo–Vezo, Vezo–Masikoro, or Vezo–Karany (see Tables 3, 7, and 9).

Intermediate Developmental Steps

One can describe adolescents, in broad strokes, as having reasoned about family resemblance in much the same way as had adults. But this is not to say that there were no differences between adolescents and adults, and it is certainly not to say that there were no individual adolescents who reasoned more like the group of children than like the group of adults. This, of course, is only to be expected if adolescence is the period during which Vezo construct an understanding of the difference between birth and adoptive parentage, and of the distinct mechanisms mediating family resemblance. One might expect some adolescents to show a pattern of reasoning somewhat intermediate between that of children and that of adults, with some concepts less deeply understood, less interrelated than others. As can be seen from Tables 2 and 8, across all scenarios there were more adolescents than adults who gave Mixed patterns, $\chi^2(1) = 5.46$, $p < .02$. These Mixed patterns are particularly interesting, for they promise to reveal the intermediate steps by which children come to construct the adult understanding of the biological inheritance of individual properties.

We compared the judgments of those adolescents who showed a Mixed pattern with the judgments of those who showed other patterns. Table 10 shows the percentage of adolescents' birth parent resemblance judgments on each type of trait as a function of their overall patterns of judgments in the Vezo–Vezo scenario (the results would be the same were we to consider the other scenarios as well). When we compare the adolescents who showed a Mixed pattern with those who showed a Differentiated pattern, we find, first, that Mixed pattern adolescents were significantly less likely to make birth parent judgments on bodily traits than were Differentiated pattern

TABLE 10

MEAN PERCENTAGE OF ADOLESCENTS' BIRTH PARENT RESEMBLANCE JUDGMENTS FOR EACH TYPE OF GROUP-NEUTRAL TRAIT IN STUDY 3 VEZO–VEZO SCENARIO, BY RESEMBLANCE JUDGMENT PATTERN

	Trait Type		
Pattern	Bodily	Beliefs	Skills
Differentiated	94	5	15
Birth	100	100	100
Adoptive	—	—	—
Mixed	69	58	25

adolescents, $t(33) = 3.76$, $p < .001$. Nonetheless, Mixed adolescents did make birth judgments on bodily traits more often than would be expected by chance, $t(12) = 2.13$, $p < .03$. Second, Mixed pattern adolescents were significantly less likely to make canonical adoptive parent judgments on beliefs than were Differentiated pattern adolescents, $t(33) = 7.80$, $p < .001$. Like children, Mixed pattern adolescents were not significantly different from chance in making resemblance judgments about beliefs. Third, the Mixed pattern adolescents were significantly more likely than chance to judge that the adopted boy would have the same skills as his adoptive father, $t(13) = 5.10$, $p < .001$. Indeed, adolescents who showed a Mixed pattern and those who showed a Differentiated pattern did not differ significantly in their judgments on skills, as both groups made predominantly adoptive parent resemblance judgments. This suggests that even the Mixed adolescents have begun to differentiate two classes of mechanisms that underlie family resemblance. To be sure, the Mixed pattern adolescents did not (by definition) categorically differentiate between bodily traits and beliefs in their resemblance judgments as the Differentiated adolescents did, and, as indicated above, they were significantly less likely than were the Differentiated adolescents to judge the bodily traits to resemble those of the birth parent. Nonetheless, it would appear that the Mixed pattern adolescents have differentiated bodily traits from skills, $t(12) = 4.68$, $p < .001$.

It is perhaps not surprising that even those adolescents who have yet to fully differentiate the mechanisms that determine a person's individual properties have made significant headway in their understanding of how skills are acquired and transmitted. Adolescents are in the midst of learning skills and customs that are necessary to their livelihood and that mark them as competent members of their communities (e.g., how to sail, how to trade fish, how to behave at funerals). We suggest that Vezo adolescents are likely to pay particular attention to the ways in which these properties are transmitted and acquired because of the heavily weighted testimony they hear about how one becomes Vezo. If true, this would imply that the differentiation between biological inheritance and social learning is partly driven by the adolescents' growing understanding of the Vezo performative theory of group identity. This hypothesis leads us to the prediction that adolescents' reasoning about group-typical properties in the Vezo–Masikoro and Vezo–Karany tasks should be even more like that of adults than their reasoning about group-neutral properties. We examine this possibility below, when we turn to the adolescents' judgments about group identity.

Justifications: All Scenarios

Adolescents fall somewhere in between children and adults in terms of their ability or willingness to articulate the reasoning behind their resemblance judgments (see Table 4 for coding criteria). A total of 71 justifications were given by adolescents, with 27 of the 38 (71%) participants producing at least one, for an average of about two justifications per participant. This compares with 108 justifications given by adults (94% of them offering at least one), and with 58 justifications given by children (60% of them offering at least one).

Adolescents always gave justifications that were consistent with the reasoning implicit in their judgments. However, only 26 of the adolescents' 71 justifications (37%) spelled out a causal mechanism to explain the resemblance between the adopted boy and his birth or adoptive father (as compared to 76% of adults' and 32% of children's justifications). Most of these causally informative justifications invoked Nurture mechanisms (16 of the 26), along with a handful of Origins (4), Spiritual Connection (5) and one Individual Intrinsic justifications. The remaining justifications did not spell out the causal mechanism underlying trait acquisition; they included simple restatements of the question or of the participant's own judgment (i.e., Like Birth Father, Generated, Like Adoptive Father, Raised), simple assertions about the truth of the belief or the desirability of the trait (i.e., Truth/Desirability justifications), or were uncodable (i.e., Other). Two experimenters coded the English translation of the justifications with 91% reliability; the first author resolved disagreements by consulting the original Malagasy version.

Like adults, adolescents were more likely to comment on the mechanism of nurture than on the mechanism of birth. Indeed, none of the adolescents ever offered an Origins justification for the judgment that the boy would resemble the birth father on bodily traits (their Origins justifications were given only for birth judgments on beliefs and skills). Some of the adolescents were able to invoke nurture as the mediating causal mechanism for the transmission of beliefs and skills. Nonetheless, we should also note that adolescents used Truth/Desirability justifications (e.g., because X is true) to explain why the adopted boy would have the same beliefs as his adoptive father (29% of the justifications ever given for this type of judgment). This is a kind of explanation that was never given by adults. Although Truth/Desirability justifications could entail a causal mechanism (i.e., because X is true, the adopted boy will discover that X is true, and will therefore believe in X), there is little evidence that adolescents who offered this type of justifications used this reasoning strategy. Rather, the researcher who interviewed them had the impression that they made their resemblance judgments (i.e., that the adopted boy will believe X) simply on the basis of their subjective decision that the belief under consideration was true.

Overall, we found that adolescents, like adults in Study 1, were significantly more likely to offer justifications when they made judgments that deviated from the canonical Differentiated pattern than they did when their judgments were consistent with it, $\chi^2(1) = 60.28$, $p < .001$. That is, they gave justifications 33% of the time they gave adoptive judgments on bodily traits or birth judgments on beliefs, as compared to only 6% of the time they gave the more canonical birth judgments on bodily traits or adoptive judgments on beliefs. Moreover, adolescents who showed a Differentiated pattern on both tasks were not significantly more likely to show this tendency than were those adolescents who showed a Mixed pattern in one or both tasks. This finding supports the suggestion that even the adolescents who did not meet our criteria for the Differentiated pattern were nonetheless somewhat sensitive to the distinctions probed by our task, insofar as they systematically chose to comment on those judgments that violated the distinction between biological and social family resemblance.

Folksociology: Group Identity Judgments and Resemblance Judgments for Group-Typical Traits

Group Identity Judgments

The majority of adolescents (94%) who participated in the Vezo–Masikoro task judged that the adopted boy would be Vezo or Masikoro like his adoptive parents. This result is not surprising, as the majority of adults (87%) and children (65%) had made similar judgments about the acquisition of these two group identities. The majority of adolescents also judged that the boy would have the group identity of his adoptive parents in the Vezo–Karany task. The 65% of adolescents making such a judgment is not significantly less than the 78% of adults who did so, but it is significantly more than the 28% of children, $\chi^2(1) = 5.66$, $p < .02$.

Although the majority of adolescents have successfully extended the causal reasoning that is implicit in what they know about Vezo and Masikoro group identities to their reasoning about Vezo and Karany identities, not all have done so. Adolescents in the Vezo–Karany task were significantly more likely to make birth parent judgments about group identity than were those who took part in the Vezo–Masikoro task, $\chi^2(1) = 4.94$, $p < .03$. This suggests that some adolescents were still in the process of working out the implications of the adult performative theory of identity. While this process unfolds the traces of children's intuition that Vezo and Karany group identities are determined by birth origins are still in evidence.

Resemblance Judgments for Group-Typical Traits

In preliminary testing, we found that adolescents overwhelming did know which particular funerary practices, marriage practices, and customs

82

were typical of the Vezo, Masikoro, or Karany (100% correctly judged which funerary practices we probed were typical of either Vezo or Masikoro people, 83% correctly judged beliefs about Vezo or Masikoro marriage practices, and 98% recognized which beliefs about funerary practices were typical of the Vezo or Karany people). As can be seen in Figure 2, adolescents, like adults and unlike children, tended to judge that the adopted boy would resemble his adoptive parent in having the acquired bodily traits, beliefs and skills typical of the adopted parent's group (whether Vezo, Masikoro, or Karany). On average, they judged that he would resemble his adopted parent 80% of the time on acquired bodily traits, 77% of the time on beliefs, and 86% of the time on skills. By contrast, adolescents on average judged that the boy would resemble his birth father 90% of the time on group-typical inborn bodily traits (i.e., skin color and hair type).

Adults, Adolescents, and Children Compared

A $3 \times 3 \times 2$ repeated-measures ANOVA examined the influences of Age, Trait, and Scenario on the percentage of birth parent resemblance judgments given for the acquired group-typical traits. There was a significant main effect of Age ($F(2, 103) = 40.35$, $p < .001$). There were no other significant main effects or interactions. Post hoc analyses indicate that the main effect of Age derives from the greater tendency of children to make birth parent judgments across traits. Adolescents' judgments were not significantly different from those of adults.

The coherence of their judgments that an adopted boy would acquire group-typical properties like those of his adoptive parents—save for inborn somatic ones—and that he would also have the group identity of his adoptive parents, confirms that the majority of the adolescents reasoned in a manner consistent with the adult performative theory of identity. They understand that an individual's group identity is mediated by the acquisition of salient group-typical properties such as occupational skills, religious practices, and beliefs.

Intermediate Developmental Steps

In Study 1, we argued that the adult performative theory of group identity depends upon the differentiation of biologically mediated and culturally mediated processes of individual trait transmission. In Study 2, we found that Vezo children did not draw on this differentiation in their reasoning about family resemblance, and that they had a very shallow understanding of how adults classify people into groups. In the present study, we

83

have found that adolescents' reasoning about the transmission of individual properties and about group identity is similar to that of the adults. Nonetheless, as noted earlier, there is a considerable group of adolescents who have yet to show the categorical differentiation between biological inheritance and social learning that was characteristic of the adult participants. As before, we can turn to these Mixed pattern adolescents to reveal some of the intermediate steps through which the adult performative theory of identity is constructed.

It would seem that, at a minimum, the adult theory requires a firm understanding of the role of learning and practice in acquiring the skills and the cultural norms and beliefs that determine whether a person is Vezo, Masikoro, or Karany. We showed in Study 2 that this understanding is beyond most children's conceptual resources. In order to discover whether Mixed pattern adolescents have the necessary concepts out of which to construct the adult understanding of group identity, we analyzed the percentages of birth parent resemblance judgments for *Group-Typical* properties in either Vezo–Masikoro or Vezo–Karany task, as a function of adolescents' overall patterns of judgments for *Group-Neutral* properties in that same task (see Table 11). Not surprisingly, the adolescents who showed a Differentiated pattern were almost categorical in judging that the adopted boy would resemble his birth parent on inborn group-typical bodily traits (e.g., skin color in the Vezo–Karany scenario), and his adoptive parent on group-typical acquired traits (including bodily properties such as having scarred hands as the result of fishing). More importantly, adolescents who showed a Mixed pattern were almost as categorical. They judged the adopted child to resemble his birth parent on features such as skin color and hair type 80% of the time, significantly more often than would be expected by chance, $t(4) = 2.45$, $p < .04$. They also judged that the adopted boy would resemble his birth parent on group-typical beliefs only 27% of the time, significantly less often than would be expected by chance,

TABLE 11

MEAN PERCENTAGE OF ADOLESCENTS' BIRTH PARENT RESEMBLANCE JUDGMENTS FOR EACH TYPE OF GROUP-TYPICAL TRAIT IN STUDY 3 VEZO–MASIKORO AND VEZO–KARANY SCENARIOS, BY RESEMBLANCE JUDGMENT PATTERN

| Pattern | Group-Typical Trait type | | | |
	Bodily Inborn	Bodily Acquired	Beliefs	Skills
Differentiated	92	17	13	6
Birth	100	100	100	100
Adoptive	—	—	—	—
Mixed	80	18	27	9

$t(10) = 2.19$, $p < .03$. This finding is in contrast to the relative lack of differentiation in their judgments for group-neutral bodily traits (67% of which were judged to be like those of the birth parent) and beliefs (a striking 55% of which were judged to be like those of the birth parent).

The above result shows that even Mixed pattern adolescents have a firm differentiated understanding of how group-typical properties are acquired. Although they do not yet fully understand why an adopted child will have pointed ears like his birth father, they seem to know why that same child will be black like him; though they would appear not to know whether an adopted child will believe what his birth or adoptive father believed about the number of teeth chameleons have, they are confident that the child will believe that funerals should be kept short, just as his adoptive father believes. This finding supports our hypothesis that adolescents begin to comprehend the difference between biological and social mechanisms of trait transmission by first making sense of the adult performative theory of group identity. That is, they first learn that, irrespective of their birth origins and skin color, people acquire their group identity by acquiring the properties that are typical of the social environment in which they grow up.

Justifications

Virtually all of the adolescents justified their group identity judgments and did so in a manner consistent with the judgments for which they were given. In the Vezo–Masikoro task, 14 justifications were given for adoptive-parent group identity judgments: 6 were coded as Upbringing, 4 as Environment, 2 as Raised, and 2 as Like Adoptive Father. In the Vezo–Karany task, 13 justifications were given for adoptive parent group identity judgments: 9 were coded as Upbringing, 1 as Environment, 2 as Occupation, and 1 as Other. The majority of these justifications reveal a causal understanding of how people become what they are: it is because of where they grow up, of the work they do, of the parents who nurture them that people turn out to be Vezo, Masikoro, or Karany.

Only one participant in the Vezo–Masikoro task gave a birth parent group identity judgment, and the justification provided was coded as Generated. In the Vezo–Karany task, 7 justifications were given for the judgment that the adopted boy would have the group identity of his birth father: 3 were coded as Origins, 1 as Spiritual Connection, 1 as Generated, 1 as Like Birth Father, and 1 as Occupation. Thus, out of the 8 adolescents across both tasks who judged the boy to have the group identity of his birth father, only one gave the kind of inconsistent Occupation justification that we found among children (i.e., she judged that the adopted boy would be Vezo like his birth father "because he knows how to sail"). Instead, most of the adolescents who made a birth parent judgment for group identity were able to articulate the view that group identity is a property of the person that is inherited at birth, through one's ancestry, and that it is impervious to change (a view shared by one-fifth of the adults in the Vezo–Karany task).

Conclusions

Three important results emerge from these analyses. First, the majority of Vezo adolescents, like adults and unlike children, were able to reproduce the adult performative theory of what it means to be Vezo. They understood that to be Vezo is to have Vezo skills, to follow Vezo ways and customs, and that these ways and customs are learned by living in a certain environment and by participating in the social life of other Vezo people. Adolescents neither essentialized Vezo identity nor naturalized it, even when they were asked to contrast it with Karany identity. Second, a minority of adolescents showed a remnant of the children's tendency to naturalize the group identity of Vezo and Karany people. As a group, adolescents, unlike adults, were significantly more likely to make birth judgments on group identity in the Vezo–Karany scenario than in the Vezo–Masikoro scenario. Third, there is evidence that adolescents work out the difference between the causal mechanism of biological inheritance and of social learning in the case of group-typical traits before they do in the case of group-neutral traits.

In view of these findings, we offer a final analysis to further explore the interrelation between the emergence of the adolescents' differentiated understanding of the biological and social mechanisms responsible for family resemblance, and their mastery of the adult performative theory of identity. We submit that to demonstrate a fully mature grasp of what it means to be Vezo, Masikoro, or Karany, a participant should have made the following interrelated and coherent set of responses: an adoptive judgment on group identity; an explicit causal justification for such judgment; at least 5 adoptive judgments on group-typical acquired properties (out of a possible total of 6); and, in the case of the Vezo–Karany task, 2 birth judgments on group-typical inborn bodily properties. A total of eleven adolescents met these very strict criteria, strikingly all adolescents who had shown a Differentiated pattern of judgments on group-neutral properties in at least one of the scenarios (within-group or across-group). This finding suggests that full mastery of the adult performative theory of group identity requires a firm and explicit differentiation between biological and social mechanisms of trait transmission. Of course, this does not mean that such a differentiated understanding guarantees the immediate and automatic construction of a fully coherent theory of identity. Nonetheless, the more consolidated the differentiated understanding becomes, the more likely it is that adolescents will meet our stringent criteria. Thus, whereas these criteria were met by 38% of the adolescents who showed a Differentiated pattern in at least one of the scenarios, they were met by 53% of the adolescents who showed a Differentiated pattern on *both* of the scenarios and, as mentioned earlier, by none of the adolescents who failed to show the Differentiated pattern on either. This result supports the hypothesis put forward in Study 1 that the differentiated understanding of the mechanisms of biological inheritance and cultural transmission is necessary, though decidedly not sufficient, for the construction of the Vezo performative theory of group identity.

DISCUSSION

Both the differentiated understanding of the biological and social transmission of individual properties and the Vezo performative construal of group identity are cultural constructions that take considerable time to develop. Although in the present Study, we found that adolescents as a group did not differ from adults—most adolescents showed a Differentiated pattern of judgments for individual group-neutral properties, they understood that group identity is determined by what people do rather than by their birth origins, even when reasoning about the unfamiliar Vezo–Karany contrast, and they gave adoptive judgments on all acquired group-typical properties—the adolescents who showed a Mixed pattern in their resemblance judgments allowed to shed light on the constructive process that drives the transition from children's to adults' understandings.

Among these Mixed pattern adolescents, we found evidence that the crucial distinction between biological and social processes of trait transmission is won, at least in part, as a result of making sense of the adult-performative theory of group identity. Adolescents who showed a Mixed pattern of judgments on group-neutral properties successfully differentiated between inborn and acquired group-typical properties. In other words, they understood that people's skin color and hair type are determined by their innate potential; babies born of Vezo parents may be as light skinned as those born of Karany parents (and they are), but Vezo babies cannot help but develop into dark skinned adults, irrespective of where and with whom they live. And they also understood that, by contrast, people's customs, religious beliefs and occupational skills are acquired through practice, learning and habituation: babies born of Vezo, Masikoro and Karany parents are equally unable to behave according to custom, are equally agnostic as to whether dead people become ancestors or whether Allah is the only God, and are equally unable to fish, cultivate or trade, but by the time they are grown up they will have learnt specific ways of behaving, believing and providing for their livelihood that are entirely dependent on where and with whom they live.

This principled differentiation between properties that develop according to one's innate potential and properties that are acquired through learning and practice is likely to be initially made for group-typical properties because it is directly and very explicitly supported by the adult testimony children are bombarded with: They are told that they are Vezo if they know how to fish; that other people are Masikoro if they know how to cultivate; that Masikoro and Vezo have different customs; that Vezo become Masikoro if they change their ways of doing things; that children themselves can be very Vezo at times—when they paddle skillfully—but Masikoro at other times—when they are sea-sick. We suggest that in the process of making sense of all of this, children's attention is drawn to the fact that those properties that are said to make people Vezo are properties that the children themselves do not yet have, but which must be learned. We suggest that Vezo children, in learning the ways of doing that make them Vezo, also learn the critical distinction between those properties that are inherited—like the color of their skin or the texture of their hair—and properties that must and can be acquired.

The realization that a person's customs, religious beliefs, and skills do not develop naturally, but are the result of a process of socially-mediated learning, appears to emerge in the face of a possible tendency of children to naturalize human group identity. We did, however, find possible evidence of a vestige of this tendency in the present Study. This is shown by the fact that the adolescents who participated in the Vezo–Karany task were more likely to naturalize group identity than were those who participated in the Vezo–Masikoro task. Consistent with the Innate Conceptual Content hypothesis, some children and adolescents demonstrated this tendency despite the fact that the adult testimony about what it means to be Vezo—and, by implication, about what it means to be Karany—does not support *this* understanding of what makes people who they are. This supports the suggestion advanced in Chapter III that reasoning in this domain may be subject to some sort of internal constraint. Although the present data do not allow us to decide between competing hypotheses concerning the nature of the constraint (see General Discussion), one possibility is that human kinds are analogized to animal species (as suggested by Atran, 1990). A first step towards evaluating this proposal is to ascertain whether Vezo children understand that birth origins are responsible for the fixation of animal kind identities. This is the aim of Study 4.

In spite of the fact that the naturalization of group identity is still in evidence among adolescents (remember, it was still in evidence among some of the adults as well), most adolescents were well along in understanding and adopting the adult performative theory of group identity. Our analysis revealed that those adolescents who had a firmer understanding of the different causal mechanisms that are implicated in the transmission of an individual's properties, also had the most mature grasp of the adult performative theory. This confirms that development in these two conceptual domains is closely intertwined.

We have first argued that adolescents begin to build a differentiated understanding of the process of biological inheritance and of socially mediated learning by drawing the distinction between inherited and acquired properties as a result of being exposed to the adult theory of group identity. We have then argued that in order to understand this theory, adolescents require the conceptual differentiation between birth and social parentage, between bodily and mental/experiential traits. This argument may appear circular, but it is precisely because the relevant concepts are interdefined such that their conceptual roles are mutually self-constituting, that they are acquired in such a coherent manner. This type of apparent circularity is typical of conceptual change, in childhood as well as in the history of science (see Smith, Solomon, & Carey, 2004 for a worked example).

Many questions of detail remain open, requiring further data to address them. These include questions such as how we should think about the constraints that lead some children to naturalize group identities in the face of adult testimony to the contrary, and what leads Vezo adults to construct a performative theory that overturns these initial constraints. Indeed, we have yet to account fully for the important discrepancy between our claim that Vezo children must come to understand the conceptual differentiation between biological and social processes of individual trait transmission in order to understand a crucial aspect of their culture (no less than who they are), and the anthropological claim that this very differentiation of biological and social processes is disallowed by the ontology of people like the Vezo. We return to these questions in Chapter VI, after presenting data on children's and adult's reasoning about animal species.

The data in Chapter III indicated that Vezo children, unlike Vezo adolescents and adults, do not understand the biological inheritance of bodily traits, even those like skin color and hair texture that are somatic markers of what in the West are construed as racial distinctions. Children did not distinguish between birth and adoptive parents in deciding which of these bodily traits a child would grow up to have, nor did they differentiate bodily traits from beliefs or skills in their resemblance judgments. However, the relevance of the distinction between birth and adoptive families was not entirely absent from their reasoning. When reasoning about group identity, the majority of children judged that a child born to Vezo parents but raised by Karany would grow up to be Vezo (birth parent judgment) and that a child born to Vezo parents but raised by Masikoro would grow up to be Masikoro (adoptive parent judgment).

One possible source of children's judgments about Vezo and Karany group identities is the analogy to species kinds, an analogy which could have been triggered by the stable morphological differences between Vezo and Karany people (see Atran, 1990). Several studies have established that in many different cultural contexts children as young as 4 years of age naturalize and essentialize animal species, that is, they understand that baby ducks hatch from the eggs laid by ducks, that they will always be ducks and that they will grow up to have the properties of ducks (see Atran et al., 2001; Gelman & Wellman, 1991; Horobin, 1997; Johnson & Solomon, 1997; Medin & Atran, in press, Sousa et al., 2002). The hypothesis that those children who judged that a baby born of Vezo parents would be Vezo even if raised by Karany parents were recruiting their understanding of animal species logically requires that Vezo children resemble their counterparts around the world in their knowledge of what determines species kind. Study 4 tests this hypothesis, using a duck–chicken "adoption" scenario adapted from Johnson and Solomon (1997). This Study also seeks to add to the already existing evidence that a naturalized understanding of species fixation emerges early in development under conditions of widely varying cultural input.

As noted in the Introduction, there are two ways of predicting the properties of an individual, human or animal. The first one is to derive them from kind membership. The inductive potential of species kind membership allows one to predict that an animal of a certain kind will have the properties that are kind dependent: properties such as the five fingers of a human hand, the soft curly fur and the "baaa" of a sheep, the stripes and the roar of a tiger. Therefore, success in predicting that an individual's kind identity and its kind-dependent properties are determined by birth parentage, while important, does not require an understanding of the mechanism of biological inheritance. All it requires is an essentialist construal of species kind and an understanding that babies resemble their parents (i.e., offspring resemble their *birth* parents simply because these are the *first* parents, and once kind is fixed, it remains constant throughout an individual's existence).

Obviously, not all of an individual's properties can be predicted from kind membership, as, for example, Jerry's brown hair or Alex's blond hair, and Mary's ignorance of poetry or Joyce's encyclopaedic knowledge of it. Success in predicting which of these properties an individual will have does require an understanding of the mechanism of biological inheritance. And this is why, if we wish to establish whether children have an understanding of biological inheritance, we must ask, as we have done in Study 2, whether they understand that Jerry's brown hair or Alex's blond hair are causally related to their birth parentage, whereas Mary's ignorance or Joyce's knowledge of poetry are not, and, in the case of animals, whether children differentiate between the biological inheritance of kind-neutral bodily properties (e.g., having one foot more yellow than the other) and the acquisition of knowledge-based properties through practice and habituation (e.g., knowing the place where rice is kept in the owner's house).

Atran et al. (2001) have criticized this diagnostic measure, pointing out that in some cultural contexts people may deny that animals are capable of learning. We agree that this is a distinct possibility among Vezo adults (see Astuti, 2000b, for ethnographic data concerning the sharp distinction Vezo draw between humans and other animals), and for this reason we have included an adult sample in Study 4 as well. If Vezo adults reject the notion that individual ducks and chickens are capable of knowing or remembering previously unknown facts, they might either assume that all the probed knowledge-based properties are kind dependent, in which case we would expect a Birth Parent Bias pattern (i.e., if mother duck knows X, it must mean that all ducks know X, and therefore the baby duck will also grow up to know X), or they might decide idiosyncratically whether a certain knowledge-based property is kind-dependent or not, in which case we would expect a Mixed pattern (e.g., the baby duck will not know how to do Y because doing Y is not something that ducks do, but it will know X because it is in ducks' nature to know X). By contrast, if Vezo adults accept the possibility that ducks and chickens learn from experience, they should differentiate between bodily and knowledge-based properties as they did in Study 1, in which case we would expect a Differentiated pattern.

In the case of Vezo children, we expect that, like the children who have been tested in other cultural contexts, they will succeed in identifying the species identity of a bird whose egg was laid by a duck but was sat upon and raised by a chicken (and vice versa). However, we do not expect them to differentiate their resemblance judgments on individual properties. In their animal adoption study, Johnson and Solomon (1997) found that North American children do not show evidence of a differentiated understanding of trait transmission in the animal context any earlier than they do in the human context. We expect to replicate this finding. That is, we predict that 6- to 13-year-olds will not differentiate bodily from knowledge-based properties in their resemblance judgments in the animal adoption scenario, just as they failed to do in the human adoption scenarios in Study 2.

The present Study has some important methodological implications. The procedure mirrors exactly that of Study 2. The scenarios are equally complex, and participants were asked several resemblance questions concerning individual properties before they were asked about species identity. Thus, if the younger participants succeed in Study 4, we can be sure that task demands and the unfamiliar testing procedure alone did not defeat our unschooled Vezo children.

METHOD

Participants

Nineteen Vezo children, 8 girls and 11 boys (mean age = 10 years, range = 6–13 years), and 15 adults, 9 women and 6 men (mean age = 35 years, range 22–60 years), took part in Study 4. Some of the children were interviewed in Lovobe, the Vezo village immediately south of Betania. None of the children had taken part in a previous study. Eight of the adults who had previously taken part in Study 1 were chosen randomly to participate in the present study. Preliminary analyses revealed no differences between adults who had and those who had not taken part in previous studies, so their data were collapsed. Participants were interviewed individually and in return received a small sum of money.

Procedure

The design of the animal adoption task used in Study 4 was almost identical to that of the human adoption tasks. Participants were told a cross-species adoption story, almost a direct translation of that used in Johnson and Solomon (1997), in which an egg laid by one animal (e.g., a duck) is placed into the nest of another animal (e.g., a hen), where it hatches and is raised by the second animal. The birth parent was said to have been sold off at the market in order to reduce the possibility that participants would assume that the offspring would have any further interaction with it (see Appendix A, Animal Adoption Scenario). Children were asked comprehension questions after the telling of the story. One child was unable to answer these questions correctly and was dropped from the study.

Participants were asked to judge resemblance on 8 feature pairs (see Appendix B, Table B6): 4 pairs of *Bodily traits* (e.g., red tongue/yellow tongue) and 4 pairs of *Knowledge-based traits* (e.g., knows where there is a hole in the fence from which to get out and look for food/does not know where there is a hole in the fence from which to get out and look for food). As the story was recited, children were shown photographs of a duck and a hen in which none of the properties probed by the task were visible. After completing the resemblance questions, participants were asked whether the little bird would be a duck or a chicken. Children were asked to justify their answers. Adults were not asked to provide such justifications as pilot testing had indicated that the answer was so obvious as to make the question tedious.

The study was balanced across participants for whether the bodily traits were presented before or after the knowledge-based traits, and for whether the duck or the hen was described as being the birth parent. Preliminary analysis indicated there to be no significant effects of these manipulations and so subsequent analyses collapsed across these factors.

RESULTS

Adults' Results

Species Identity Judgments

As expected, all 15 adults judged that the offspring would have the kind identity of its birth parent (see Figure 3). This is significantly different from the judgments made by adults in Study 1, in which 13% of the participants made a birth parent judgment on group identity in the Vezo–Masikoro scenario ($\chi^2(1) = 22.94$, $p < .001$), and 25% did so in the Vezo–Karany

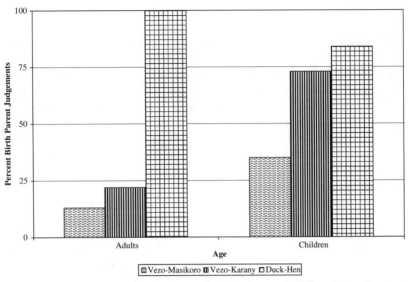

FIGURE 3. Percentage of adults in Studies 1 and 4, and children in Studies 2 and 4 judging the offspring to have the group or species identity of its birth parent in the Vezo–Masikoro, Vezo–Karany, and Chicken-Duck scenarios.

scenario ($\chi^2(1) = 18.36$, $p < .001$). Vezo adults, in other words, did not extend their performative theory about the determination of human group identity to their reasoning about animal species identity. This is hardly surprising, given their differentiated understanding of biological inheritance revealed in Study 1.

Resemblance Judgments for Individual Properties

Participants' judgments were characterized according to the same pattern categories as had been used in the human adoption studies, with Knowledge-based traits used in place of Beliefs. Thus, participants were said to have shown a *Differentiated Pattern* if they judged the bird to resemble its birth mother on at least three of the four Bodily traits and on none of the four Knowledge-based traits, or on all four Bodily traits and on not more than one of the four Knowledge-based traits ($p < .04$); they were said to have shown a *Birth Parent Bias* if they judged the bird to resemble its birth mother on at least 7 of the 8 features ($p < .04$), and to have shown an *Adoptive Parent Bias* if they judged the bird to resemble its adoptive mother on at least 7 of the 8 features ($p < .04$). As can be seen in Table 12, a majority of adults (53%) showed a Differentiated pattern, significantly more than

TABLE 12

PERCENTAGE OF PARTICIPANTS IN STUDY 4 SHOWING EACH RESEMBLANCE JUDGMENT
PATTERN, BY AGE

	Age	
Pattern	Adults	Children
Differentiated	53	16
Birth	13	42
Adoptive	0	16
Mixed	34	26

would be expected by chance ($p < .001$). Thirteen percent of adults provided Birth Parent Bias patterns, as would be expected if they interpreted
the knowledge-based properties to be species-dependent. The rest (34%)
provided Mixed patterns in which bodily traits were predicted on the basis
of birth parentage, whereas judgements on knowledge-based properties
were made idiosyncratically.

The differentiation of the two types of traits was seen not only in the
high proportion of differentiated patterns, but also in the group means for
the trait types (see Table 13). All adult participants judged that the bird
would resemble its birth mother on all bodily traits. In contrast, for only
32% of the knowledge-based traits did adults judge that the baby would end
up resembling the birth mother. Overall, adults reasoned about the inter-
generational transmission of properties in the case of animals as they had
for humans, contrary to the hypothesis that they might consider animals
incapable of learning. Nonetheless, details of our results give partial support to that hypothesis: first, deviations from the canonical differentiated
pattern always involved judgments that the bird would resemble its birth
mother in the knowledge-based properties; and second, as we shall see
below, the view that ducks and chickens are incapable of learning was
sometimes explicitly articulated in the justifications for these birth mother
resemblance judgments.

TABLE 13

MEAN PERCENTAGE OF ADULTS' AND CHILDREN'S STUDY 4 BIRTH PARENT RESEMBLANCE
JUDGMENTS FOR EACH TYPE OF TRAIT IN STUDY 4

	Age	
Trait type	Adults	Children
Bodily	100	72
Knowledge-based	32	54

Justifications

When asked whether a bird hatched from the egg of a duck would be a duck or a chicken, Vezo adults were bemused. Only one adult offered a justification for this obvious judgment ("It was a chicken because it came out of a chicken's egg"). Similarly, as we saw above, adults judged that the baby bird would have the bodily properties of its birth mother 100% of the time, but they never offered a justification for these judgments. The answers must have seemed too obvious to warrant elaboration.

By contrast, adults offered a total of 19 justifications for their resemblance judgments on knowledge-based properties, with 73% of the adults producing at least one justification (a mean of 1.3 justifications per participant). All of the six justifications given in support of an adoptive judgment were coded as Nurture, accounting for 32% of all justifications given (e.g., "It will learn from the duck where the food is kept and will steal it"). By contrast, the 13 justifications given by participants who judged that the little bird would resemble its birth mother were coded either as Kind (47% of all justifications), Origins (16% of all justifications), or Like Birth Parent (5% of all justifications). As in the human scenarios, adults were significantly more likely to comment spontaneously on their judgments when they deviated from the canonical pattern than when they were consistent with it. That is, they offered justifications 15% of the time they judged that the bird would resemble its adoptive mother on knowledge-based properties, as opposed to 68% of the time they judged that the bird would resemble its birth mother, $\chi^2(1) = 17.36, p < .001$.

The Kind justifications are of particular interest here. They invoked the intrinsic nature of the chicken or the duck as explanation for the baby bird's development of a certain property, irrespective of the bird's nurturing environment (e.g., "The bird will be like its birth mother because it is the way of being of ducks that they don't find holes in fences, that they don't look for a way out."). They thus express the view that different animal species have different innate potentials, or different instincts that guide their species-specific behaviors. Note that we intentionally chose knowledge-based properties which, in the piloting of the study, had not been judged to be species typical, and most informants were happy to treat them as such. However, a third of the time, adult participants interpreted these properties to be more typical of either ducks or chickens. The fact that there was no consensus as to which trait was typical of either bird species makes it even more remarkable that such traits nonetheless were associated with essentialist reasoning for some of the participants.

In most cases, this reasoning strategy was accompanied by the denial that animals are capable of learning. In the debriefing of the task, participants who had made at least one birth judgment for knowledge-based properties were asked whether they thought that a chicken or a duck could ever learn a certain behavior (e.g., how to steal rice or find a hole in the fence). Of the 5 adults who offered Kind justifications, 4 asserted that the bird would not be able to learn anything. Some of these participants acknowledged that the bird can know things, but that "it will not have learnt them" while others asserted that "chickens have no thoughts" and that "birds can't learn anything, they don't know anything." We can therefore conclude that about a third of the adult participants have integrated the view that an animal's innate potential determines its species-specific behavior with the view that ducks and chickens—unlike people—are incapable of learning through imitation, practice, and habituation.

In sum, as expected, adults reasoned in an explicitly essentialist manner about animals' species identity and about some animal properties. Adults overall also extended to animals their differentiated understanding of how individual human traits are acquired, though a minority of participants did consider some of the knowledge-based properties probed by our task to be part of the animals' innate potential rather than something that is learned. Both of these findings are significant, as they show that Vezo adults do have access to an essentialist mode of reasoning about identity and about properties. The fact that they did not deploy such essentialist reasoning when considering contrasting human groups is therefore all the more striking.

Children's Results

Species Identity Judgments

Vezo children were also overwhelmingly more likely to judge that the offspring would have the same kind identity of its birth mother than of its adoptive mother (see Figure 3). The proportion of children (84%) who did so is not significantly different from that of adults. Again like adults, children in the animal task were significantly more likely to make birth parent identity judgments than were those children who participated in the Vezo–Masikoro task, in which only 35% judged that the adopted boy would be the kind of his birth parents, $\chi^2(1) = 9.75, p < .005$.

Resemblance Judgments for Individual Properties

Most children failed to differentiate the two classes of mechanisms for trait transmission on the animal adoption task (see Table 12), just as a comparable proportion had failed to show a Differentiated pattern on the human adoption tasks in Study 2 (see Table 6). The children in this study were

97

also not significantly more likely to show a Birth Parent Bias pattern than were the children in Study 2.

Notably, children's resemblance judgments on bodily traits and beliefs for humans in Study 2 were not significantly different from children's judgments on bodily traits and knowledge-based traits for animals in Study 4. Moreover, children's judgments on knowledge-based traits did not differ significantly from chance. Given that children showed no understanding of the role of learning, practice and habituation in humans, it should not be surprising that they failed to do so in animals.

As can be seen in Table 13, children reasoned about the transmission of an animal's individual traits differently than the adults. A 2×2 repeated-measures ANOVA, crossing the 2 levels of the between-subjects factor of Age (children vs. adults) with the 2 levels of the within-subjects factor of Trait (bodily vs. knowledge-based traits) indicated that there was a main effect of trait, $F(1, 32) = 41.09$, $p < .001$, and a significant interaction of age by trait, $F(1, 32) = 13.60$, $p < .001$, on the number of birth parent resemblance judgments. Post hoc analyses show that this interaction is due to the fact that children were significantly less likely than the adults to give birth judgments for bodily traits ($t(32) = 2.38$, $p < .03$) and significantly more likely than the adults to give birth judgments for knowledge-based traits ($t(32) = 1.83$, $p < .04$).

There was one respect in which children as a group performed better on individual kind-neutral animal traits than they did on individual group-neutral human traits in Study 2. As can be seen in Table 13, children in the present study judged that the baby bird would have the bodily features of the birth mother 72% of the time, significantly more than chance, $t(18) = 2.18$, $p < .03$. This finding is consistent with two possible interpretations: first, children understand that animal kind is fixed at birth, and reason about the bird's bodily properties as if they were kind typical and therefore fixed by kind (e.g., the color of a bird's tongue could be a kind-dependent morphological feature rather than an idiosyncratic property of the individual); or, second, children are beginning to understand the biological inheritance of bodily features.

Justifications

Children's overall performance in the animal adoption task should allay methodological concerns about the viability of our protocol. While it is certainly true that our tasks required Vezo children to interact with the researcher in a manner to which they were not accustomed, the justifications they provided in the course of the animal task indicate that they were not defeated by the procedure. Seventy-four percent of Vezo children justified

98

their species identity judgments. Although none of the children who made an adoptive judgment produced a justification, 88% of the children who made a birth judgment did so. Of these justifications, 50% were coded as Origins, 28% were coded as Generated or Like Birth Parent, 7% as Kind, and the remaining 14% were coded as Other. All of the Origins justifications explicitly mentioned the egg which had been laid by either duck or hen as the reason why the bird was of the same species as its birth mother (e.g., "it will be a chicken because the hen laid the egg and the duck only sat on it" or "the bird will be a chicken because the hen brought it out, it came from the hen's egg"). These children, half of those providing justifications, successfully recruited their knowledge of a causal mechanism that goes beyond mere resemblance to parents in explaining why offspring are of the same species kind as their birth parent.

Recall that in the human adoption scenarios presented in Study 2, the only children who had offered Origins justifications as explicit as those offered in the present study were those who were explaining their judgment that the boy would be Vezo or Karany like his birth father (e.g., "because he is Karany on his father's side, he came from the tummy of his [father's] wife, he is white, and he is Karany"). This is consistent with the claim that children's birth kind judgments in the animal task and their birth group identity judgments in the Vezo–Karany task were motivated by a similar appreciation of the role of origins and procreation in determining kind in both animals and people.

Children in Study 4 demonstrated a greater causal understanding of the mechanisms involved in the transmission of an individual's properties than did children in Study 2, as revealed by the fact that, as already noted, their judgements on bodily properties differed from chance, and by their justifications. A total of 30 justifications of property judgments were produced by 84% of the children in this study, for an average of 1.6 per participant. Of all the justifications produced, 37% were coded as Origins, 23% as Nurture, 3% as Kind, 10% as Like Birth Parent or Generated, 10% as Like Adoptive Parent or Raised, and 17% as Other.

Children in the animal task provided a higher proportion of causally informative justifications for their judgments on individual properties than did those in the human task (60% as compared to 32%), with 67% of children ever giving such a causal justification in Study 4 as opposed to 18% of the children in Study 2, significantly more than would be expected by chance. Moreover, children in the animal task gave Origins justifications for 12% of their birth judgments on individual properties, significantly more than the 0.2% of such justifications given for birth judgments in the human task, $\chi^2(1) = 45.28, p < .001$. Unlike the Origins justifications offered in the human task, more than half of those produced on the animal task contained a reference to either the offspring's "line of descent," to the egg, or to the fact that the birth mother is the one "who brought the bird out into the world." We saw earlier that adults gave explicit Kind justifications for their birth judgments on individual properties 69% of the time, indicating that they inferred the properties from species kind. Unlike adults, children gave Kind justifications only 5% of the time. Of course, children's Origins justifications may have been providing one important link in the same chain of reasoning, but we have no direct evidence that this is so.

One might argue that the reason children performed better in the animal task is not that they know more about animals than about humans, but that they know more about mothers than about fathers. Indeed, Springer (1995, 1999) proposed that North American children's realization that babies grow inside their mothers is a crucial step towards the elaboration of a biological (as opposed to social) conception of how offspring come to resemble their parents. One could argue that the reason Vezo children were so less likely to explicitly invoke birth as the mechanism responsible for the transmission of bodily trait in our human task than in our animal task is that they are not yet aware of the role that *fathers* play in reproduction. To test this hypothesis, we ran a version of the Vezo–Vezo adoption task in which the adopted child was a girl, and the birth and adoptive parents were mothers. Nineteen children, 10 boys and 9 girls aged 6–13, participated in this study. In accordance with the findings of a similar study with North American children (Solomon et al., 1996), we found that Vezo children's responses (overall patterns of judgments and overall percent of birth judgments) were not significantly different from those of the children who participated in Study 2.

In sum, when children were asked to justify their birth judgments on animal species identity, they were able to invoke the bird's birth origins and to refer explicitly to relevant aspects of the reproductive process. The only other instance when children were so confident in their judgments and so articulate in their justifications was when they answered the group identity question in the Vezo–Karany task. In the animal task, children were also more likely than in Study 2 to invoke the animal's origins to explain why it comes to have the same individual properties as its birth mother.

DISCUSSION

As expected, adults demonstrated a naturalized and essentialized understanding of species kind, both in their judgments and justifications. In addition, they recruited their differentiated understanding of birth-mediated and nurture-based processes of trait determination to reason about the transmission of kind-neutral properties from parents to offspring. Nonetheless, it is evident that some of the adults occasionally deployed a different reasoning strategy: Not only they construed some of the properties probed by our task as kind dependent and therefore intrinsic to the baby bird, but they also argued that animals such as chickens and ducks are unable to acquire any knowledge or skill that is not intrinsic to their species. In such cases, the mechanisms that mediate the acquisition of beliefs and skills in humans—teaching, practice, imitation—were not thought to apply to animals.

The findings about children are of particular importance. Methodologically, the results indicate that Vezo children are up to this task, in spite of being unschooled and not used to being questioned systematically by adults. Theoretically, these data establish that an understanding of the role of birth parentage in determining animal kind is available as an analogical base for extension to human group identity. Also, these data extend those of Atran et al. (2001), Gelman and Wellman (1991), Johnson and Solomon (1997), Medin and Atran (in press), Sousa et al. (2002) to yet another cultural context. In all cultural contexts studied so far, young children have been shown to understand the role of birth parentage in fixing species kind. In this case, therefore, we find supporting evidence for the Innate Conceptual Content hypothesis: cross-cultural universality in the adult state plus early acquisition in the face of culturally variable input. In Chapter VI, where we will consider side by side the three patterns of development we have explored in this monograph—the understanding of the determination of species kind, of human group identity, and of species/group-neutral properties—we will discuss the merits and limitations of the Innate Conceptual Content hypothesis. We will then contrast it with an alternative account of the nature of the innate constraints on learning in this domain (the Constrained Conceptual Construction hypothesis).

Here we limit ourselves to highlight three important aspects of the children's data. First, these data overall confirm those of Johnson and Solomon (1997) concerning the much earlier emergence of the understanding of the role of birth parentage in the fixation of species kind than of the role of birth parentage in the transmission of within-species individual traits. Vezo children were almost as undifferentiated in their projection of family resemblance of bodily vs. knowledge-based traits in this animal adoption scenario as they were in the human case, and in this they differed from the adults with respect to both their birth parent resemblance judgments on bodily traits and their adoptive parent judgments on knowledge-based traits. This finding is consistent with the suggestion that the birth parent resemblance judgments on kind may have been driven by children's essentialist construal of animal species, which posits that kind identity must remain constant throughout an individual's existence. Thus, the reason children predicted that the baby bird was a duck like its birth mother may not have been that they have a concept of *innate potential*; rather, the baby is a duck because it must have already been a duck when it was born.

Second, children's justifications show that their understanding of the role of birth parentage in determining species kind goes beyond a mere understanding of family resemblance; half of the children explicitly mentioned the role of the mother in generating the egg. Still, this understanding falls short of a full understanding of biological inheritance: the child could be reasoning, as Springer (1995) suggested, that the birth mother is the only animal who could have any causal effect on the baby. We shall return to this proposal in the General Discussion.

Third, the species adoption study suggested the first nascent understanding of biological inheritance in a stronger sense, one in which offspring are understood to get a template from their birth parents, which determines innate potential with respect to individual bodily traits. This understanding has not reached the adult consolidated state even by age 13, but both in the non-random resemblance judgements for individual bodily traits and in the justifications for these judgments, we see some evidence that children are beginning to work out *why* being born of a duck makes a baby a duck.

In Chapter IV we argued that it is in the process of understanding the adult performative theory of Vezo identity that Vezo adolescents come to differentiate biological inheritance from social mechanisms of trait transmission. Chapter V underscores that, as they enter adolescence, Vezo children already have access to one important piece of the differentiation—an understanding that birth parentage fixes species kind, even if they have not yet fully worked out why this is so.

VI. GENERAL DISCUSSION

In the two domains that have been the subject of our studies, folk-biology and folksociology, we have found evidence *both* for constrained development and for extended processes of conceptual construction. Many questions remain concerning the nature of the constraints and the details of the constructive processes. We conclude our *Monograph* with a discussion of these issues, beginning with the domain of folkbiology. We believe our findings and the discussion that follows to be of equal significance to both psychologists and anthropologists. However, we especially address the last section of this chapter to anthropologists.

FOLKBIOLOGY: ON UNDERSTANDING WHY DUCKS HAVE BABY DUCKS

In the introduction to this *Monograph*, we laid out two predictions of the Innate Conceptual Content hypothesis: cross-cultural universality in adult representations and early emergence in development. Our data on the representations of species as naturalized (i.e., as inherited from birth parents) and essentialized (i.e., as having rich inductive potential) would seem to give some support to both these predictions.

Even the youngest Vezo children we were able to test (age 6) succeeded in the animal adoption task: they predicted that a bird that emerges from an egg laid by a duck will be a duck, even if hatched and raised by a chicken. In this regard, Vezo children resemble those (even younger children) who have been tested on this task in a number of other cultural contexts (un-schooled Yukatek Maya children in Mexico, Atran et al., 2001; middle-class children in Brazil, Sousa et al., 2002; urban and rural, Native American and majority lower- and middle-class children in the United States, Johnson & Solomon, 1997, Medin & Atran, in press). Moreover, in all of these cultural venues, adults also shared the same intuitions.

The evidence therefore indicates that the knowledge that species kind is fixed at birth arises relatively early in development, continues to articulate adult representations, and appears to be cross-culturally universal. Crucially, this knowledge emerges under widely divergent conditions of input (e.g., Vezo children have direct experience with animal reproduction, whereas North American children have limited exposure to it), as would be expected if its acquisition were constrained by cognitive capacities that the child brings to the task of conceptual development. We accept this conclusion. The nature of these constraints, however, remains very much an open question.

Two quite different possibilities are consistent with the available data. The first (the Innate Conceptual Content hypothesis) is that the child is endowed with innate knowledge of species kinds, in which kind membership is both naturalized and essentialized. That is, the child assumes animal species to have rich inductive potential and expects species kind to be fixed by biologically relevant mechanisms. In other words, the child is equipped with a folkbiological module, as Medin and Atran (Atran, 1998; Medin & Atran, in press) suggest.

The second possibility (the Constrained Conceptual Construction hypothesis) is that the child is endowed with powerful but domain-general theory-building mechanisms that underlie the capacity to recognize and essentialize natural kinds and to analyze and construct causal explanatory theories of the essential features of such kinds. However, each child must discover anew which kinds in the world are natural kinds, including biological kinds, and must construct theory-specific causal mechanisms for the domain of biology (see Carey, 1985, 1999, and Gelman, 2003, for a defense of this view). One such biological mechanism is the inheritance of species kind.

Following this second line of reasoning, Springer (1995, 1999) has sketched the process through which children might construct a biological understanding of inheritance, which we elaborate here, drawing also from Gelman's analysis (2003). The rich inductive potential of animal kinds is amply available to young children, who learn many properties that can be reliably predicted from kind membership. In addition, parents often use generics in talking about animal kinds. North American parents make such statements as "dogs can be vicious; lions hunt and eat antelopes; salmon are delicious to eat," and Vezo parents say such things as "mackerel are very smart and are not fooled by poorly prepared bait; chameleons have ugly faces; geckoes are useful because they eat mosquitoes"). These cues enable the child to identify species kinds as natural kinds, that is, as falling within the scope of psychological essentialist reasoning (Medin & Ortony, 1989).

Significantly, the identification of species kinds as natural kinds entails analyzing them as "substance sortals" (Carey & Xu, 1999): kinds that trace identity throughout the existence of an individual and for which there are hidden, unknown causal processes that explain their existence and surface properties. In turn, identification of species kinds as substance sortals leads children to focus on origins—on the onset of that identity that will persist through time. As Springer pointed out, once children have represented "duck" as a substance sortal, they know that any individual duck is a duck throughout its whole existence. Moreover, as soon as children learn about the facts of birth, they will also know that the duck's existence begins before birth (i.e., the animal existed inside the egg that grew in the mother's tummy). At this point, domain-general assumptions about causal processes (e.g., that causes act locally and by proximity) may lead children to realize that the kind of the mother determines the kind of the baby growing inside her. Springer (1995) provided evidence for this analysis, showing that only children who knew that babies grow inside their mothers solved certain switched at birth tasks, and that teaching uninformed children the facts of birth led them to succeed where they had previously failed (but see Solomon & Johnson, 2000, and Williams & Affleck, 1999 for qualifications of this finding). On this account, it is entirely possible that the understanding of the fixation of animal kind observed universally by ages 4–6 years does not reflect innate knowledge with specifically biological content, but rather is the result of a process of learning and discovery that is constrained by powerful domain-general theory-building capacities and is supported by the testimony that children receive and use to make sense of the world.

The two possibilities outlined above are importantly different: one posits innate conceptual constraints with biological content (i.e., the concepts *animal*, *species*, and *biological inheritance*), whereas the other posits powerful domain-general constraints on theory building (the capacity for causal analysis, a commitment to psychological essentialism, the capacity to recognize natural kinds). However, they are also importantly similar—by comparison with the Unconstrained Learning hypothesis—insofar as the output of the developmental process is, by ages 4–6, a biological theory of animal species that further constrains conceptual development.

We consider the exact nature of the constraints that support the early naturalization and essentialization of species kind in all cultural contexts studied to date to be an open question. Data in support of the Constrained Conceptual Construction hypothesis would include within-child consistency in understanding animals as living things, death as the breakdown of the bodily machine, and birth parentage as determining species kind (see Slaughter & Lyons, 2003; Solomon & Johnson, 2000). Insofar as 3-year-olds truly lack these concepts, and insofar as these concepts are mutually constructed in the course of development, the Constrained Conceptual Construction hypothesis would be favored. Insofar as *young* preschool children are shown to possess these concepts in a variety of different cultural contexts, and to acquire them independently from other aspects of folkbiological knowledge, the Innate Conceptual Content hypothesis would be favored instead.

105

Although we believe both possibilities to be open, we favor the Constrained Conceptual Construction hypothesis for several reasons. First, as mentioned in the Introduction, there is evidence that North American 4–6-year-olds do not possess a robust understanding of biological inheritance even in the case of species kind fixation (see Keil's 1989 transformation and discovery studies). Second, North American children do not construct other biological concepts (e.g., *living thing*, *death*) until around age 5 or 6 (Slaughter et al., 1999), while they cannot represent animal species as *living things* until they have created a vitalist biology at the end of the preschool years (Inagaki & Hatano, 2002). Third, several studies (reviewed in the Introduction) have shown that young children do not differentiate biological inheritance from social learning mechanisms of inter-generational trait transmission until around age 6 or 7 (in the North American samples) or until adolescence or even later (in the Tamil, Zafimaniry and Vezo samples). This is exactly what we would expect if children had an initial understanding that ducks can only ever be ducks and have baby ducks, while not yet fully understanding the deeper biological reason for why this is so. As Johnson and Solomon (1997) put it, children can understand that dogs have baby dogs before they grasp that the baby is a dog *because* its birth parent were dogs. Only when children understand that birth parents pass on to their offspring the potential to become a dog, and the potential to develop certain dog-like properties, have they fully fleshed out their understanding of this biological process.

The Constrained Conceptual Construction hypothesis makes sense of *both* aspects of the results from these cross-cultural studies: the early emergence of a naturalized and essentialized construal of species kind and the protracted process by which children come to understand that some of an individual's traits are determined by biological inheritance and some by learning, teaching, and habituation. On this story, preschool children identify animal species as natural kinds, attend to their origins before birth, and thus realize that birth parentage determines species kind. Then, over the next several years, they construct an understanding of how people and animals come to have their individual properties. This will require them to differente biological inheritance from socially mediated learning.

FOLKBIOLOGY: ON UNDERSTANDING A CRUCIAL DIFFERENCE

The results of our within-species adoption tasks paint a very different picture concerning innate constraints on the developmental process. We found cross-cultural convergence in the adults' understanding of biological inheritance—contrary to the prediction of the Unconstrained Learning hypothesis—but we did not observe the early emergence and universal developmental trajectory predicted by the Innate Conceptual Content hypothesis.

In our adoption tasks, Vezo adults systematically differentiated between two causal mechanisms for the inter-generational transmission of different kinds of properties. Like North American adults, they held the view that bodily properties are inherited through links of filiation (hence the child's resemblance to the birth parent), and that beliefs and skills are transmitted through learning and teaching (hence the child's resemblance to the adoptive parent). Vezo adults showed a remarkable consistency in their reasoning irrespective of whether the adoption was said to have taken place among Vezo people or between Vezo and Masikoro or Karany families, whether it was said to have taken place among unrelated people or among close relatives, or whether our questions targeted the transmission of properties from father to son or from mother to daughter (as in Astuti et al., in preparation). We shall have more to say about the significance of this finding in the final section.

Vezo children aged 6 to 13, however, did not differentiate between birth or adoptive parentage or between family resemblance on bodily traits and family resemblance on beliefs and skills. This failure was repeatedly observed in separate scenarios in Study 2, irrespective of whether the traits were group neutral (e.g., the shape of the ears, the ability to make ropes, or beliefs such as how many teeth chameleons have) or group typical (e.g., skin color, occupational skills, and customary beliefs). The same failure was also observed in the animal adoption scenario of Study 4. This robust finding is not simply the result of unrealistic task demands. Consider that both in the species adoption task and in the Vezo–Karany task children were able to coordinate consistently and systematically their species- and group-identity judgments and justifications. This shows that, after a long series of questions, the children were still with us.

Our results replicate the findings of Bloch et al. (2001) among the Zafimaniry and those of Mahalingham (1998) in India, both of which showed that it was not until adolescence or later that the majority of participants succeeded on this task. They are also consistent with the finding that the great majority of North American and European children do not differentiate biological inheritance from social learning before the age of 6–7 (Gimenez & Harris, 2002; Solomon, 2002; Solomon et al., 1996; Springer, 1996; Springer & Keil, 1989; Weissman & Kalish, 1999; Williams & Affleck, 1999). We take these data as evidence against the claim that preschool children have a *biological* understanding of family resemblance (e.g., Atran et al., 2001; Hirschfeld, 1996). And this, in turn, we take as a challenge to the hypothesis that concepts such as *biological inheritance*, *birth parentage*, *innate potential* are part of children's innate conceptual repertoire.

Consistent with this conclusion is the finding that differences in input conditions have a dramatic influence on the emergence of these concepts, as shown by the fact that Vezo children take so much longer than their North American counterparts to construct a differentiated understanding of family resemblance. As we discussed in Chapter IV, there are a number of possible reasons for this developmental difference, among them the fact that Vezo children are virtually unschooled, and that they are actively discouraged from asking questions and from engaging in analytical reasoning. Moreover, as reported in the Introduction, Vezo children receive testimony that systematically confounds the distinction between the effects of birth and nurture (e.g., babies resemble people befriended or disliked by their mothers) so that their parents, in effect, train them *not* to see that people who are biologically related resemble one another. Indeed, in the face of such systematic input, it is a remarkable testimony to Vezo children's theory-building capacities that by adolescence they construct the same differentiated understanding of inter-generational trait transmission that has been documented in India, Europe, and the U.S.

Apart from indicating that this constructive process takes considerably longer in Madagascar than it does in North America, our data also suggest that the cultural environment that scaffolds the conceptual development of Vezo children may exert some influence on the specific steps that they take towards constructing and consolidating a differentiated understanding of family resemblance.

There are likely to be several inputs into children's constructive process, some of which we do not expect to vary across cultural contexts. For example, representations of intentional agents ought to be part of the relevant input, as these are implicated in the understanding of teaching and learning. The cross-cultural universality of theory of mind, which would support such representations, has not been the focus of this *Monograph* (see Avis & Harris, 1991), but given the evidence for conceptual representations of intentional agents in preverbal infants (Csibra et al., 1999; Gergely et al. 1995; Gopnik & Meltzoff, 1997; Johnson, Slaughter, & Carey, 1998; Johnson, 2000; Woodward, 1998), conceptual content in this domain may be innately specified. Another source of input is the understanding of the biological determination of animal kinds. As shown in Study 4, Vezo children are in the midst of deepening their understanding that birth parentage determines species kind, as they begin to recognize that something inherited from birth parents also determines species-specific somatic traits and some somatic traits that vary within species. As discussed above, whether this understanding is in turn the result of innate conceptual content constraints or of a constrained process of construction is still open to debate. What the existing cross-cultural evidence reveals, however, is the remarkable uniformity in the emergence of this understanding.

Granted these similarities, we were able to identify one source of the constructive process that appears to be specific to the cultural environment

108

in which Vezo children grow up. By looking at those adolescents who were still in the throes of working out a fully differentiated understanding of the causal role of birth parentage and social learning in the transmission of an individual's properties, we found that they first seemed to gain their conceptual purchase on this differentiation through an understanding of the acquisition of skills. Notwithstanding that children, in fact, tend to share the skills of their birth parents who commonly raise them, even those adolescents who showed an overall Mixed pattern of judgments (and hence did not have a fully differentiated understanding of the transmission of an individual's properties) had come to realize that skills are learned, not inherited. Similarly, they knew that customs, religious beliefs, and occupational specializations are acquired through practice and habituation, rather than by descent. It should not be surprising that Vezo adolescents begin by reflecting on, and understanding the transmission of skills and customary "ways of doing things", because these are the properties that are said to determine a person's group identity. If there is one thing that is afforded by the Vezo cultural environment, by Vezo adults' testimony, it is the notion that people learn, get used to, and take on the livelihood, skills, and customs of the place where they live. It is likely that Vezo adolescents find it particularly easy to recruit this notion in theory building.

We do not know whether this is a universal pattern of development, but we suggest that probably it is not. It is likely that in other cultural contexts, children's attention is drawn to the transmission of other properties. For example, in societies where the inheritance of a certain kind of blood or of a certain kind of bones is taken to mediate people's affiliation to specific descent or ethnic groups, children may come to realize the significance of birth origins in the transmission of bodily traits before they understand the role of learning and habituation in the acquisition of skills. This, of course, is an empirical question, that could be answered with more comparative work.

FOLKSOCIOLOGY: ON UNDERSTANDING WHAT KIND OF PEOPLE THEY ARE

Our data on how Vezo children learn the adult performative theory of group identity present us with yet another developmental trajectory. In this case, we have found evidence of early emerging constraints on conceptual development, which are transcended as a result of a protracted process of cultural construction.

As before, we shall start with the adult end-state: Vezo adults' performance in our across-group adoption scenarios supported Astuti's (1995a, 1995b) ethnographically based claim that Vezo define group identity in terms of the occupational activities that people perform, the customary practices they follow, and the religious beliefs they hold, rather than in terms of their birth origins and ancestral roots. Vezo adults explicitly and often apply this way of reasoning to Vezo children (and how it is that they become Vezo) or to the neighboring Masikoro (and how it is that they could become Vezo). Crucially, our adult informants also extended their performative way of categorizing people to the Karany: they reasoned that a child born of Vezo parents and adopted by Karany parents would become Karany (or vice versa). In keeping with their differentiated understanding of family resemblance, adults judged that the adopted child would have the same skin color and hair type as his birth parents, but that he would learn how to behave, what to believe, and how to earn a living from his adoptive parents. Because of these acquired properties, they judged that he would have the same group identity as his adoptive parents, be they Vezo or Karany.

It is of consequence that Vezo adults did *not* extend their performative theory of identity to animal species. This finding underscores the fact that Vezo adults categorically differentiate between human groups and animal species, and that they do not treat the former as if they were natural biological kinds. Although we did not test them on a task involving an adoption across human and non-human animal species, Vezo adults' performance in the species adoption task (plus their understanding of biological inheritance) makes it almost certain that they would construe humans qua humans as a natural kind. Like chickens and ducks, humans are what they were born to be (although, unlike chickens and ducks, they may need other humans to realize their potential humanity; see Lambek, 1981, p. 150). However, the group identity of humans, as opposed to the species identity of humans, turns out to be determined by the culturally constituted environment in which people grow up, rather than by their innate potential for developing into certain kinds of people.

This finding challenges the Innate Conceptual Content hypothesis, which claims that, as a result of their evolutionary history, humans are bound to apprehend the social world as made up of distinct natural kinds. Like the ethnographic data (Astuti, 1995a, 1995b), our experimental data do not support either Hirschfeld's or Gil-White's hypothesis. Given the social, economic and cultural context of Madagascar, we chose the Karany—people of Indo-Pakistani descent, who are somatically, economically, and religiously distinct from the Vezo and do not inter-marry with them—as the most likely group to trigger Hirschfeld's Human Kind Competences or to prime Gil-White's hypothesized tendency to treat endogamous groups as if they were animal species. Our results strongly suggest that not all *adult* human minds are bound to partition the social world into naturalized human kinds. However, our data also suggest that, despite the cultural input they receive, the minds of Vezo *children* are inclined to do so.

A majority (14 of 20) of Vezo children judged that a child born to parents belonging to one group (the Vezo) and raised by parents belonging to another (the Karany) would be Vezo (or vice versa); in other words, they reasoned that people are what they were born to be. The relatively early emergence of this way of reasoning and, crucially, the fact that it is unsupported by—in fact, it flies in the face of—the cultural input that children receive about how one becomes Vezo, suggest that it may be constrained by cognitive capacities that the child brings to the task of making sense of the social world. To be sure, the group of people who are explicitly targeted by adult testimony are the Masikoro, not the Karany, but if learning to sail, to fish, and to participate in Vezo cultural practices is what makes one Vezo, then this should apply to all people. Indeed, this was the view expressed by our adult participants. The child's understanding, it would seem, derives from a source other than adult testimony, and the constraints under which it emerges are powerful enough to withstand that testimony, at least until adolescence.

This leads us to ask what these constraints might be. As before, there are two quite different answers to this question. On the one hand, children's reasoning about the Karany could reflect an innate system of knowledge that places content-rich constraints on the representations of human kinds (the Innate Conceptual Content hypothesis); on the other hand, this same reasoning could be the output of domain-general theory-building capacities (the Constrained Conceptual Construction hypothesis).

The first possibility, then, is that either Hirschfeld (1996) or Gil-White (2001) is right in claiming that reasoning about human kinds is constrained by an evolved mental disposition that delivers the concept *natural human kind*. On Hirschfeld's proposal, the Human Kind Competence would account for the fact that Vezo children naturalize *some* human kinds, while the political economy of the region would explain why the Karany (rather than the Masikoro) is the group that is in fact naturalized in this context (e.g., children may be sensitive to the fact that the interaction between Vezo and Karany is markedly hierarchical, as when Vezo approach Karany shops or offer their fish to Karany buyers). Gil-White's proposal is more problematic. He argues that endogamy is the crucial trigger that leads people to "mistake" ethnic groups for animal species, but it is not clear what kind of developmental account is implied by his claim. We know that Vezo *adults* do not make this "mistake," and it is unlikely that *children* as young as 6 would realize, and find salient, the fact that Vezo and Karany people do not intermarry (see Gelman, 2003, p. 304 for a similar point).

The second possibility is that children's reasoning reflects domain-general theory-building capacities. As described by students of the history of science (Gentner et al., 1997; Nersessian, 1992), the bootstrapping processes that lead to theory construction often involve analogical thinking. Children, as suggested by Atran (1990), may analogize human kinds to species kinds not because of some evolved tendency to do so (as Gil-White would have it), but because of the productive use of analogy in building explanatory understanding in general.

We consider both the Innate Conceptual Content hypothesis and the Constrained Conceptual Construction hypothesis still open, although, as before, we favor the latter one for some of the same reasons. First, our data did not support Hirschfeld's claim (1995, 1996) that even preschool children understand that skin color and other racial somatic markers are determined by birth parentage and that, therefore, kind identity is also thus determined; it was not until adolescence that Vezo participants had worked out the biological inheritance of skin color and hair type (see also Solomon, 2002). Given the pivotal role played by the early emergence of this understanding in Hirschfeld's overall argument, the fact that it takes Vezo children a laborious and drawn-out process to construct such an understanding militates against his proposal. By contrast, the finding that Vezo children understand that species kind is determined by birth parentage is certainly consistent with the Constrained Conceptual Construction hypothesis, because it indicates that children command the base domain for analogizing the difference between Vezo and Karany to a species difference. Similarly, the fact that children's justifications of their birth judgments in the Vezo–Karany and in the animal tasks were strikingly similar (they explicitly invoked the process of reproduction, e.g., the mother's tummy or the egg) is also consistent with the hypothesis that children were recruiting their understanding of the role of birth parentage in fixing animal kind when reasoning about the contrast between Vezo and Karany.

The proposal that children analogize human to species kinds needs an account of why this analogy is present for some human groups and not others. Recall that Vezo children tend to naturalize the difference between Vezo and Karany but not the difference between Vezo and Masikoro. A possible explanation for this finding is that, as suggested by Atran (1990, p. 78), "apparent morphological distinctions between human groups are easily (but not necessarily) conceived as apparent morphological distinctions between animal species." Quite simply, whereas marked and stable morphological differences exist between Vezo and Karany (e.g., skin color), none exist between Vezo and Masikoro. If morphological differences motivate the analogy between animal species and human groups, children should have no reasons to construe the Masikoro as a different species—and indeed they did not.

Other factors, however, may account for the naturalization of a human kind. Rothbart and Taylor (1992) suggested that social categories are often perceived more like natural kinds, despite the fact that they are more like human artifacts, because of their rich inductive potential. In the same way in which people expect the category "tiger" to be predictive of an almost infinite number of tiger properties, people assume that if a social category

112

has an almost infinite number of properties, then it must be of the tiger kind, that is, it must be a natural kind. Vezo, Masikoro, and Karany are inductively rich categories; hence, to label individuals as Vezo, Masikoro, or Karany is predictive of an almost infinite number of properties: where they live, their occupations, whether they are rich or poor, whether they are literate, what rituals they perform, their hairstyle, their demeanor, their clothes, their speech, their cuisine, and so on and so forth. True, it is likely that children are not aware of *all* the properties that are typical of Vezo, Masikoro, and Karany people, but they are certainly aware of the fact that these labels are predictive of *many* properties, and this may be enough for them to construe the groups as natural kinds. On this story, children would be expected to naturalize the Masikoro as well as the Karany, because both are equally inductively rich categories. The reason our children did not in fact naturalize the Masikoro could be that they have learned—rather, that they were learning—not to do so. In other words, were it not for the massive cultural input they receive, which specifically targets their immediate neighbors, children might have naturalized *both* Masikoro and Karany group identities.

There are thus two hypotheses concerning what may account for the analogy between animal species and human kinds: first, the stable somatic differences between Vezo and Karany (which would explain why the Vezo–Masikoro was not naturalized) and second, the inductive richness of the categories (in which case direct adult testimony regarding the Masikoro would explain why the Vezo–Masikoro contrast was not naturalized). Further studies could decide between these two hypotheses. Children could be introduced to a novel and unfamiliar group of people, whose morphological features are identical to those of the Vezo, but whose place of residence, livelihood, skills, religious beliefs, and customs are markedly different. At issue is whether, in the absence of adult testimony and in the absence of morphological differences, but in the presence of a rich cluster of typical properties, children would naturalize this novel group as they did the Karany. If they did, the inductive richness hypothesis would be supported.

One aspect of our existing data seems to offer some support to the hypothesis that, irrespective of morphological similarity, children might construe the Masikoro just as they construe the Karany (i.e., as a natural kind) were it not for the cultural induction they receive. In Chapter III, we described the pervasiveness of the testimony that Vezo children receive from adults regarding how people—the children themselves—become Vezo or Masikoro. Children are told that they are becoming Vezo when they learn how to swim, or when they successfully catch and sell fish, and whenever they fail to act in Vezo fashion they are taunted that they are Masikoro. In light of this, it is certainly not surprising that by age 6 most children have learned something important about the nature of their group identity, as was demonstrated by their adult-like answers to our group identity question in the Vezo–Masikoro scenario. They knew that a Vezo boy raised by Masikoro would become Masikoro and that a Masikoro child raised by Vezo would become Vezo. More surprising, however, is that, despite this massive cultural input, a third of the children flatly contradicted that input and judged that the adopted boy would be Vezo or Masikoro like his *birth* father. Moreover, the rest of the children failed to show evidence of the coherent causal reasoning that is implicit in the adult testimony (i.e., they failed to attribute to the adopted boy the properties that make him a member of his adoptive group). We speculate that one of the reasons for this shaky performance is that the children who participated in the Vezo–Masikoro task were still influenced by the same strong intuition that guided children who participated in the Vezo–Karany task: that human kinds are natural kinds.

This finding forcefully illustrates the point that children are not passive recipients of ready-made cultural beliefs, but are actively engaged in the process of making culture. In this process, they may create representations that conflict with the adult cultural consensus. As suggested by our studies, these representations are likely to influence the way children construe (and distort) the testimony they receive from their cultural environment, and to significantly constrain and enable the process of cultural transmission. This should make children's representations, and the children who produce them, far more central to anthropological research than they have been (as noted by, for example, Boyer, 1994; Hirschfeld, 2002; Schwartz, 1981; Toren, 1999).

We know, for example, that in many parts of the world adults continue to subscribe to the idea that human kinds are natural kinds, which are inherently different from each other because of their different underlying essences (e.g., Abu-Lughod, 1986; Empson, 2002; Errington, 1989; Fortes, 1945; Gil-White, 2001). Granted that there are bound to be a variety of historical, political, and economic factors—"mind-external factors," as Sperber (2001) would call them—that explain why some populations construe human groups as natural kinds, while others construe them performatively, as the Vezo do. However, it follows from our findings that a comparative analysis of these different outcomes must take into account the knowledge that children bring to the task of learning about the social world. The aim of the analysis would be to explain how, in different historical and cultural contexts, children's understanding is transformed, reinforced, or overturned.

It is somewhat ironic, in view of the anthropological claim that many non-western peoples are ontological monists (i.e., that they do not distinguish biological from social processes), that understanding the difference between biological inheritance and socially mediated learning plays a crucial role in the developmental process that leads Vezo children to overturn the intuition that human groups are natural kinds and to embrace the adult performative theory of group identity. Our data show that only those adolescents whose resemblance judgments on individual properties fully differentiated between the causal roles of birth parentage and learning were like Vezo adults in all aspects of their reasoning about group-identity and group-typical properties. This suggests that understanding the difference between birth and nurture is necessary for understanding what it means to be Vezo. Conversely, making sense of what it means to be Vezo may motivate children to differentiate between birth and nurture. The fact that Vezo children initially subscribe to the view that birth parentage fixes human group identity may explain why the discovery that birth origins are irrelevant to the determination of this property of the person would lead them to reflect on, and to discover, which other properties (the shape of the ears, the color of the skin) are instead thus determined. And hence, as Vezo children learn how and why they are Vezo, they also learn how and why babies resemble their *birth* parents in their physiognomy. What they will have to understand next is why their parents and elders find it so important to deny that resemblance. It is to this last issue that we now turn.

ON ANTHROPOLOGICAL INTERPRETATION

Vezo adults who participated in our studies systematically took the view that the bodily properties of adopted children resemble those of their birth parents because, for example, that is where they got their "template" from, and that adopted children share the beliefs and skills of their adoptive parents because, for example, these parents are their "school." In other words, Vezo adults clearly and explicitly differentiated between different mechanisms for the inter-generational transmission of properties.

We have taken the understanding of the distinct causal roles of birth parentage and socially-mediated learning as evidence that participants have a theory of biological inheritance, and that this theory is predicated on the ontological distinction between "facts of biology" and "facts of sociality." As discussed in the Introduction, it is common for anthropologists to claim that this distinction is a peculiar feature of the western intellectual tradition and that it is foreign to most non-western peoples. Our data do not support this claim.

It is important to stress that by concluding that Vezo make the same ontological cut as do North Americans, we do not wish to imply that their concepts of biological inheritance and socially mediated learning map exactly onto the equivalent concepts held by North American adults. Given the different intellectual traditions and socio-economic contexts in which these concepts get constructed, this claim would be daft. Indeed, the analysis of our participants' justifications has revealed some significant differences.

Recall, for example, that those informants who judged that the adopted boy would share the same beliefs as his birth father invoked a variety of supernatural and psychological interventions, such as spirits or God acting as messengers for the dead father, or the child's intuitive resistance towards the beliefs of his adoptive parents. We surmise that North American adults would not share these views. On their part, few Vezo adults elaborated on the causal mechanism by which children come to resemble their birth parents in their bodily properties; whenever they did, they gave no indication of being familiar with western accounts of biological inheritance in terms of genetic coding. Notwithstanding these differences, we stand by the claim that Vezo and North American concepts of biological inheritance and socially mediated learning are commensurable to one another, insofar as they play the same inferential role in adult reasoning about family resemblance.

In the Introduction, we reported a number of striking statements articulated by Vezo adults regarding the physiognomy of their babies (e.g., that babies come to resemble people who are not biologically related to them). It is important to appreciate that these (or similar) statements could be interpreted as evidence that Vezo (or other non-western peoples) are ontological monists: that they do not draw the distinction between "facts of biology" and "facts of sociality." The significance of our data lies in the challenge they pose to this way of interpreting the ethnographic evidence, which has arguably become the dominant one in contemporary anthropology. Against this background, our conclusion that, despite what they say, Vezo adults are *not* ontological monists has at least two important theoretical implications for anthropologists (see also Astuti, 2001).

First, recall that much of the critique of the study of kinship was predicated on the claim that kinship theorists had based their comparative work on the ethnocentric distinction between the biological ties engendered by human reproduction (e.g., the biological tie between birth parents and their offspring) and the social and cultural meanings attributed to them (e.g., the extension of the terms father and mother to people other than the birth parents): a distinction between "biology" and "sociality" that the people whose kinship was the object of study allegedly did not make. By showing that Vezo adults in fact discriminate between "facts of biology" and "facts of sociality," our results suggest that the claim of ontological incommensurability has been greatly exaggerated, and that therefore cross-cultural comparison is not impossible.

Second, our discovery that Vezo adults know why offspring resemble their birth parents (statements about their babies' looks notwithstanding) should compel anthropologists to recognize that informants' explicit discourse may not be a reliable indication of their conceptual knowledge and ontological commitments. This point has been made before, in different forms and contexts (e.g., Bloch, 1977, 1998; Bourdieu, 1985; Boyer, 2001;

Firth, 1985; Leach, 1966; Sperber, 1985, 1996, 1997; Spiro, 1993). None-theless, it is still common for anthropologists to rely on the commonsense assumption that people's concepts can be inferred from everyday discourse, and to miss the point that much cultural practice and discourse is a reflec-tion and commentary on people's knowledge, not its articulation (see Bloch, 1998; in preparation). This point, we believe, applies to our case study, as we hope to demonstrate herewith.

Clearly, as far as the interpretative aim of anthropology is concerned, the conclusion that Vezo adults have constructed an understanding of bi-ological inheritance should be taken as no more than a starting point, for we are left to explain why, if adults know that human physiognomy is deter-mined by the "template" that babies inherit from the parents who gener-ated them, they insist that their children resemble people other than their birth parents. One possibility is that our adoption task taps a systematically different type of mental representation than does everyday discourse, per-haps more implicit and less accessible to conscious reflection. We accept that intrinsic differences between types of mental representations exist. For ex-ample, the representations that articulate early emerging knowledge in the domains of intuitive physics, intuitive psychology, and number, are the output of dedicated perceptual input analyzers (Carey & Spelke, 1994), and it is most unlikely that they can find expression in a linguistic format. However, we doubt that the mismatch between Vezo adults' performance in our adoption paradigm and their explicit cultural discourse is due to the different nature of the mental representations involved, as is suggested by the fact that, in their justifications, Vezo adults were fully capable of explic-itly articulating the knowledge tapped by our task.

Rather, we speculate that the apparent conflict in conceptual repre-sentations is caused by people's *deliberate* contradiction of their understand-ing of biological inheritance. In other words, when Vezo adults say that a baby looks like the person his mother befriended when she was pregnant, or that a wandering spirit has changed the baby's features, they elect to ignore their knowledge that the baby looks like the birth parents. If so, the inter-pretative aim becomes to explain why Vezo adults contradict, ignore, or do not attend to what we know they know.

We suggest that Vezo statements about babies' physiognomy should be interpreted as one instance of a much wider strategy by which Vezo avoid drawing attention to the exclusivity of the biological relations between birth parents and their children. As argued elsewhere (Astuti, 2000a), the notion that children "belong" to more people than their birth parents (and that grandchildren and great grandchildren "belong" to more people than their grandparents and great grandparents) is central to Vezo kinship and to the realization of people's most valued aim in life: to reach old age surrounded by a vast number of descendants. While this objective is inherent to the Vezo undifferentiated system of kinship reckoning, which is inclusive rather than exclusive, people also actively pursue this end in their everyday practices. For example, although children tend to be raised by their birth parents, it is considered highly immoral and unforgivingly rude for such parents to assert their unique rights or duties over *their* children. By contrast, every effort is made to break down the biological boundaries that demarcate individual family units—for example, by encouraging children to eat from any of the kitchens of their numerous "parents" (e.g., mother's sisters, mother's brothers, father's sisters, father's brothers, and so on). Although there is a well-understood practical advantage in sharing children in this way, an important effect of this practice is that it minimizes the significance of the distinctions created by biological kinship (e.g., between one's birth parents and other classificatory parents, between one's full and one's classificatory siblings). Exactly the same effect is achieved when people do *not* attend to the resemblance between babies and their birth parents, but choose to see it elsewhere.

This point was brought into focus by a 43-year-old man who was interviewed during the piloting stage. He strongly dissented with the majority of Vezo adults who choose not "to see" the resemblance between babies and their birth parents and stated instead that the adopted boy would resemble the birth father in the shape of his ears "because in the case of human beings there must be a sign, a proof, that your child is *yours*." Granted that such signs exist, most Vezo adults strive to erase them as best as they can.

From this interpretative perspective, Vezo adults' statements about their babies' looks take on an important moral connotation, for they are part of people's efforts to create a community in which children are generated, nurtured, and molded by a much larger network of relations than the ones demarcated by their birth parents. But such efforts, we propose, can be fully appreciated only if we recognize the background against which they are made: Vezo do differentiate between relations engendered by birth and relations created through nurture, but they are committed to speaking and acting as if they do not. The claim that Vezo ontology is monistic is not only factually wrong; paradoxically, in making such a claim, anthropologists risk blinding themselves to the meaning, moral valence, and psychological force of what Vezo adults want to say about their babies.

VEZO–VEZO ADOPTION SCENARIO

There was a man and a woman; they were Vezo people from a village in the North. They gave birth to a baby-boy, and when the child was still very small, when he was still a tiny baby, they went to the interior to consult a diviner. And they took the baby with them.

When they got well inside the forest, something very bad happened to them: some bandits crossed their way. When the woman, the baby's mother, saw the bandits approaching, she was scared as she understood what was going to happen to them ... and so very quickly she took the baby off her back and hid him in the grass. When the bandits got hold of them, they took them far away into the forest, and killed them—both the woman and the man, the mother and father who generated the baby, were thus dead. But the baby was left hidden in the grass, still alive.

After a little while, the baby started to cry, and he cried and cried. When a man from a Vezo village in the South went by, he heard the baby cry. He looked and looked and finally he saw the baby hidden in the grass, and he picked him up, he held him in his arms. He was very surprised to see the baby, and he waited there in the forest for he thought that someone would come to fetch the baby. But when it got dark and nobody had come, he had no choice but to return home, taking the child with him to his own village in the South.

His wife was very surprised when she saw that her husband was carrying the baby, and she asked: "Where is this baby from?" And her husband explained the whole story. Both of them were convinced that some one would come to fetch the baby, and so they waited and waited, but after many days had gone by and nobody had come to get him, finally they knew that the baby was going to be their child. And they were very happy, because they didn't have children of their own, and so they were happy to have got a child—a male child. After some time, they called on the ancestors— the dead people—and informed them that they had got a son, and they received the ancestors' blessing.

And so the child grew up in the village in the South, he grew up strong and healthy, he was happy, he liked his father and mother, and the father and mother who raised him, who brought him up and looked after him, were really parents to him.

Now my questions are going to be like this: the child is no longer a child but is a grown up person. And the questions about him are going to be like this:

> The father who generated the boy, the one from the northern village who died, he had longish and narrow feet. The father who raised the boy, the one from the southern village, he had shortish and wide feet. In your opinion, when the child is fully grown up: will he have longish and narrow feet like the father who generated him, or will he have shortish and wide feet like the father who raised him?

ANIMAL ADOPTION SCENARIO

There was a woman who raised ducks and chickens. When winter came, she was very cold, as she didn't have a blanket. She wanted to buy one, but didn't have any money. She was so cold that finally one day she decided she had to do something: "I'll take this duck [hen] to the market and I'll sell it, and with the money I'll buy myself a blanket". And so she left and went to the market, and when she got there, she sold the duck, got the money, and off she went to the Karany shops to buy herself a blanket. On her way back to the village she was happy, because of her new blanket. When she got to the village, she was very surprised to find that, hidden in the grass in her courtyard, was an egg that had been laid by the duck [hen] she had just sold at the market. She hadn't known the duck [hen] was about to lay eggs! Now that the duck [hen] was no longer there, she was left with her egg.

However, the woman also had a hen [a duck] that had laid her eggs and was actually already sitting on them. This is a picture of the hen [duck]. So the woman took the duck's egg and put it under the hen and the hen sat on it. The hen sat and sat on it, until the egg finally hatched. The bird that was inside the duck's egg spent all its time with the hen, and it was the hen who led the little bird around, who raised it together with her other offspring: They ate together, slept together, and played together the whole time until the bird was all grown up.

Now my questions are going to be like this. Let's say that the little bird is no longer little, but is all grown up. My questions are about this bird:

> The duck that generated the bird had a red tongue. The hen that sat on the egg and then raised the little bird had a yellow tongue. In your opinion,

when the bird is fully grown up: will it have a red tongue like the duck that generated it, or will it have a yellow tongue like the hen that raised it?

Finally, in your opinion, what is this bird going to be when it's all grown up: a duck or a chicken?

TABLE B1

VEZO–VEZO SCENARIO

Bodily traits	*Bodily traits*
Longish, narrow feet	Shortish, wide feet
Longish, narrow nose	Broad, flat nose
Roundish kidneys	Longish kidneys
Cross-eyed	Straight eyes
Beliefs	*Beliefs*
Believed that cows have stronger teeth than horses	Believed that horses have stronger teeth than cows
Believed that papaya is healthier than pineapple	Believed that pineapple is healthier than papaya
Believed that there are kinds of dogs that can't see at night	Believed that there are kinds of lemurs that can't see at night
Believed that frogs have black hearts	Believed that frogs have green hearts
Skills	*Skills*
Knew how to be a mechanic but not a carpenter	Knew how to be a carpenter but not a mechanic
Knew how to whistle	Didn't know how to whistle
Knew how to fish with the line	Knew how to fish with nets
Knew how to fell trees for canoe making	Didn't know how to fell trees for canoe making

TABLE B2

VEZO–MASIKORO SCENARIO

Group-Neutral Bodily traits	*Group-Neutral Bodily traits*
Pointed ears	Roundish ears
Roundish appendix	Flat appendix
Long, slender hands	Short, wide hands
Small lips	Big lower lip
Group-Typical Bodily traits (Vezo)	*Group-Typical Bodily traits (Masikoro)*
Had scarred fingers from the fishing line	Had hard calluses on his palms from hoeing
Had a callous on the top of his foot from sitting on the canoe	Had calluses on his toes from walking on hard soil

Table B2. (Contd.)

Group-Neutral Beliefs	*Group-Neutral Beliefs*
Believed that chameleons have 20 teeth	Believed that chameleons have 30 teeth
Believed that duck liver is harder than chicken liver	Believed that chicken liver is harder than duck liver
Group-Typical Beliefs (Vezo)	*Group-Typical Beliefs (Masikoro)*
Believed that corpses should not be kept for long at the village before burial	Believed that corpses should be kept for long at the village before burial
Believed that an offering of rum is enough to complete the marriage ritual	Believed that the marriage ritual can't be completed unless one head of cattle is sacrificed
Group-Neutral Skills	*Group-Neutral Skills*
Knew how to roll cigarettes but doesn't know how to make ropes	Knew how to make ropes but doesn't know how to roll cigarettes
Knew how to cut hair	Didn't know how to cut hair
Group-Typical Skills (Vezo)	*Group-Typical Skills (Masikoro)*
Knew how to sail	Knew how to ride a cart
Knew how to fish	Knew how to cultivate rice

TABLE B3

VEZO–KARANY SCENARIO

Group-Neutral Bodily traits	*Group-Neutral Bodily traits*
Pointed ears	Roundish ears
Roundish appendix	Flat appendix
Long, slender hands	Short, wide hands
Small lips	Big lower lip
Group-Typical Inborn Bodily traits (Vezo)	*Group-Typical Inborn Bodily traits (Karany)*
Black skin	Light skin
Curly hair	Straight hair
Group-Typical Bodily traits (Vezo)	*Group-Typical Bodily traits (Karany)*
Had scarred fingers from the fishing line	Didn't have scarred fingers because didn't fish
Had a callous on the top of his foot from sitting on the canoe	Didn't have a callous on the top of his foot because he didn't sit on the canoe
Group-Neutral Beliefs	*Group-Neutral Beliefs*
Believed that chameleons have 20 teeth	Believed that chameleons have 30 teeth
Believed that duck liver is harder than chicken liver	Believed that chicken liver is harder than duck liver
Group-Typical Beliefs (Vezo)	*Group-Typical Beliefs (Karany)*
Believed that corpses should be kept overnight inside the house before burial	Believed that corpses should not be kept overnight inside the house before burial
Did not believe that one should fast each year	Believed that one should fast each year

Group-Neutral Skills	Group-Neutral Skills
Knew how to sing but didn't know how to dance	Knew how to dance but didn't know how to sing
Didn't know how to cut hair	Knew how to cut hair
Group-Typical Skills (Vezo)	Group-Typical Skills (Karany)
Knew how to fish	Knew how to trade
Knew how to sail	Knew how to drive

TABLE B4

ANIMAL SCENARIO

Bodily traits	Bodily traits
Red tongue	Yellow tongue
Yellow eyes	Black eyes
14 ribs	16 ribs
One foot more yellow than the other	Both feet the same colour
Knowledge-based properties	Knowledge-based properties
Knew where there is a hole in the fence from which to get out to look for food	Didn't know where there is a hole in the fence from which to get out to look for food
Didn't know how to steal rice from inside the house	Knew how to steal rice from inside the house
Knew how to find shade	Didn't know how to find shade
It was used to get close to people's houses because it didn't know that it might get hurt	Didn't go near people's houses because it knew it might get hurt

REFERENCES

Abu-Lughod, L. (1986). *Veiled sentiments. Honor and poetry in a Bedouin society.* Berkeley: University of California Press.

Arterberry, M. E., Barrett, E., & Hudspeth, D. (1999). *Preschoolers' understanding of the inheritance of biological vs. social traits.* Paper presented at the biennial meeting of the Society for Research in Child Development, Albuquerque, New Mexico.

Astuti, R. (1993). Food for pregnancy: Procreation, marriage and images of gender among the Vezo of western Madagascar. *Social Anthropology: The Journal of the European Association of Social Anthropologists*, **1**, 277–290.

Astuti, R. (1995a). *People of the sea: Identity and descent among the Vezo of Madagascar.* Cambridge, England: Cambridge University Press.

Astuti, R. (1995b). "The Vezo are not a kind of people": Identity, difference, and "ethnicity" among a fishing people of western Madagascar. *American Ethnologist*, **22**, 464–482.

Astuti, R. (1998). 'It's a boy!', 'It's a girl!'. Reflections on sex and gender in Madagascar and beyond. In M. Lambek & A. Strathern (Eds.), *Bodies and persons. Comparative perspectives from Africa and Melanesia* (pp. 29–52). Cambridge, England: Cambridge University Press.

Astuti, R. (2000a). Kindreds, cognatic and unilineal descent: A view from Madagascar. In J. Carsten (Ed.), *Cultures of relatedness* (pp. 90–103). Cambridge, England: Cambridge University Press.

Astuti, R. (2000b). Les gens ressemblent-ils aux poulets? Penser la frontière homme/animal à Madagascar. *Terrain*, **34**, 89–105.

Astuti, R. (2001). Are we all natural dualists? A cognitive developmental approach. (The Malinowski Memorial Lecture 2000). *Journal of the Royal Anthropological Institute*, **7**, 429–447.

Astuti, R., Solomon, G. E. A., & Carey, S. (2003). Full text of adoptions scenarios, and sample protocols. Available on-line: http://www.wjh.harvard.edu/~lds/pdfs/vezo.pdf

Astuti, R., Solomon, G. E. A., & Carey, S. (in preparation). On combining psychological and anthropological methods among the Vezo of Madagascar. Manuscript.

Atran, S. (1990). *Cognitive foundations of natural history: Towards an anthropology of science.* Cambridge, England: Maison des Sciences de l'Homme and Cambridge University Press.

Atran, S. (1998). Folkbiology and the anthropology of science: Cognitive universals and cultural particulars. *Behavioral and Brain Sciences*, **21**, 547–609.

Atran, S. (2001). Comment on Gil-White, "Are ethnic groups biological 'species' to the human brain?" *Current Anthropology*, **42**, 537–538.

Atran, S., Estin, P., Coley, J., & Medin, D. L. (1997). Generic species and basic levels: Essence and appearance in folkbiology. *Journal of Ethnobiology*, **17**, 22–45.

Atran, S., Medin, D., Lynch, E., Vapnarsky, V., Ek', E. U., & Sousa, P. (2001). Folkbiology doesn't come from folkpsychology: Evidence from Yukatek Maya in cross-cultural perspective. *Journal of Cognition and Culture*, **1**, 3–42.

Au, T. K.-F., & Romo, L. F. (1996). Building a coherent conception of HIV transmission: A new approach to AIDS education. In D. Medin (Ed.), *The psychology of learning and motivation*. New York: Academic Press.

Au, T. K.-F., Romo, L. F., & DeWitt, J. E. (1999). Considering children's folkbiology in health education. In M. Siegel & C. Peterson (Eds.), *Children's understanding of biology and health* (pp. 209–234). Cambridge, England: Cambridge University Press.

Avis, J., & Harris, P. (1991). Belief-desire reasoning among Baka children: Evidence for a universal conception of mind. *Child Development*, **62**, 460–467.

Baillargeon, R., Kotovsky, L., & Needham, A. (1995). The acquisition of physical knowledge in infancy. In D. Sperber, D. Premack & A. Premack (Eds.), *Causal cognition: A multidisciplinary debate* (pp. 79–116). Oxford, England: Clarendon Press.

Bernstein, A., & Cowan, P. (1975). Children's concepts of how people get babies. *Child Development*, **46**, 77–91.

Bibace, R., & Walsh, M. E. (1980). Development of children's concept of illness. *Pediatrics*, **66**, 912–917.

Bloch, M. E. F. (1977). The past and the present in the present. (The Malinowski Memorial Lecture 1976). *Man*, **12**, 278–292.

Bloch, M. E. F. (1993). Zafimaniry birth and kinship theory. *Social Anthropology. The Journal of the European Association of Social Anthropologists*, **1**, 119–132.

Bloch, M. E. F. (1998). *How we think they think: Anthropological approaches to cognition, memory and literacy*. Boulder, CO: Westview Press.

Bloch, M. E. F. (in preparation). Anthropology and the cognitive challenge. Manuscript.

Bloch, M. E. F., Solomon, G. E. A., & Carey, S. (2001). An understanding of what is passed on from parents to children: A cross-cultural investigation. *Journal of Cognition and Culture*, **1**, 43–68.

Bloch, M. E. F., & Sperber, D. (2002). Kinship and evolved psychological dispositions: The mother's brother controversy reconsidered. *Current Anthropology*, **43**, 723–748.

Bourdieu, P. (1985). *Outline of a theory of practice*. Cambridge, England: Cambridge University Press.

Boyer, P. (1994). *The naturalness of religious ideas: A cognitive theory of religion*. Los Angeles: University of California Press.

Boyer, P. (2001). *Religion explained: The evolutionary origins of religious thought*. New York, NY: Basic Books.

Carey, S. (1985). *Conceptual change in childhood*. Cambridge, MA: MIT Press.

Carey, S. (1988). Conceptual differences between children and adults. *Mind and Language*, **3**, 167–181.

Carey, S. (1995). On the origin of causal understanding. In D. Sperber, D. Premack & A. Premack (Eds.), *Causal cognition: A multidisciplinary debate* (pp. 268–302). Oxford, England: Clarendon Press.

Carey, S. (1999). Sources of conceptual change. In E. K. Scholnick, K. Nelson, S. A. Gelman & P. Miller (Eds.), *Conceptual Development: Piaget's Legacy* (pp. 293–326). Hillsdale, NJ: Erlbaum.

Carey, S., & Spelke, E. S. (1994). Domain specific knowledge and conceptual change. In L. Hirschfeld & S. Gelman (Eds.), *Mapping the mind: Domain specificity in cognition and culture* (pp. 169–200). Cambridge, England: Cambridge University Press.

Carey, S., & Xu, F. (1999). Sortals and kinds: An appreciation of John Macnamara. In R. Jackendoff, P. Bloom & K. Wynn (Eds.), *Language, logic and concepts* (pp. 311–336). Cambridge, MA: MIT Press.

Carsten, J. (1991). Children in between: Fostering and the process of kinship on Pulau Langkawi, Malaysia. *Man (ns)*, **26**, 425–443.

Carsten, J. (1995). The substance of kinship and the heat of the hearth: Feeding, personhood, and relatedness among Malays in Pulau Langkawi. *American Ethnologist*, **22**, 223–241.

Carsten, J. (1997). *The heat of the hearth: The process of kinship in a Malay fishing community.* Oxford, England: Clarendon Press.

Carsten, J. (2000). Introduction. Cultures of relatedness. In J. Cartsen (Ed.), *Cultures of relatedness: New approaches to the study of kinship* (pp. 1–36). Cambridge, England: Cambridge University Press.

Crider, C. (1981). Children's conceptions of the body interior. In R. Bibace & M. Walsh (Eds.), *Children's conceptions of health, illness, and bodily functions.* San Francisco, CA: Jossey-Bass.

Cole, M. (1996). *Cultural psychology: A once and future discipline.* Cambridge, MA: The Belknap Press of Harvard University Press.

Cole, M., & Scribner, L. (1974). *Culture and thought: A psychological introduction.* New York: Wiley.

Coley, J. (2000). On the importance of comparative research: The case of folkbiology. *Child Development*, **71**, 82–90.

Csibra, G., Gergely, G., Biro, S., Koos, O., & Brockbank, M. (1999). Goal attribution without agency cues: The perception of "pure reason" in infancy. *Cognition*, **72**, 237–267.

Dehaene, S. (1997). *The number sense: How the mind creates mathematics.* New York: Plenum Press.

Diesendruck, G. (2001). Essentialism in Brazilian children's extension of animal names. *Developmental Psychology*, **37**, 49–60.

Empson, R. (2002). *Integrating transformations: A study of children and daughters-in-law in a new approach to Mongolian kinship.* Unpublished doctoral dissertation, University of Cambridge, England.

Errington, S. (1989). *Meaning and power in a Southeast Asian realm.* Princeton, NJ: Princeton University Press.

Feigenson, L., Carey, S., & Hauser, M. (2002). The representation underlying infants' choice of more: Object files versus analog magnitudes. *Psychological Science*, **13**, 150–156.

Firth, R. (1985). Degrees of intelligibility. In J. Overing (Ed.), *Reason and morality* (pp. 29–46). London and New York: Tavistock Publications.

Fortes, M. (1945). *The dynamics of clanship among the Tallensi.* Oxford, England: Oxford University Press.

Freeman, L. (2001). *Knowledge, education and social differentiation amongst the Betsileo of Fisakana, Highland Madagascar.* Unpublished doctoral dissertation, London School of Economics and Political Science.

Geertz, C. (1973). *The interpretation of cultures.* New York: Basic Books.

Gelman, S. A. (2003). *The essential child: Origins of essentialism in everyday thought.* Oxford, England: Oxford University Press.

Gelman, S. A., & Hirschfeld, L. A. (1999). How biological is essentialism? In S. Atran & D. Medin (Eds.), *Folkbiology* (pp. 403–446). Cambridge, MA: MIT.

Gelman, S. A., & Wellman, H. M. (1991). Insides and essences: Early understandings of the nonobvious. *Cognition*, **38**, 213–244.

Gentner, D., Brem, S., Ferguson, R. W., Markman, A. B., Levidow, B. B., Wolff, P., & Forbus, K. D. (1997). Analogical reasoning and conceptual change: A case study of Johannes Kepler. *The Journal of the Learning Sciences*, **6**, 3–40.

Gergely, G., Nadasdy, Z., Gergely, C., & Biro, S. (1995). Taking the intentional stance at 12 months of age. *Cognition*, **56**, 165–193.

Gil-White, F. J. (2001). Are ethnic groups biological "species" to the human brain? Essentialism in our cognition of some social categories. *Current Anthropology*, **42**, 515–536.

Gimenez, M., & Harris, P. L. (2002). Understanding constraints on inheritance: Evidence for biological thinking in early childhood. *British Journal of Developmental Psychology*, **20**, 307–324.

Good, B. J. (1994). *Medicine, rationality and experience: An anthropological perspective*. Cambridge, England: Cambridge University Press.

Gopnik, A., Glymour, C., Sobel, D., Schulz, L., Kushnir, T., & Danks, D. (2004). A theory of causal learning in children: Causal maps and Bayes nets. *Psychological Review*, **111**, 3–32.

Gopnik, A., & Meltzoff, A. (1997). *Words, thoughts and theories*. Cambridge, MA: MIT Press.

Hair, J. F., Anderson, R. E., Tatham, R. L., & & Black, W. C. (1998). *Multivariate data analysis*. Upper Saddle River, NJ: Prentice Hall.

Hergenrather, J. R., & Rabinowitz, M. (1991). Age-related differences in the organization of children's knowledge of illness. *Developmental Psychology*, **27**, 952–959.

Hirschfeld, L. A. (1995). Do children have a theory of race? *Cognition*, **54**, 209–252.

Hirschfeld, L. A. (1996). *Race in the making: Cognition, culture, and the child's construction of human kinds*. Cambridge, MA: MIT Press.

Hirschfeld, L. A. (1997). The conceptual politics of race: Lessons from our children. *Ethos*, **25**, 63–92.

Hirschfeld, L. A. (1998). Natural assumptions: Race, essence and taxonomies of human kinds. *Social Research. An International Quarterly of the Social Sciences*, **65**, 331–349.

Hirschfeld, L. A. (2002). Why don't anthropologists like children? *American Anthropologist*, **104**, 611–627.

Horobin, K. D. (1997). *Children's understanding of biological inheritance: Nature, nurture, and essentialism*. Paper presented at the meeting of the Society for Research in Child Development, Washington, DC.

Inagaki, K., & Hatano, G. (1993). Young children's understanding of the mind-body distinction. *Child Development*, **64**, 1534–1549.

Inagaki, K., & Hatano, G. (2002). *Young children's naïve thinking about the biological world*. New York: Psychology Press.

Ingold, T. (1991). Becoming persons: Consciousness and sociality in human evolution. *Cultural Dynamics*, **4**, 355–378.

Ingold, T. (2001). From the transmission of representations to the education of attention. In H. Whitehouse (Ed.), *The debated mind: Evolutionary psychology versus ethnography* (pp. 113–153). Oxford, England and New York: Berg.

Jaakkola, R. O. (1997). *The development of scientific understanding: Children's construction of their first biological theory*. Unpublished Ph.D. thesis, Massachusetts Institute of Technology, Cambridge, MA.

Jeyifous, S. W. (1992). Developmental changes in the representation of word meaning: Cross-cultural findings. *British Journal of Developmental Psychology*, **10**, 285–299.

Johnson, S. C. (2000). The recognition of mentalistic agents in infancy. *Trends in Cognitive Sciences*, **4**, 22–28.

Johnson, S. C., & Carey, S. (1998). Knowledge enrichment and conceptual change in folk biology: Evidence from people with Williams syndrome. *Cognitive Psychology*, **37**, 156–200.

Johnson, S. C., Slaughter, V., & Carey, S. (1998). Whose gaze will infants follow? The elicitation of gaze-following in 12-month-olds. *Developmental Science*, **1**, 233–238.

Johnson, S. C., & Solomon, G. E. A. (1997). Why dogs have puppies and cats have kittens: The role of birth in young children's understanding of biological origins. *Child Development*, **68**, 404–419.

Keil, F. C. (1989). *Concepts, kinds, and conceptual development*. Cambridge MA: MIT Press.

Keil, F. C. (1992). The origins of an autonomous biology. In M. R. Gunnar & M. Maratsos (Eds.), *Modularity and constraints in language and cognition: Minnesota symposia on child psychology* (Vol. XXV, pp. 103–138). Hillsdale, NJ: Erlbaum.

Kelemen, D. (1999). The scope of teleological thinking in preschool children. *Cognition*, **70**, 241–272.

Kitcher, P. (1988). The child as parent of the scientist. *Mind and Language*, **3**, 217–228.

Kripke, S. (1972). *Naming and necessity*. Cambridge, MA: Harvard University Press.

Koocher, G. (1973). Childhood, death and cognitive development. *Developmental Psychology*, **9**, 369–375.

Kuhn, T. S. (1983). Commensurability, comparability, and communicability. In P. Asquith & T. Nickles (Eds.), *PSA 1982* (pp. 669–688). East Lansing, MI: Philosophy of Science Association.

Kuper, A. (1999). *Culture: The anthropologists' account*. Cambridge, MA: Harvard University Press.

LaFontaine, J. (1986). An anthropological perspective on children. In M. Richards & P. Light (Eds.), *Children social worlds: Development in a social context* (pp. 10–30). Cambridge, England: Polity Press.

Lambek, M. (1981). *Human spirits: A cultural account of trance in Mayotte*. Cambridge, England: Cambridge University Press.

Lambek, M. (1998). Body and mind in mind, body and mind in body: Some anthropological interventions in a long conversation. In M. Lambek & A. Strathern (Eds.), *Bodies and persons: Comparative perspectives from Africa and Melanesia* (pp. 103–123). Cambridge, England: Cambridge University Press.

Laurendeau, M., & Pinard, A. (1962). *Causal thinking in the child: A genetic and experimental approach*. New York: International Universities Press.

Leach, E. (1961). *Rethinking anthropology*. London School of Economics Monographs on Social Anthropology, No. 22. London: The Athlone Press.

Leach, E. (1966). Virgin birth. *Proceedings of the Royal Anthropological Institute of Great Britain and Ireland*, No. 1966, 39–49.

Leslie, A. M. (1994). ToMM, ToBy, and Agency: Core architecture and domain specificity. In L. Hirschfeld & S. Gelman (Eds.), *Mapping the mind: Domain specificity in cognition and culture* (pp. 119–148). Cambridge, England: Cambridge University Press.

LeVine, R. A., Dixon, S., LeVine, S., Richman, A., Leiderman, P. H., Keefer, C. H., & Brazelton, T. B. (1994). *Childcare and culture: Lessons from Africa*. Cambridge, England: Cambridge University Press.

Lingenfelter, S. (1985). Review of the book. A critique of the study of kinship. *American Ethnologist*, **12**, 372–374.

Linnekin, J., & Poyer, L. (Eds.) (1990). *Cultural identity and ethnicity in the Pacific*. Honolulu, HI: University of Hawaii.

Lopez, A., Atran, S., Coley, J., Medin, D., & Smith, E. (1997). The tree of life: Universal of folk-biological taxonomies and inductions. *Cognitive Psychology*, **32**, 251–295.

Lutz, C. A. (1988). *Unnatural emotions: Everyday sentiments on a Micronesian Atoll and their challenge to western theory*. Chicago, IL: Chicago University Press.

Mahalingam, R. (1998). *Essentialism, power, and representation of caste: A developmental study*. Unpublished doctoral dissertation, University of Pittsburgh.

Mandler, J. (2000). Perceptual and conceptual processes in infancy. *Journal of Cognition and Development*, **1**, 3–36.

Marriott, M. (1976). Hindu transactions: Diversity without dualism. In B. Kapferer (Ed.), *Transaction and meaning* (pp. 109–1412). Philadelphia, PA: ISHI Publications.

Marshall, M. (1977). The nature of nurture. *American Ethnologist*, **4**, 642–643.

McKinnon, S. (2002). *Comments for the panel entitled "The genealogical method reconsidered".* Paper presented at the 101st Annual Meeting of the American Anthropological Association, New Orleans, LA.

Medin, D. L., & Atran, S. (in press). The native mind: Biological categorization and reasoning in development and across cultures. *Psychological Review.*

Medin, D. L., & Ortony, A. (1989). Psychological essentialism. In S. Vosniadou & A. Ortony (Eds.), *Similarity and analogical reasoning* (pp. 179–195). Cambridge, England: Cambridge University Press.

Middleton, K. (1999). Introduction. In K. Middleton (Ed.), *Ancestors, power and history in Madagascar* (pp. 1–36). Leiden: Brill.

Middleton, K. (2000.). How Karembola men become mothers. In J. Carsten (Ed.), *Cultures of relatedness: New approaches to the study of kinship* (pp. 104–127). Cambridge, England: Cambridge University Press.

Montgomery, H. (2001). *Modern Babylon?: Prostituting children in Thailand.* Oxford, England: Berghahn.

Nagy, M. (1953). Children's conceptions of some bodily functions. *Journal of Genetic Psychology,* **83**, 199–216.

Needham, R. (Ed.) (1971a). Introduction. In *Rethinking kinship and marriage* (pp. xiii–cxvii). London: Tavistock.

Needham, R. (Ed.) (1971b). Remarks on the analysis of kinship and marriage. In *Rethinking kinship and marriage* (pp. 1–34). London: Tavistock.

Nersessian, N. J. (1992). How do scientists think? Capturing the dynamics of conceptual change in science. In R. N. Giere (Ed.), *Cognitive Models of Science: Minnesota studies in the philosophy of science* (Vol. 15, pp. 3–44). Minneapolis: University of Minnesota Press.

Nuttall, M. (2000). Choosing kin: Sharing and subsistence in a Greenlandic hunting community. In P. Schweitzer (Ed.), *Dividends of kinship: Meanings and uses of social relatedness* (pp. 33–60). London, England: Routledge.

Ortner, S. B. (1996). *Making gender.* Boston, MA: Beacon Press.

Perrin, E. C., Sayer, A. G., & Willett, J. B. (1991). Sticks and stones may break my bones . . . Reasoning about illness causality and body functioning in children who have a chronic illness. *Pediatrics,* **88**, 608–619.

Rivers, W. H. R. (1968). The genealogical method of anthropological enquiry. In W. H. R. Rivers (Ed.), *Kinship and social organization.* LSE Monographs on Social Anthropology No. 34 (pp. 97–109). New York: The Athlone Press.

Rogoff, B. (1990). *Apprenticeship in thinking: Cognitive development in social context.* New York: Oxford University Press.

Rogoff, B. (2003). *The cultural nature of human development.* New York: Oxford University Press.

Rothbart, M., & Taylor, M. (1992). Category labels and social reality: Do we view social categories as natural kinds? In G. Semin & K. Fieder (Eds.), *Language and social cognition* (pp. 11–36). Thousand Oaks, CA: Sage.

Rothbart, M., & Taylor, M. (2001). Comment on Gil-White, "Are ethnic groups biological 'species' to the human brain?" *Current Anthropology,* **42**, 544–545.

Safier, G. (1964). A study in relationships between the life and death concepts in children. *Journal of Genetic Psychology,* **105**, 283–294.

Scheffler, H. W. (1991). Sexism and naturalism in the study of kinship. In M. di Leonardo (Ed.), *Gender at the crossroads of knowledge: Feminist anthropology in the postmodern era* (pp. 361–382). Berkeley, CA: University of California Press.

Scheper-Hughes, N., & Lock, M. (1987). The mindful body: A prolegomenon to future work in medical anthropology. *Medical Anthropology Quarterly,* **1**, 6–41.

Schneider, D. (1965). Kinship and biology. In A. J. Coale, L. A. Fallers, M. J. Levy, D. Schneider & S. S. Tomkins (Eds.), *Aspects of the analysis of family structure* (pp. 83–101). Princeton, NJ: Princeton University Press.

Schneider, D. (1984). *A critique of the study of kinship*. Ann Arbor, MI: University of Michigan Press.

Schwartz, T. (1981). The acquisition of culture. *Ethos*, **9**, 4–17.

Shweder, R. A., Goodnow, J., Hatano, G., LeVine, R. A., Markus, H., & Miller, P. (1998). The cultural psychology of development: One mind, many mentalities. In W. Damon, D. Kuhn & R. S. Siegler (Eds.), *Handbook of child psychology, Vol. 2: Cognition, perception, and language* (5th ed., pp. 865–937). New York: Wiley.

Slaughter, V., Jaakkola, K., & Carey, S. (1999). Constructing a coherent theory: Children's biological understanding of life and death. In M. Siegel & C. Peterson (Eds.), *Children's understanding of biology and health* (pp. 71–98). Cambridge, England: Cambridge University Press.

Slaughter, V., & Lyons, M. (2003). Learning about life and death in early childhood. *Cognitive Psychology*, **43**, 1–30.

Smith, C., Solomon, G. E. A., & Carey, S. (2004). Getting to zero: Elementary school students' understanding of the infinite divisibility of number and matter. Manuscript submitted for review.

Solomon, G. E. A. (2002). Birth, kind, and naïve biology. *Developmental Science*, **5**, 213–218.

Solomon, G. E. A., & Cassimatis, N. L. (1999). On facts and conceptual systems: Young children's integration of the understandings of germs and contagion. *Developmental Psychology*, **35**, 113–126.

Solomon, G. E. A., & Johnson, S. C. (2000). Conceptual change in the classroom: Teaching young children to understand biological inheritance. *British Journal of Developmental Psychology*, **18**, 81–96.

Solomon, G. E. A., Johnson, S. C., Zaitchik, D., & Carey, S. (1996). Like father, like son: Children's understanding of how and why offspring resemble their parents. *Child Development*, **67**, 151–171.

Sousa, P. (2003). The fall of kinship: Towards an epidemiological explanation. *Journal of Cognition and Culture*, **3**, 265–303.

Sousa, P., Atran, S., & Medin, D. (2002). Essentialism and folkbiology: Evidence from Brazil. *Journal of Cognition and Culture*, **2**, 195–223.

Southall, A. (1986). Common themes in Malagasy culture. In C. P. Kottak, J. A. Rakotoarisoa, A. Southall & P. Verin (Eds.), *Madagascar, society, and history* (pp. 411–426). Durham, NC: Carolina Academic Press.

Speece, M., & Brent, S. (1985). Children's understanding of death: A review of three components of a death concept. *Child Development*, **55**, 671–686.

Spelke, E. S., Breilinger, K., Macomber, J., & Jacobson, K. (1992). Origins of knowledge. *Psychological Review*, **99**, 605–632.

Spelke, E. S., Phillips, A., & Woodward, A. L. (1995). Infants' knowledge of object motion and human action. In D. Sperber, D. Premack & A. Premack (Eds.), *Causal cognition: A multidisciplinary debate* (pp. 44–78). Oxford, England: Clarendon Press.

Sperber, D. (1985). *On anthropological knowledge*. Cambridge, England: Cambridge University Press.

Sperber, D. (1996). *Explaining culture: A naturalistic approach*. Oxford, England: Blackwell Publishers.

Sperber, D. (1997). Intuitive and reflective beliefs. *Mind and Language*, **12**, 67–83.

Sperber, D. (2001). Conceptual tools for a natural science of society and culture (Radcliffe-Brown Lecture in Social Anthropology 1999). *Proceedings of the British Academy*, **111**, 297–317.

Sperber, D., & Hirschfeld, L. (1999). Evolution, cognition, and culture. In R. Wilson & F. Keil (Eds.), *The MIT encyclopedia of the cognitive sciences* (pp. cxi–cxxxii). Cambridge, MA: MIT Press.

Spiro, M. E. (1993). Is the Western conception of the self "peculiar" within the context of the world cultures? *Ethos*, **21**, 107–153.

Springer, K. (1995). Acquiring a naive theory of biology through inference. *Child Development*, **66**, 547–558.

Springer, K. (1996). Young children's understanding of a biological basis for parent-offspring relations. *Child Development*, **67**, 2841–2856.

Springer, K. (1999). How a naive theory of biology is acquired. In M. Siegal & C. C. Peterson (Eds.), *Children's understanding of biology and health* (pp. 45–70). Cambridge, England: Cambridge University Press.

Springer, K., & Keil, F. C. (1989). On the development of biologically specific beliefs: The case of inheritance. *Child Development*, **60**, 637–648.

Springer, K., & Keil, F. C. (1991). Early differentiation of causal mechanisms appropriate to biological and nonbiological kinds. *Child Development*, **62**, 767–781.

Springer, K., & Ruckel, J. (1992). Early beliefs about the cause of illness: Evidence against immanent justice. *Cognitive Development*, **7**, 429–443.

Strathern, M. (1988). *The gender of the gift: Problems with women and problems with society in Melanesia*. Berkeley, CA: University of California Press.

Strauss, C., & Quinn, N. (1997). *A cognitive theory of cultural meaning*. Cambridge, England: Cambridge University Press.

Thagard, P. (1992). *Conceptual revolutions*. Princeton, NJ: Princeton University Press.

Toren, C. (1999). *Mind, materiality and history: Explorations in Fijian ethnography*. London: Routledge.

Toren, C. (2001). The child in mind. In H. Whitehouse (Ed.), *The debated mind: Evolutionary psychology versus ethnography* (pp. 155–179). Oxford, England: Berg.

Trautmann, T. R. (1987). *Lewis Henry Morgan and the invention of kinship*. Berkeley, CA: University of California Press.

Vosniadou, S. (1994). Universal and cultural-specific properties of children's mental models of the earth. In L. Hirschfeld & S. Gelman (Eds.), *Mapping the mind: Domain specificity in cognition and culture* (pp. 412–430). Cambridge, England: Cambridge University Press.

Walker, S. (1999). Culture, domain-specificity, and conceptual change: Natural kind and artefact concepts. *British Journal of Developmental Psychology*, **17**, 203–219.

Waxman, S. (1999). The dubbing ceremony revisited: Object naming and categorization in infancy and early childhood. In D. L. Medin & S. Atran (Eds.), *Folkbiology* (pp. 233–283). Cambridge, MA: MIT Press.

Weissman, M. D., & Kalish, C. (1999). The inheritance of desired characteristics: Children's view of the role of intention in parent-offspring resemblance. *Quarterly Journal of Experimental Child Psychology*, **73**, 245–265.

Wellman, H. M., & Gelman, S. A. (1998). Knowledge acquisition in foundational domains. In D. Kuhn & R. S. Siegler (Eds.), *Handbook of child psychology, Vol. 2: Cognition, perception, and language* (5th ed., pp. 523–573). New York: Wiley.

Williams, J. M., & Affleck, G. (1999). The effects of an age-appropriate intervention on young children's understanding of inheritance. *Educational Psychology*, **19**, 259–275.

Witherspoon, G. (1975). *Navajo kinship and marriage*. Chicago, IL: University of Chicago Press.

Woodward, A. L. (1998). Infants selectively encode the goal object of an actor's reach. *Cognition*, **69**, 1–34.

Wynn, K. (1992). Addition and subtraction by human infants. *Nature*, **358**, 749–750.

Xu, F., & Spelke, E. (2000). Large number discrimination in 6-month-old infants. *Cognition*, **74**, B1–B11.

Yanagisako, S. J., & Collier, J. F. (1987). Towards a unified analysis of gender and kinship. In J. F. Collier & S. J. Yanagisako (Eds.), *Gender and kinship: Essays towards a unified analysis* (pp. 14–50). New York: Routledge.

ACKNOWLEDGMENTS

Because of its interdisciplinary nature and the logistics of fieldwork, this project has required intellectual and financial support from many sources. Maurice Bloch, anthropologist at the London School of Economics, was instrumental in initiating his and Astuti's collaboration with Susan Carey and Gregg Solomon. He piloted the adoption study with Zafimaniry children and adults in Madagascar, paving the way for our study among the Vezo. He has continued to contribute to our research in all of its stages, with moral support (especially when Astuti was in the field), insight, comments, and humor. Larry Hirschfeld's work on race has inspired much of our work. At the outset, we discussed our project with him and we thank him for his intellectual input and for his patience in awaiting its outcome. Sean Epstein, Astuti's son, was in Madagascar during the period of data collection and he proved an excellent research assistant. He not only took a keen interest in the topic of biological inheritance, but also greatly facilitated Astuti's work with Vezo children. Our warmest thanks go to all the Vezo children, adolescents and adults who agreed to take part in our studies. As ever, Astuti greatly appreciated Gion Cabalzar's hospitality in Morondava. During the extended period of data analysis, the CNRS and the Institute Jean Nicod sponsored a series of interdisciplinary workshops in Paris in which all three authors participated. Thanks are due to the organizer, Dan Sperber, for these interesting meetings and for providing a venue for face-to-face work. Finally, we wish to thank the anonymous reviewers and the SRCD *Monographs'* editor for their careful reading of the manuscript, for their criticisms and suggestions.

Astuti wishes to thank the Anthropology Department at the London School of Economics, in particular its then convener Johnny Parry, for allowing her to take time off from her teaching and administrative duties. This project could not have been completed without the extended period of research leave that Astuti has been allowed to enjoy. She would also like to thank her colleague and friend Charles Stafford for carrying a heavy load, without resenting her freedom. The *Monograph* was written at the

Laboratory of Developmental Studies at Harvard, where Astuti spent a sabbatical year. She is grateful for the assistance she received from Andrew Baron and from all the other members of the Carey, Spelke, and Snedeker Labs, who made her stay an outstanding and fully enjoyable experience. Many thanks also to Paul Harris, Melissa Koenig, Fabrice Clement, and Laurence Kaufmann for lively and stimulating discussions. Finally, Astuti wishes to thank Lorenzo Epstein who, as always, has shared the frustrations, the excitement, and the joys of her work.

Astuti was supported by the Economic and Social Research Council, U.K. (Research Grant R000237191, 1997–1998, and Research Fellowship R000271254, 2002–2005), the Nuffield Foundation (Social Science Research Foundation Fellowship, 1997–1998), the Leverhulme Foundation (Study Abroad Fellowship, 2002–2003). She thanks all of these institutions for their generous support.

Solomon wishes to thank the National Science Foundation and the Fondation Fyssen for their support. Thanks also to Bill Gerin, Ted Gibson, Fati Khosroshahi, and Jean-Michel Roy.

COMMENTARY

CONCEPTUAL DEVELOPMENT IN MADAGASCAR: A CRITICAL COMMENT

Tim Ingold

This study has much to commend it. Through its focus on children's conceptual development in a non-western setting, it engages a critical interface between psychology and anthropology that should be of considerable interest to scholars in both fields. The fact that one of the authors (Astuti) has a deep and intimate knowledge of this setting, gained through previous long-term ethnographic fieldwork, allows the study to be grounded in a sensitivity to the nuances of cultural context that is quite rare in developmental inquiries of this kind. Nevertheless I have to confess that I am one of those anthropologists who remain profoundly sceptical of the approach taken here. The authors are aware that the appeal to innate conceptual structures or learning mechanisms, universal to human infants, is unlikely to find favor with anthropological readers. Indeed their style of presentation seems almost calculated to repel such readers. They will be put off by the robotic and dehumanizing depiction of children as solitary ratiocinating devices, by the reduction of creative thought to the operation of preprogrammed mechanisms on external "inputs," and by the self-confirming circularity that leads the authors to find in the heads of their experimental subjects the very same ontological assumptions that frame their own study. Indeed there is more than a hint of double standards here. For if it were really true that thought and its development are universally constrained in the ways the authors claim, then they should be just as constrained in their thinking as everyone else. Yet only by freeing themselves from such constraints can their possible existence and influence upon the thought of others be put to the test.

I divide my comments into two sections. In the first, I review the assumptions underlying the authors' theory of conceptual development. In the second, I review the assumptions they claim to find in the thinking of the people studied—the Vezo of Madagascar. The two sets of assumptions turn out to be suspiciously similar.

136

THEORIZING CONCEPTUAL DEVELOPMENT

From the start the study assumes that the way the world is known by human beings is through representing it in the mind, by means of concepts. These concepts, the authors insist, cannot simply be inferred from what people say. For everyday discourse offers no more than an extended commentary on the bedrock of a priori conceptual knowledge, if not actually concealing it behind a smokescreen of disclaimers and denials. Comprising a system of "structured mental representations," people are supposed to carry this knowledge around with them wherever they go, and to use it to make sense of whatever scenarios they happen to be presented with, whether these be in the form of narratives or actual events. To take one example that plays a prominent role in this study: if I have the concept "biological inheritance," then on observing a physiognomic resemblance between two persons who claim to be related as parent and child, I will automatically infer that this is due to the replication and transmission at birth of an innate character template. I might of course explicitly deny this inference, and attribute the resemblance to parental involvement in the child's training and upbringing, or to a history of shared activity. I might even claim that on closer inspection, the child also resembles a number of other people, besides the parents, with whom he or she has had something to do. Such claims might be driven by a strong moral conviction about the importance of nurture, or by a sense that children should not be connected too exclusively to their birth parents at the expense of the wider community. But in my heart of hearts I know that I am deluding myself, and that *really* bodily traits are inherited from birth parents, and from them alone.

This, according to the authors of the present study, is the predicament in which most Vezo adults find themselves. What they say is one thing; what they know is another. Sayings enjoy a currency within the public sphere of social interaction; knowledge is internal and private to the individual. Thus the process by which Vezo adults come to have a knowledge of the world around them, and specifically of other people, is categorically removed from their engagements with these others in the ordinary course of social life. The same is assumed to be true of children, although for them the concept of biological inheritance is apparently not so firmly established, nor are they under such a strong moral compunction as their elders to deny it. This assumption, however, flies in the face of a considerable body of work in the field of cultural psychology that has shown how cognition is itself a social process that goes on in the practical and discursive contexts of people's engagements both with one another and with non-human components of the environment. Most of this work goes uncited here (see, e.g., Bruner, 1986; Rogoff & Lave, 1984; Lave, 1988; Lave & Wenger, 1991; Carrithers, 1992; Chaiklin & Lave, 1993; Hutchins, 1995; Keller & Keller, 1996, and many more). Much of its inspiration comes from the developmental psychology of Lev Vygotsky. It was Vygotsky's fundamental insight that children *grow* in knowledge and understanding, just as they do in strength and stature, within a field of relations that is structured and scaffolded by the presence and support of others. This field is what he called the "zone of proximal development" (Vygotsky, 1978).

Only once do the authors of this study mention "Vygotsky-inspired cultural psychology," referring to the seminal work of Barbara Rogoff (1990) on children's cognitive development. But the reference is made merely in passing, and to make the banal point that any study of development must be culturally situated. The point is taken no further; indeed the authors seem not to understand what the cultural situatedness of conceptual development actually entails. So far as they are concerned, the "situation" is no more than a source of external environmental *inputs* to development. Thus according to what they call the "Constrained Conceptual Construction" hypothesis, each child constructs his or her concepts anew, interpreting the input from the cultural environment by means of a suite of innate learning mechanisms. As the inputs can be expected to vary from one situation to another, so will the developmental outcomes, though within uniform parameters set by the innate mechanisms. Why should we assume, however, that "each child" constructs concepts on his or her own? Vygotsky's argument, quite to the contrary, was that the process of construction is inherently social and collaborative. Children construct their concepts together, and with adults, incorporating into their own understanding ways of thinking and knowing forged in currents of shared activity and communication. In a nutshell, they do not *undergo* development but rather *participate* in it. The generative source of concepts, in this view, lies neither in innate mechanisms nor in environmental inputs, nor in the interaction between the two, but in the dynamic potential of the entire system of relations established through the presence of the child in a specific social and historical context. And by the "situation," here, is meant nothing less than a moment in the unfolding of this total developmental system.

If the authors are unable to comprehend development as a social and historical process, it is because their thought is securely locked within the terms of a dichotomy between innate and acquired knowledge. This leads them to conclude that any anthropologists who have trouble with the idea that knowledge or its construction is constrained by innate structures must be of the opinion that all knowledge is simply picked up from the surrounding environment. "Most mainstream anthropologists," we are told, adhere to the position labelled here as the "Unconstrained Learning" hypothesis. According to this hypothesis conceptual development is governed wholly by sociocultural inputs to the mind, and not at all by its evolved architecture. I do not know of any anthropologists who presently adhere to this view (no names are mentioned), though there have been one or two famous advocates in the past. Today, "Unconstrained Learning" is a straw man. The significant difference is rather between those who would accept some variant of the "Constrained Conceptual Construction" hypothesis, arguing that culturally specific knowledge is acquired by means of innate learning mechanisms or acquisition devices, and those who hold, to the contrary, that knowledge is not acquired at all but continually co-created within fields of relationships. I am myself of this latter view, and am even quoted to this effect: "[human] capacities are neither innately pre-specified nor externally imposed, but arise within processes of develop-ment, as properties of dynamic self-organization of the total field of relationships in which a person's life unfolds" (Ingold, 2001, p. 131). Yet rather than taking issue what I and others have argued along these lines, the authors are content merely to state their own belief that no a priori con-siderations rule out the hypothesis that innate constraints guide conceptual development.

The issue, however, is not the relative balance of innate and acquired knowledge; it is whether it makes any sense to distinguish between these two kinds of knowledge in the first place. And this issue cannot be tested em-pirically by way of a research design that has the distinction already built into it. There are, in fact, good a priori reasons why the distinction, and any hypothesis based on it, *should* be rejected. If the acquisition or construction of concepts depends on innate learning mechanisms, where do these mech-anisms come from? They are commonly assumed to have arisen in the course of human evolution, and therefore to be effectively installed in every individual mind, as part of its suite of "phylogenetic properties", in advance of—and as a precondition for—its subsequent development. The fact is, however, that minds do not come as kits of parts ready-made for assembly. Like the organisms to which they belong, minds *grow*. And any mechanisms that might be attributed to these minds have to grow too. At whatever stage in life we might identify a particular mechanism, even at birth, a history of growth in a particular environment already lies behind it. In short, the very learning mechanisms that are supposed to enable and constrain conceptual development must themselves develop. How, then, are we to distinguish the development of the innate mechanisms from the development of the con-cepts that are acquired thereby? Attempts in the literature to answer this question are confused and contradictory, but boil down to two distinct claims. One is that the mechanisms that underwrite learning are reliably constructed under all possible circumstances. The other is that these uni-versal mechanisms proceed to work on variable inputs from the environ-ment to produce the diversity of manifest developmental outcomes. Both of these claims are entailed in the hypothesis of "Constrained Conceptual Construction."

In effect, the hypothesis models cognitive development as a two-stage process. In the first, the innate mechanisms are constructed; in the second, they are put into service to furnish the universal capacities so established with specific cultural content. This model, however, depends on factoring out those features of the environment that are constant, or reliably present, in every conceivable developmental context, from those that represent a source of variable input from one context to another. Only the former are relevant in the first stage (the construction of innate mechanisms); only the latter are relevant in the second (the acquisition of culturally specific concepts). Of course for comparative analytic purposes it is sometimes helpful, even essential, to sift the general from the particular, or to establish a kind of "lowest common denominator" of development. But real environments are not partitioned in this way. It is inconceivable that the infant, either before or after birth, should encounter exclusively those aspects of the environment that are common to infants everywhere, and only subsequently, once its "mechanisms" are established, encounter the environment's more contingent aspects. On the contrary, the environment encountered in early life is just as rich and varied as that encountered later on. We should not, then, regard the learning environment as a source of variable input for preconstructed mechanisms. Rather, it furnishes variable conditions for the growth or self-assembly, in the course of both early and later development, of the child's ability to think in the particular ways that he or she does. That ability is neither innate nor acquired. It is the outcome of a process of growth, within a field of relations that cuts across the emergent boundary between the learner and the world.

THE VEZO THEORY OF HUMAN DEVELOPMENT

Let me now return to the Vezo, and to the central proposition of this study, namely that innate mechanisms guide conceptual development such that by the time they reach adulthood, Vezo people are led to distinguish between inherited and acquired traits in the same way that people generally do, not just in the West but perhaps the world over. Vezo adults, it is claimed, are just as prone to dualistic thinking as are their counterparts in Europe or North America. Accordingly, they understand the human being to be constituted as a compound of bodily characteristics fixed at birth through biological inheritance and of mental characteristics (beliefs and skills) established through a subsequent period of nurture and transmitted by social learning. The evidence for this claim comes from Vezo responses to a story about a baby boy who was adopted at birth. For a range of characteristics, ranging from somatic traits to beliefs and skills, respondents were asked to state whether, when grown up, the boy would come to resemble the "father who generated him" or the "father who raised him." Most attributed somatic traits to the former, and beliefs and skills to the latter. Although the story tells of "generating" and "raising," the language in which it is couched makes no mention of the dichotomies between body and mind, between birth and nurture, and between the biological and the social. In that respect, the authors are justified in their contention that while the task was constructed around these dichotomies, they were not forced on respondents, who would have had no difficulty in completing it whether they thought in these terms or not. The issue lies, rather, in the interpretation of the results. Do they show that Vezo adults make the same "ontological cut" as westerners? Or does the cut have its source in the analytic language of the researchers? To answer these questions, I shall consider each of the three dichotomies in turn: first, body versus mind; second, birth versus nurture, and third, biology versus society.

I could find no evidence in the material presented to suggest that in their selection of characteristics typically fixed by the time the baby is born and of those established later on while the child is being raised, Vezo adults are categorically distinguishing between body and mind. It seems rather that they are distinguishing, reasonably enough, between the kinds of characteristics that develop early and are relatively unaffected by the practical activities in which children become involved as they grow up, and those that develop later and are relatively dependent on these activities for their formation. Vezo men fish for a living, and among their distinctive bodily traits are scarred fingers from working with fishing lines and calluses on the upper foot from sitting in canoes. Doubtless the lives people lead and the skills they habitually practice leave many other traces on the body. How, then, can the authors of this study infer that by distinguishing traits fixed at birth from traits fixed later on, Vezo are also distinguishing mind from body? The inference can only be sustained by reclassifying all such traces as mental! When it comes to skills such as whistling, fishing and felling trees, which are at once deliberative and intentional, but also call for developmentally enhanced dexterity, it is impossible to say whether they are bodily or mental, since they are clearly both. The practice of a skill is indeed a matter of "thinking through the body" (Jackson, 1989). Again there is no evidence, from their responses, that Vezo regard skills learned in childhood as of mind *rather than* body. The source of this idea seems rather to lie in the authors' own conviction that skilled practice involves nothing more than the biomechanical implementation of mental templates or schemata.

What, then, of the distinction between birth and nurture? I wonder how many people, even in the West, really believe that nurture begins at birth. As Dent (1990, p. 693) points out, "birth is a transition, not a magic starting point before which experience cannot play a role." In their explicit

141

pronouncements, Vezo would agree. They assert that the unborn child is not only nourished by the mother's blood and the father's semen, but is also liable to be shaped in its physiognomy by virtue of its vicarious immersion in a wider field of social relations with other persons and even spirits. Thus when they say that certain features are given at birth, they are *not* implying that they are "fixed" by inheritance rather than by nurture. What they are saying is that they are fixed by the nurture that precedes birth, rather than by the nurture that carries on after it. According to the authors, however, what Vezo people say is not a reliable guide to their conceptual knowledge and ontological commitments. They point out that none of their respondents suggested "prenatal *social* influences" as a possible reason for the resemblance between the child in the story and its birth father. There may however be a simple explanation for this. In the story the birth father is described as the man who "generated" the child, as opposed to the man who "raised" him. From what we know of Vezo understandings of procreation, it appears that the generation of children is regarded not as a one-off event at the point of conception, but rather as a process that continues throughout pregnancy. Thus in their responses, Vezo would have no cause to single out prenatal paternal nurture as an alternative or additional reason for the physiognomic resemblance between father and child, since such nurture is already subsumed by the idea of generation. For Vezo people, it appears, "generation" and "raising" are successive phases in a continuous, life-historic process that is merely punctuated, not initiated, by the event of birth. Thus *birth is a milestone of nurture*, it does not preconstitute the human being in advance of nurture. When Vezo distinguish between characteristics established by the time of birth from characteristics established later in life, they are doing just that, they are not setting up nurture and birth as distinct formative influences.

Finally, the authors infer that by separating out traits established at birth from those established through subsequent upbringing, Vezo are also distinguishing between the domains of biological and social relations. But this distinction between the biological and the social is the authors' own; it has no equivalent in Vezo conceptions. Quite what the authors mean by "biology" is unclear, but the term seems to stand for some fixed essence of the human individual, given at the moment of conception, independently and in advance of that individual's development in an environment. Thus the authors say that they take the alleged Vezo "understanding of the distinct causal roles of birth parentage and socially mediated learning as evidence that participants have a theory of biological inheritance." This can only imply that in the researchers' scheme of things, all processes of development are ipso facto non-biological. This is a strange idea. Would they say that the growth of a child in strength and stature, following birth, is a non-biological process? And what of development before birth? We have already seen how the authors take respondents' failure to cite any influences of a specifically *social* nature as a reason to discount the paternal contribution to prenatal development. But the idea that such influence should be exclusively social is a corollary of their own assumption that biology precedes development. There is absolutely no evidence to suggest that the Vezo people themselves concur with the apparent belief of some people in western societies (including the authors of this study), that bodily traits are inherited by some magical process of replication *prior to* prenatal development, and plenty of evidence to suggest that they do not. In short, to distinguish between characteristics that develop respectively before and after birth is *not* to presuppose an ontological distinction between "facts of biology" and "facts of sociality." Anthropologists are right to question the validity of this distinction, and nothing in the data presented here suggests otherwise.

CONCLUSION

I conclude that the alleged convergence between Vezo and western thought upon a fundamental ontological dualism is wholly spurious. The inferences the authors draw from their data are unjustified and in some cases even vitiated by the evidence presented. They derive these inferences by filtering Vezo responses through their own, markedly dualistic categorical framework. What they consequently discover in these responses are the very same assumptions that underlie their own theorizing. Naturally, if all responses are filtered through the same frame, then this frame is bound to be reflected back in the responses. No wonder the authors find universals everywhere! According to their theory, the *biological inheritance* of certain cognitive mechanisms is prerequisite for the transmission, by *social learning*, of culturally specific concepts. And what do they find? They find that the concepts so transmitted universally encode a distinction between biological inheritance and social learning. For universality, read circularity. Apparently, all you have to do to establish a universal is to show that "despite what they say" people in this or that non-Western culture think like assorted North Americans. There is, of course, no reason to believe that all North Americans think in the same way. But even if they did, and even if it turned out that the people of the selected "other culture" were closet dualists, two cases—one western, the other non-western—do not make a universal. Or if they did, then it would take only a third case to refute it. There exists, in fact, an abundance of ethnographic evidence—some of it even from western societies (e.g., Edwards, 2000)—that would drive a coach and horses through the arguments advanced here. The authors' claim to have

143

identified a common substrate for human conceptual development remains unsubstantiated. Indeed their study provides an object lesson in how *not* to do cultural psychology.

References

Bruner, J. (1986). *Actual minds, possible worlds*. Cambridge, MA: Harvard University Press.

Carrithers, M. (1992). *Why humans have cultures*. Oxford: Oxford University Press.

Chaiklin, S. & Lave, J. (Eds.) (1993). *Understanding in practice: Perspectives on activity and context*. Cambridge: Cambridge University Press.

Dent, C. H. (1990). An ecological approach to language development: An alternative functionalism. *Developmental Psychobiology*, **23**, 679–703.

Edwards, J. (2000). *Born and bred: Idioms of kinship and new reproductive technologies in England*. Oxford: Oxford University Press.

Hutchins, E. (1995). *Cognition in the wild*. Cambridge, MA: MIT Press.

Ingold, T. (2001). From the transmission of representations to the education of attention. In H. Whitehouse (Ed.), *The debated mind: Evolutionary psychology versus ethnography* (pp. 113–153). Oxford: Berg.

Jackson, M. (1989). *Paths toward a clearing: Radical empiricism and ethnographic inquiry*. Bloomington: Indiana University Press.

Keller, C. M., & Keller, J. D. (1996). *Cognition and tool use: The blacksmith at work*. Cambridge: Cambridge University Press.

Lave, J. (1988). *Cognition in practice*. Cambridge: Cambridge University Press.

Lave, J., & Wenger, E. (1991). *Situated learning: Legitimate peripheral participation*. Cambridge: Cambridge University Press.

Rogoff, B. (1990). *Apprenticeship in thinking: Cognitive development in social context*. Oxford: Oxford University Press.

Rogoff, B. & Lave, J. (Eds.) (1984). *Everyday cognition*. Cambridge, MA: Harvard University Press.

Vygotsky, L. (1978). *Mind in society: The development of higher psychological processes*. Cambridge, MA: Harvard University Press.

COGNITIVE DEVELOPMENT: HERE, THERE, AND EVERYWHERE

Patricia H. Miller

This *Monograph* is important and provocative in several ways. First, it is an excellent model for multidisciplinary research. Although psychologists recognize the value of doing such research, few actually carry out a truly multidisciplinary project. Such research is difficult, time-consuming, and often frustrating. When it works, however, it provides a rich, complex, and multifaceted perspective and even opens up new areas of inquiry. In the present study, it works. An anthropologist who has conducted ethnographic research in Madagascar and two cognitive psychologists who have studied conceptual development collaborated to test whether there are innate universal "habits of mind."

Combining anthropology and cognitive-developmental psychology led to an interesting set of questions based on competing hypotheses. Each discipline provided prior evidence for its hypothesis. Anthropological research suggested that Madagascar would be an ideal cultural laboratory for testing a critical question from cognitive psychology: Is the acquisition of folkbiological knowledge about hereditary transmission of traits biologically constrained in some way, and thus universal, or is it acquired through experience and thus variable? Anthropologists have evidence from field-work that Vezo adults in Madagascar believe that a mother's experiences with other people during pregnancy can affect her child's appearance. The Vezo also seem to see kinship and group identity as something achieved rather than simply inherited. The psychologists' contribution was to provide an established paradigm for answering this question, which is of great interest to psychologists as well. A central question for both disciplines concerns universal or diverse beliefs about origins and group identity. Thus, this research serves as a guide to how to do multidisciplinary research: Identify questions of interest to both disciplines, compare the available data from both disciplines, typically generated by different methods, construct a set of competing hypotheses, identify the appropriate population for testing the hypotheses, select a method that draws on the best from both disciplines, and draw appropriate conclusions in light of the knowledge base of both disciplines. As the present research demonstrates, this is a win–win situation.

A second main strength of this *Monograph* is its elegant and nuanced presentation of each theoretical position from psychology and anthropology, the predictions of each position, prior evidence for and against it, and the sort of evidence from the present research that would support or refute it. The Unconstrained Learning hypothesis, from cultural anthropology and cultural psychology, is that there are few if any constraints on what sort of folkbiology and folksociology can be developed. At the other extreme, the Innate Conceptual Content hypothesis is that children are endowed with a domain-specific folkbiological module dedicated to guiding the construction of intuitive biological concepts (e.g., Medin & Atran, in press). Thus, this position argues for strong biological constraints on cognition. In between these two positions, the Constrained Conceptual Construction hypothesis is that children are endowed with powerful but domain-general theory-building mechanisms for recognizing and essentializing natural kinds and constructing causal explanations about such kinds. However, each child must discover which kinds are natural kinds, including biological kinds, and must construct theories specifying causal mechanisms in their folkbiology (e.g., Carey, 1999; Gelman, 2003). One biological causal mechanism is the inheritance of species kind. Children could, for example, learn about natural kinds by listening to adults talk about the attributes of various sorts of animals.

A third, obvious, strength of this research is that it examined a non-western culture, particularly one rarely studied by psychologists. The data seem to have been gathered in ways that were sensitive to the Vezo culture.

THE QUESTIONS

The issue of the biological and experiential influences on human behavior and development is one of the oldest and most central ones in psychology. This research asked: Are there universal concepts, emerging early, that would suggest biological constraints on human thought? More specifically, the research addressed two questions about Vezo children, adolescents, and adults. One is "What do they believe about the transmission of individual traits?" A person might or might not understand that physical traits are mainly influenced by heredity and that beliefs are mainly influenced by experience. The other question is "What do they believe determines a person's group identity?"

THE ISSUE OF UNIVERSAL CONSTRAINTS

The authors considered two sorts of evidence essential for the claim of the Innate Conceptual Content hypothesis concerning the understanding of biological inheritance. One is that adults in quite different cultures hold similar beliefs. It turned out, for example, that Vezo adults, like those in other cultures studied, represent a species' bodily traits as naturalized (inherited from birth parents) and essentialized, but behavioral and psychological traits as learned. They apparently also differentiate conceptually between human groups and animal species. The other sort of supporting evidence for biological constraints would be the early emergence of a belief in various cultures. Although, like young children in a variety of cultures, even the youngest Vezo children (age 6) predicted that a duck that emerges from an egg laid by a duck will be a duck even if hatched and raised by a hen, it takes years for them to fully understand which traits are determined by biological inheritance and which by learning. Thus, the authors favor the Constrained Conceptual Construction hypothesis over the Innate Conceptual Content hypothesis. That is, the specific folkbiology of a culture must be constructed.

In my view, although the results are consistent with the Constrained Conceptual Construction hypothesis, they do not eliminate positions hypothesizing even weaker constraints, such as the Unconstrained Learning hypothesis. Regarding the adult data, adult similarity could come from the similarity of critical human experiences rather than from any sort of biologically based constraint. Regarding the child data, it is not clear what age of emergence of understanding would favor one of these two hypotheses over the other. None of the participants were younger than age 6 and much can happen in six years. If children's first beliefs about transmission and identity are evidence for constraints, then one cannot be sure that the present study has not missed their first set of beliefs. It would be useful to have this information when comparing the Vezo children to young children in other cultures. Moreover, even the preschoolers in other cultures showing, for example, an essentialist belief, still have had several years of experience for constructing their beliefs. The authors, however, make the important point that the Vezo children seem to hold beliefs that contradict what they hear adults say. That is, children reason that people are born to be Vezo or Karany even though adults' talk emphasizes how Vezo become Vezo by doing Vezo things. Piaget made this point decades ago when he found, for example, that even directly telling a child that amounts are unchanged despite changes in appearance had no effect on preschoolers' beliefs in nonconservation. The authors' evidence that children think in ways that are not simply taught to them by adults reminds us yet again that children construct, rather than simply receive, their views of the world. It is not

147

known whether there are other aspects of their experience that cancel out the effect of hearing this talk.

In addition to current debates over whether there are constraints at all, there are various positions on the mechanisms underlying constraints on constructing essentialist categories. Constraints can range from a biologically-based content-specific module, to biases based on one's current conceptual structure, to limitations based on limited information-processing abilities. In my view, it could be, for example, that essentializing is simply a cognitive strategy used by a limited capacity mind to simplify a complex world. Regardless of whether one agrees with the authors that there is some sort of constraint on humans' folkbiology and folksociology, though not a strong module-based constraint, this impressive set of studies should spark an interesting debate between psychologists and anthropologists and between psychologists holding various positions on this issue.

THE ISSUE OF METHODS

The results from psychologists' assessments with adoption scenarios did not support the kinds of child concepts expected from anthropological ethnographies showing that Vezo people talk about how children come to resemble people not related to them, as when a baby looks like a person his mother befriended while pregnant. The authors' interpretation of this is that informants' discourse may not be a reliable indication of their knowledge and beliefs. Their fascinating hypothesis is that denying that only parents contribute to their children's physical traits is a strategy for creating a community in which children are generated by a much larger social network. Alternatively, to me, some of the examples suggest that the adults' remarks could reflect little moral tales. One example was that a mother who as a child had made fun of someone with a clubfoot consequently gave birth to a child with a clubfoot. Another example is that a baby can resemble someone whom the mother disliked. Suck talk may be intended to teach a lesson to others. In any case, one important implication of these sorts of social explanations is that researchers must consider the social goals and motives in the particular setting when interpreting data about people's knowledge.

This apparent motive-based inconsistency in Vezo adults' behavior has implications for a current theme in the field of cognitive development, namely, observed intra-individual variability in strategies, concepts, and reasoning (e.g., Rosengren & Braswell, 2001; Siegler, 1996). Such variability may not simply show the uneven ability to apply knowledge across settings, or competition among strategies, but sometimes may reflect differing social purposes in different settings. Variability sometimes may indicate different social goals rather than the jockeying for dominance of a more advanced and less advanced way of reasoning.

The use of the adoption scenario to examine concepts about the biological versus environmental origins of traits raises an interesting question: Does the biology–environment dichotomy, so salient in the Western mind have less hold in some cultures? Perhaps this is a dichotomy salient in the Western mind but less salient in the Vezo mind. Perhaps other dimensions are important to the Vezo or perhaps they even are less inclined to dichotomize at all.

BONUS RESULTS

This *Monograph* focuses on the results pertaining to cross-cultural and cross-age similarities and differences, which can address the issue of cognitive universality. This research, like most research on cultures other than North American or Western European ones, shows how the culture differs from these heavily studied cultures. Such research has produced much valuable information. However, research on non-Western cultures can make another sort of contribution. Instead of taking the authors' focus on differences and similarities, we could use the Vezo beliefs as a *starting point* for thinking about cognition. That is, if we are concerned less with comparing Vezo beliefs with Western beliefs and temporarily try to forget everything we know about cognition and cognitive development based on research in the West and just focus on the Vezo beliefs, what would cognitive development look like? I believe that we would ask different questions and perhaps develop different models of development.

In particular, I was intrigued by the finding that, for Vezo adults, a person's activities and skills play a central role in their beliefs about that person's identity. Thus, the authors report that Vezo adults seem to have a "performative theory of group identity." That is, the Vezo consider group identity to be determined by what people do, what customs they follow, what they eat, and so on, rather than their birth origins and ancestry. You are a Vezo because you do Vezo things—fish, sail, and participate in Vezo religious customs. You are what you *do* more than who gave birth to you.

This focus on the "lived world" is in sharp contrast to most current Western models of adult identity and its development. Western models emphasize an essence-based identity: you are what you *are*. The focus is on the individual, autonomy, and abstract personal attributes. Such research examines people's self concepts and their concepts about the personal characteristics of others rather than what a person does. Western developmental social cognitive research focuses on children's understanding of other people's traits—what people are, not what they do; what sort of person someone is, not what sorts of activities in which he or she engages. Similarly, the most active area of research on social cognition in children—theory of mind—examines children's understanding of mental states such as beliefs and desires rather than their understanding of behaviors and skills—a theory of behavior, what people do. Or perhaps more accurately, children's theory of behavior is studied in terms of its relation to mental states rather than to an activity-based identity. Western folk psychology includes the belief that mental states lead to behavior; developmentalists rarely study children's understanding of how behavior might shape permanent belief systems about the identity of self and others. Thus, if Western developmentalists started a line of research based on the Vezo perspective they might ask how children and adolescents come to understand other people in terms of what they do, how engagement in cultural practices leads to the development of a self.

The Vezo performative theory of identity also challenges the Western mind–body split. A body that does Vezo or Karany activities and follows Vezo or Karany customs makes a person a Vezo or a Karany. It seems that in Vezo culture the mind is not abstracted, disembodied, and decontextualized. Identity is not something that exists only in the mind; it exists in the larger indivisible unit of person-in-context. In the Vezo performative theory of identity there is both mind in body and body in mind. People in the West may think about minds in general and bodies in general, but a Vezo adult cares about specific bodies doing specific activities in specific communities. It is an empirical question whether Western people do not hold a performative theory of identity or psychologists just do not use methods that would reveal such a theory.

The Vezo emphasis on aspects of identity connected with the cultural group opens up Western research on social cognition about individuals in yet another way. Children's developing understanding of the defining features of one's culture, so important for the Vezo conception of identity, is rarely studied by social cognitive developmentalists, who tend to study children's concepts about other people—their traits and mental states. Information about the understanding of features of a culture, as well as the understanding of individuals, would enhance our theories of cognitive development. Information about what Western children understand about the different customs, occupational activities, and skills of different cultural groups is essential for any society that is becoming increasingly multicultural. In short, the bonus results of the present *Monograph* add an important sociological dimension to research on social cognitive development. By using a Vezo perspective as a launching point for a model of social cognitive development, we see phenomena that our current models and methods have not revealed. The present research thus makes an important contribution to building new theories and methods.

METHODOLOGICAL LIMITATIONS

One methodological limitation stems from the fact that the investigators had to decide whether to devote their limited amount of time to using only one type of adoption vignette to study beliefs about numerous traits or using several types of vignettes to study a smaller set of traits. They chose the former route. Although this was a reasonable decision, the problem with the use of only one type of vignette for human adoption and one vignette for hen–duck adoption is that any comparison of the two must be done cautiously. Specifically, although the stories were similar they varied in ways that might be important. Differences include, for the human and hen–duck stories respectively, father versus mother, boy versus unknown gendered offspring; body traits-beliefs-skills (neutral or typical) versus body traits–knowledge (neutral). For example, would using a human mother rather than a father lead to more answers based on the biological parent rather than upbringing since children may be more aware of children coming from their mother's body than from their fathers' genes? (The authors refer to an unpublished study showing the same results for adults when mothers and girls were in the story instead.) I also wondered whether the Vezo emphasis on skills, especially doing Vezo things, might have encouraged more answers based on upbringing in the hen-duck stories if the children had been told that the duck did hen things just as they were told that the Vezo child did the things that the adoptive father and his group did. Moreover, in the case of the hen and duck, a visible means of biological transmission was provided—an egg—whereas in the human case no means of transmission was provided. This lack of a plausible biological mechanism in the human story may be especially likely since they were asked about the father rather than the mother who may be known to give birth.

A related problem for comparing the vignettes is that the hen–duck vignettes included only a cross-species adoption. In contrast, the human vignettes were all within the human species: two Vezo groups differing only in geography (we are told that this has no significance to the Vezo), the Vezo and Masikoro who are similar physically but live very different sorts of lives (fishing versus cultivating rice), and the Vezo and Karany who are both physically and culturally different. It would have been useful, for drawing appropriate conclusions, to know whether children would state more resemblance of the duck to an adoptive parent if the biological and adoptive parents were both ducks who simply lived in different areas of the country (analogous to the Vezo–Vezo human story) or lived different sorts of lives. That is, the authors found that the children seemed to treat the Vezo–Karany difference as a species difference. Would a similar parallel emerge if the other two sorts of human stories had their counterparts in the duck vignettes?

151

In the vignettes that compared the Vezo, Masikoro, and Karany peoples, one missing consideration is the influence of social location, with its associated power or lack of power, on beliefs about the biological or social origins of attributes of other groups. For example, Mahalingam (2003) found that Brahmins in India believed that a poor man's brain transfer to a rich man would not affect the rich man's behavior but that a rich man's brain transfer to a poor man would affect the poor man's behavior. In contrast, Dalits (former "Untouchables") showed less essentialism and did not have these asymmetrical beliefs. Thus, dominant groups may be more likely to invoke a biological notion of essence than are marginalized groups. The differences in the social location and power of the Vezo, Masikoro, and Karany groups may influence the obtained results in unknown ways.

A final limitation of the design is that there were not enough child participants to examine age differences between age 6 and 13. If age of emergence of a concept is important for differentiating among competing hypotheses, then it would be important to have a more refined picture of development during this age range, particularly the gradual versus abrupt nature of change.

CONCLUSIONS

This intriguing set of studies should encourage psychologists to look outside their discipline for ideas and collaborators. The rich set of data and the careful analysis of theoretical positions is an important contribution to developmental psychology, cognitive science, and anthropology. Further such work will continue to tell us how we all are alike and yet different.

References

Carey, S. (1999). Sources of conceptual change. In E. K. Scholnick, K. Nelson, S. A. Gelman & P. H. Miller (Eds.), *Conceptual development: Piaget's legacy* (pp. 293–326). Hillsdale, NJ: Erlbaum.

Gelman, S. (2003). *The essential child*. Oxford: Oxford University Press.

Mahalingam, R. (2003). Essentialism, culture, and power: Representations of social class. *Journal of Social Issues*, **59**, 733–749.

Medin, D. L., & Atran, S. (in press). The native mind: biological categorization and reasoning in development and across cultures. *Psychological Review*.

Rosengren, K. S., & Braswell, G. S. (2001). Variability in children's reasoning. In H. W. Reese & R. Kail (Eds.), *Advances in child development and behavior* (pp. 1–40). San Diego, CA: Academic Press.

Siegler, R. S. (1996). *Emerging minds: The process of change in children's thinking*. New York: Oxford University Press.

REPLIES TO COMMENTARIES

Rita Astuti and Susan Carey

In this reply, we will first address the concerns raised by Tim Ingold. Following this, we will turn our attention to issues raised by Patricia Miller.

Ingold puts words in our mouths and views in our heads that are completely antithetical to what we believe and argue in this *Monograph*. We will divide our reply into two sets of comments. First, we address Ingold's general concerns about what he takes to be our view of cognitive development and its consequences for a vision of human nature. Second, we address his concerns about the project of interdisciplinary cooperation between anthropologists and psychologists, and his specific criticisms of our analysis of how Vezo adults and children construe human and animal kinds and the processes through which humans and animals become unique individuals.

CONCEPTUAL DEVELOPMENT IN GENERAL

We were appalled by what Ingold thinks we would (or do) deny. We too hold dear the tenets that he holds dear: human knowledge is socially situated and culturally constructed, that is, children acquire it from interacting with their elders and peers and by participating in their culture. We are constructivists, as we make clear repeatedly in our *Monograph*. We absolutely believe that children actively participate in the process of their own conceptual development. Indeed, our focus is on something that is needed to understand this socially constructive process—something that Ingold entirely leaves out of his discussion—namely, what the child brings to the process. What is it about the human mind that makes the cultural construction of knowledge possible?

Ingold is upset by the distinction between innate and acquired knowledge, and between innate and acquired learning mechanisms. We, like him, do not believe that people are made up of one bit that is innate, and one bit that is acquired. The innate and the acquired are intertwined in complicated ways from the start. What we are doing is precisely to try to understand and study empirically this complicated process and interaction, to understand what is more-or-less negotiable in the course of development, what is more-or-less easily learned and constructed, what are the conceptual resources (innate *and* acquired) that are needed to live and act in one's historically constituted environment.

In his extended commentary, Ingold never mentions any developmental phenomena, which is strange since *these* are the focus of our studies and the basis for our argument. It is impossible to engage Ingold (or any other anthropologist who thinks the notion of innate constraints is confused) in productive debate about development *unless* they will in turn *engage with the data*. Ingold appears satisfied with a theoretical position that largely ignores empirical studies of the process of cognitive development. But how exactly do Ingold's empirically untested views make sense of the apparently cross-culturally universal construction of an understanding of the biological inheritance of species kind by the end of the preschool years (this now found in at least six very diverse cultural settings)? How do his views make sense of Vezo children's utter failure to understand Vezo adults' performative theory of group identity, as well as their failure to understand Vezo adults' theories about how individual traits are determined? How do his views help make sense of Vezo children's robust belief that a child born to Karany parents but raised by Vezo parents will grow up to be Karany, in spite of daily scaffolding by adults of the Vezo performative theory of group identity?

Ingold's mischaracterization of our view of cognitive development leads seamlessly to a caricature of our picture of human nature. Do we depict children as solitary ratiocinating robotic devices? No, of course not. We give great weight to the social nature of children's learning and development. But cognitive psychology has provided considerable evidence for mechanistic components to the child's—and adult's—mind, and it would be foolish to close one's mind to this. Does entertaining the possibility that human infants are born with rich innate knowledge and with complicated learning mechanisms dehumanize children? No, of course not. Ultimately, it is an empirical question, and it would be foolish to ignore the mounting evidence. Rather than finding them dehumanizing, we find thrilling the discoveries of innate knowledge of number, objects, and intentional agents, and of rich learning mechanisms that support language learning and that support learning about the causal structure of the world. Indeed, we see these discoveries as providing part of the answer to what separates us from other primates, part of the characterization of what makes us human.

Ingold repeatedly says that minds grow, that learning processes are grown. Of course, and what we are studying is how they grow. To deny that some learning processes are innate (associative mechanisms, mechanisms for computing causality from patterns of covariation, and so on) is to ignore an absolutely voluminous body of data. The claim that richer learning mechanisms (e.g., bootstrapping processes, theory building mechanisms) may also have innate support is more controversial, although we believe it is likely to be correct (and in the *Monograph* we refer to the relevant supportive literature). But believing in innately specified learning mechanisms, and some innate conceptual content, does *not* have the consequences Ingold thinks it has, such as the consequence that learning mechanisms themselves cannot develop. Like him, we believe that minds grow. We document this growth in the *Monograph*, and we try to relate an explanatory story for how this is possible in the case study at hand.

Ingold seems to think that we support the view that the adult differentiation of biological inheritance from learning mechanisms develops under innate conceptual constraints—as if there are innate concepts with biological content. Although there are people who hold this position, our *Monograph* is an extended argument against it. (To remind the reader: we think there are innate concepts with psychological and physical content, but not with biological content. We are arguing *against* thinkers like Hirschfeld and Atran on this point.)

Finally, Ingold wonders why we do not discuss the Vygotsky-inspired literature on development, the writings of Bruner, Rogoff, Lave, Hutchins, and others. We admire these writers' work, and the only reason we do not discuss it is that it has not been concerned with the content domains under investigation in our *Monograph*. True, our intellectual project derives more from Piaget than from Vygotsky, but the two perspectives are not incompatible.

Nonetheless, there is one set of claims generally associated with these authors (well reflected in Ingold's comments) that we do want to deny. This is the view that sometimes goes under the label "situated cognition." Again, under some formulations, we find this view entirely compatible with our own, but not when it is claimed that one cannot distinguish internal from external representations, and not when it is claimed that one cannot study the mind on its own. In fact, the fascinating empirical work by these authors does not require these hyperbolic claims. And at the risk of sounding like a broken record, Ingold's insight that "children grow within a field of relations that is structured and scaffolded by the presence and support of others" (p. 138) is not inconsistent with our focus here—namely, on what the child brings to the process of learning within this structured and scaffolded field of relations.

One final methodological point: Ingold notes that we, the theorizers, are as constrained as our subjects, and he concludes that our project is impossible because only by—impossibly—freeing ourselves "from such constraints can their possible existence and influence upon the thought of others, be put to the test" (p. 136). But this is a glib criticism. For example, we are all constrained by certain limits on working memory, but humans can and have plumbed those limits (See any cognition textbook!). The human mind is wonderfully capable of studying constraints that it is itself subject to.

THE VEZO IN PARTICULAR

Ingold takes high moral ground and makes the most damning criticism in anthropology—that we have misunderstood the Vezo because we saw them through the blinders of our own conceptual system. Ironically, his commentary is filled with confident pronouncements on what Vezo *really* think, even though his own ethnographic research has been carried out with Arctic people. His confident views are based on Astuti's ethnography. But if he trusts her "deep and intimate knowledge" of the ethnographic setting (p. 136), why does he reject out of hand our interpretation of Vezo comments on their babies' looks? Does he really think that her collaboration with two psychologists has led to the inevitable corruption of her ethnographic skills? On her part, Astuti thinks that what she has gained from this collaborative project is a far deeper understanding of her informants' sophisticated minds, a point to which we shall return shortly.

But first, we suggest a different reason why Ingold rejects out of hand our interpretation of the ethnographic data. The reason is simply that, in this instance, we have found that Vezo intuitions are essentially the same as our own. It follows, claims Ingold, that we have imposed them on our informants. In the current anthropological climate, it is no doubt a bonus to find that non-western people think differently from us—about bodies, minds, emotions, persons, gender, birth, growth, time, space . . . But surely, whether they do or not is an empirical question, and anthropologists *must* be allowed to discover—without being damned—that sometimes the people they study are not so different from them.

Let us be clear. Ingold clinches his critique by revealing the convergence between our theory of conceptual development and the intuitions we attribute to our Vezo informants. And isn't that suspicious? Ingold's revelation, however, is simply ridiculous. We do not think—and never claim—that Vezo have a theory about innate conceptual constraints on cognitive development. All we claim is that when they make inferences about an individual's properties and kind identity, Vezo adults distinguish between the causal role of birth parentage and the causal role of socially mediated learning. What theory of conceptual development the Vezo have is undoubtedly a fascinating question, but it was not the one we were addressing in the *Monograph*.

Ingold seems to think that we deny the possibility of discovering what people believe from what they say, but actually we hold the subtler view that people's representations of the world are highly context-dependent. Has he failed to notice that our data entirely consist of what Vezo adults, adolescents, and children *said* in response to our questions? The grain of truth in Ingold's charge is that we think it is naïve to assume that *everything* that is said is a transparent reflection of what is known and believed, and that the process of uncovering people's knowledge and beliefs requires many inferential steps, for which systematic data must be sought. But is this point really so controversial?

Throughout the second half of his commentary, Ingold gives the impression that our depiction of Vezo adult inferential reasoning is solely based on our informants' patterns of judgments. But this ignores our extensive (indeed some reviewers deemed it tedious) engagement with their *justifications*. How can Ingold question that Vezo adults distinguish between a bodily and a mental component of the person when they *say* that "when it comes to believing things, the child will follow the father who raised him, but when it comes to the ways of his body, this will depend on the father who generated him. These things are determined by blood," or when they *say* that "the child will be like the father who raised him [i.e., he will believe that chameleons have 20 teeth] because this is about his character and not about his body, and he will believe like the father who brought him up because he hears his words"?

Ingold supposes that we think that people say one thing but that, in their heart of hearts, they know that they are deluding themselves. Do we think that when Vezo adults say that a child is born with a clubfoot because his mother made fun of somebody with a clubfoot they are deluding themselves? Of course not, and we never said so. Rather, we attribute to Vezo adults a far subtler and more articulated mind than Ingold does, and we adopt a much more differentiated view of social discourse and socially constituted knowledge than his. We believe that people can simultaneously hold different, even incompatible, representations of the same phenomenon (i.e., the process by which an individual comes to be what s/he is). We never claim that one representation is truer than the other, or that only one is held in people's heart of hearts while the other is a mere delusion. Rather, we claim that different representations are deployed in different social contexts and for different reasons. We suggest that anthropologists are ill advised to base their claims about their informants' knowledge and beliefs solely on the social context they happen to access more easily: those moments in which people, rather than making inferences about the world, self-consciously reflect on how they want the world to be.

There is one place where, thankfully, Ingold engages with our data, and this is where he offers an alternative interpretation of the results of our adoption task with Vezo adults. He argues that what we take as a distinction between bodily traits that are determined by biological inheritance

157

and mental/experiential traits that are determined by learning, practice, and habituation, is really a distinction between characteristics that develop early and those that develop later. In other words, the responses of our adult informants merely indicate that they recognize that certain characteristics are present at birth or soon after, while others take time to develop. However, most of the bodily traits that we tested are *not* present at birth and do *not* develop soon after (e.g., long, slender hands; small lips; black skin; curly hair). When Vezo adults judged that the adopted boy in our story would grow up to resemble his birth father in his bodily traits, they made an inference about innate potential: they judged that a baby's chubby hands (or light skin) have the potential to become long and slender (or black) because of the "template" that the baby has received from his birth parent.

Again, Ingold has misinterpreted some of our claims for these data. We do not think that all changes that occur with development implicate learning, or that all bodily traits are determined by mechanisms of biological inheritance or that all mental traits are determined by learning. This is why we included the range of bodily traits, talents, preferences, and beliefs that we did. He is quite right that the acquisition of skills requires both mental and bodily mechanisms of growth, and that aspects of each of these are inherited from one's biological parents and learned by practice, imitation, and explicit tuition. What we discovered is that Vezo adults think about the acquisition of skills in these same terms. Individual North American adults differ among themselves in where they would place their bets with respect to any given trait; so do individual Vezo adults. Indeed, the distinct classes of causal mechanisms we uncovered in our Vezo informants' reasoning leave room for much idiosyncratic theorizing, as we document in the protocols we collected (and have posted on the web).

Finally, Ingold suggests that when Vezo adults state that an adopted child will have the bodily characteristics of the birth parents, they do not imply that these characteristics are fixed by inheritance rather than by nurture. Instead, what they are saying is that the child's bodily characteristics "are fixed by the *nurture* that precedes birth, rather than by the nurture that carries on after it" (p. 142). Maybe—although our informants' justifications and Astuti's ethnographic data do not seem to support such a view. But at last this is an empirical question. Ingold offers an alternative interpretation, which leads to empirical predictions, which can be tested. And *this* we gratefully accept.

METHODOLOGICAL ISSUES

Turning to Patricia Miller's commentary: we found little to disagree with in Miller's generous and interesting comments; thus our reply will be brief. We address her comments in the reverse order in which she made them, beginning with methodological points and then turning to the theoretical ones.

In her section titled *Methodological Limitations*, Miller produced a wish-list of data she would have liked to see, had we had more time. Of course, more research is *always* called for; any published paper or *Monograph* is really a progress report. But we were puzzled by her desire to see more children in the 6–13-year-age range, for most of the transitions we document occurred during the adolescent years. Nonetheless, we certainly agree that focused studies on the adolescents would be necessary to really understand what is changing, when exactly, and why. The "when exactly" question is actually the least interesting of the three.

We agree, resoundingly, with Miller's observation that we did not explore the possibility that Vezo children's tendency to naturalize the contrast between Karany and Vezo group identities identities may reflect their awareness of the socio-economic disparities that exist between Vezo and Karany. This might explain why children did not naturalize the contrast between Vezo and Masikoro, since these are equally poor, equally marginal folks. This is an alternative account to that which proposes that children's responses reflect their sensitivity to somatic differences that exist between Vezo and Karany (and are absent between Vezo and Masikoro). We too would like to see, and are intending to carry out, more studies to decide between these alternative accounts.

The other methodological points raised by Miller presuppose more substantive criticisms, and we welcome the opportunity to clarify our position. She points out, correctly, that the duck–hen scenario cannot be directly compared with the Vezo–Karany scenario. Of course, people differ from ducks and hens in many ways that make our human and animal adoption scenarios inevitably different. But our goal was not to directly compare Vezo children's responses to the duck–hen scenarios with those to the Vezo–Karany scenario, but rather to compare Vezo children's responses with those of other children tested in a variety of different cultural contexts. Our argument in the *Monograph* is based on the following observation: Vezo children as young as 6, like their North American, Brazilian, and Yukatek Mayan counterparts, answered the question about species determination just like Vezo, North American, Brazilian, and Yukatek Mayan adults. By contrast, it is not until middle adolescence that they answered questions about individual properties or group identity in similar adult fashion. Thus, we were not directly comparing the human adoption stories with the species adoption story, but we were investigating whether Vezo children's understanding of species kind resembled that of the 4–6-year-olds who have been studied elsewhere in the world. For this, we needed to do the same task that has been done elsewhere in the world.

159

We were perplexed by Miller's complaint that the duck–hen scenario only included a cross-species comparison. That was its point. We were simply asking whether Vezo children know that species kind is inherited from birth parents to establish whether this aspect of biological understanding can be an analogical basis for children's reasoning about human group identity in the Vezo–Karany scenario. We were not asking whether participants, children and adults alike, think that individual animal traits are determined by the same mechanisms that determine individual traits in humans. This is an interesting question, and Vezo adults' justifications suggest that the answer is no, since they claimed that animals, unlike humans, are unable to learn from explicit teaching, nor from imitation and other specifically human mechanisms of knowledge transmission. It would indeed be interesting to explore this issue systematically, but this was not the goal of our animal study.

CONCEPTUAL CONSTRUCTION HYPOTHESIS

We turn now to more theoretical points. Miller argues that while we support the Constrained Conceptual Construction hypothesis, our data are actually consistent with a weaker hypothesis: Unconstrained Learning. Her main argument is that our data do not bear on the processes through which preschool children construct their understanding of the phenomena we investigate because our youngest children are 6-years-old. This is undeniable, but Miller has misunderstood the Constrained Conceptual Construction hypothesis. We are happy to take the opportunity to clarify it, for we believe that our position is pretty much what she herself would advocate.

The Constrained Conceptual Construction hypothesis does not require that the constraints be innate. Accordingly, the evidence we provide shows that Vezo children have constructed the conceptual resources to naturalize the contrast between Vezo and Karany, not just in the face of contrasting adult beliefs, but in the face of contrasting adult beliefs that are articulated in conversation, praising, and teasing on a daily basis. We agree with Miller that there are many examples of resistance to learning. In the case under consideration, we suggest that some of the constraints may be innate, referring to the relevant literature on core knowledge, on causal reasoning, and on psychological essentialism. But we agree that this question is not addressed by the data we present here. By contrast, Miller merely alludes to children's several years of unspecified experience during which they could be constructing their essentialist beliefs. But if one believes that essentialist commitments are learned, one needs to offer, at least in principle, some suggestions about what input and what mechanisms yield the learning.

Miller's suggestion that "essentializing is simply a cognitive strategy used by a limited capacity mind to simplify a complex world" (p. 148) is not an alternative to the hypothesis that psychological essentialism is an innate domain general constraint—why *this* strategy when faced with a complex world? Where do the components of children's essentializing strategy come from? How does one account for the fact that even infants distinguish kind contrasts from mere property contrasts, and weigh causal information more centrally in the case of the former (c.f., Xu, Carey, and Quint, 2004, for discussion). It appears that the skeleton of children's strategy is in place by 12 months of age.

ON CROSS-CULTURAL RESEARCH

Finally, we obviously agree with Miller's endorsement of the importance of cross-cultural research. In making this point, she drew some of the same conclusions that anthropologists have drawn from the ethnographic data we have presented. For example, she suggests that the Vezo performative theory of identity challenges the Western mind–body split (p. 150). We note that such a conclusion (shared by many anthropologists) is challenged by our data (see also Astuti, 2001, which develops this point at length; see also Ingold's commentary and our above reply), and that this challenge is one of the significant outcomes of our interdisciplinary collaboration, which Miller also very generously endorses.

References

Astuti, R. (2001). Are we all natural dualists? A cognitive developmental approach. (The Malinowski Memorial Lecture 2000). *Journal of the Royal Anthropological Institute*, **7**, 429–447.
Xu, F., Carey, S., & Quint, N. (2004). The emergence of kind-based object individuation in infancy. *Cognitive Psychology*, **49**, 155–190.

CONTRIBUTORS

Rita Astuti (Ph.D., 1991, LSE) is Reader in Anthropology at the London School of Economics and Political Science. She has conducted extensive fieldwork among the Vezo of Madagascar, and her writings have focused on issues of gender, ethnic identity, and kinship. In her more recent work, she has combined anthropological and psychological methods to explore how Vezo children construct the adult understanding of the social world. Her next project will focus on Vezo children's acquisition of supernatural concepts.

Gregg E. A. Solomon (Ph.D., 1988, Harvard University) is Program Director for Research on Learning and Education in the Directorate for Education and Human Resources at the National Science Foundation. His research with children explores their understandings of folkbiology and their understandings of rational numbers. His research with adults investigates the nature and acquisition of expertise. He is also active in developing ties between the cognitive science and educational research communities.

Susan Carey (Ph.D., 1972, Harvard University) is Professor of Psychology at Harvard University. Her research concerns conceptual development across three different time scales: evolutionary, historical, and individual ontogenesis. She has carried out case studies of the acquisition of representations of natural number, of folkbiological concepts, and of representations of the physical and social worlds. She also works on language acquisition, especially on the relations between lexical and conceptual development.

Tim Ingold (Ph.D., 1976, University of Cambridge). Professor of Social Anthropology at the University of Aberdeen. Ingold has carried out ethnographic fieldwork among Saami and Finnish people in Lapland, and has written extensively on comparative questions of environment, technology and social organization in the circumpolar North, as well as on evolutionary theory in anthropology, biology and history, on the role of animals in human society, and on issues in human ecology. His current research interests are in the anthropology of technology and in aspects of environmental perception. His major publications include *Evolution and Social Life* (1986), *The Appropriation of Nature* (1986), *Tools, Language and Cognition in Human Evolution* (co-edited with Kathleen Gibson, 1993) and *Key Debates in Anthropology* (1996). His latest book, *The Perception of the Environment*, was published by Routledge in 2000.

Patricia H. Miller (Ph.D., 1970, University of Minnesota) is Professor of Psychology and Women's Studies and Director of Women's Studies at the University of Georgia. She is the author, co-author, or co-editor of 4 books: *Theories of Developmental Psychology, Cognitive Development, Conceptual Development: Piaget's Legacy,* and *Toward a Feminist Developmental Psychology.* She also is Associate Editor of *Child Development*.

STATEMENT OF EDITORIAL POLICY

The *Monographs* series is devoted to publishing developmental research that generates authoritative new findings and uses these to foster fresh, better integrated, or more coherent perspectives on major developmental issues, problems, and controversies. The significance of the work in extending developmental theory and contributing definitive empirical information in support of a major conceptual advance is the most critical editorial consideration. Along with advancing knowledge on specialized topics, the series aims to enhance cross-fertilization among developmental disciplines and developmental sub fields. Therefore, clarity of the links between the specific issues under study and questions relating to general developmental processes is important. These links, as well as the manuscript as a whole, must be as clear to the general reader as to the specialist. The selection of manuscripts for editorial consideration, and the shaping of manuscripts through reviews-and-revisions, are processes dedicated to actualizing these ideals as closely as possible.

Typically *Monographs* entail programmatic large-scale investigations; sets of programmatic interlocking studies; or—in some cases—smaller studies with highly definitive and theoretically significant empirical findings. Multi-authored sets of studies that center on the same underlying question can also be appropriate; a critical requirement here is that all studies address common issues, and that the contribution arising from the set as a whole be unique, substantial, and well integrated. The needs of integration preclude having individual chapters identified by individual authors. In general, irrespective of how it may be framed, any work that is judged to significantly extend developmental thinking will be taken under editorial consideration.

To be considered, submissions should meet the editorial goals of *Monographs* and should be no briefer than a minimum of 80 pages (including references and tables). There is an upper limit of 175–200 pages. In exceptional circumstances this upper limit may be modified. (Please submit four copies.) Because a *Monograph* is inevitable lengthy and usually substantively complex, it is particularly important that the text be well organized and written in clear, precise, and literate English. Note, however, that authors from non-English-speaking countries should not be put off by this stricture. In accordance with the general aims of SRCD, this series is actively interested in promoting international exchange of developmental research. Neither membership in the Society nor affiliation with the academic discipline of psychology are relevant in considering a *Monographs* submission.

The corresponding author for any manuscript must, in the submission letter, warrant that all coauthors are in agreement with the content of the manuscript. The corresponding author also is responsible for informing all coauthors, in a timely manner, of manuscript submission, editorial decisions, reviews received, and any revisions recommended. Before publication, the corresponding author also must warrant in the submission letter that the study has been conducted according to the ethical guidelines of the Society for Research in Child Development.

Potential authors who may be unsure whether the manuscript they are planning would make an appropriate submission are invited to draft an outline of what they propose, and send it to the Editor for assessment. This mechanism, as well as a more detailed description of all editorial policies, evaluation process, and format requirements can be found at the Editorial Office web site (http://astro.temple.edu/-overton/monosrcd.html) or by contacting the Editor, Wills F. Overton, Temple University-Psychology, 1701 North 13th St. – Rm 567, Philadelphia, PA 19122-6085 (e-mail: monosrcd@temple.edu) (telephone: 1-215-204-7360).

Monographs of the Society for Research in Child Development (ISSN 0037-976X), one of two publications of Society of Research in Child Development, is published three times a year by Blackwell Publishing, Inc., with offices at 350 Main Street, Malden, MA 02148, USA, and 9600 Garsington Road, Oxford OX4 2XG, UK. Call US (800) 835-6770 or (781) 388-8206, UK +44 (0) 1865 778315; fax US (781) 388-8232, UK +44 (0) 1865 471775; e-mail US subscrip@bos.blackwellpublishing.com, UK customerservices@oxon.blackwellpublishing.com. A subscription to *Monographs of the SRCD* comes with a subscription to *Child Development* (published bimonthly).

INFORMATION FOR SUBSCRIBERS   For new orders, renewals, sample copy requests, claims, change of address, and all other subscription correspondence, please contact the Journals Subscription Department at your nearest Blackwell office.

INSTITUTIONAL PREMIUM RATES* FOR MONOGRAPHS OF THE SRCD/CHILD DEVELOPMENT 2004   The Americas $420, Rest of World £298. Customers in Canada should add 7% GST to The Americas price or provide evidence of entitlement to exemption. Customers in the UK and EU should add VAT at 5% or provide a VAT registration number or evidence of entitlement to exemption.

*Includes print plus premium online access to the current and all available backfiles. Print and online-only rates are also available. For more information about Blackwell Publishing journals, including online access information, terms and conditions, and other pricing options, please visit www.blackwellpublishing.com or contact our customer service department, tel: (800) 835-6770 or (781) 388-8206 (US office); +44 (0)1865 778315 (UK office).

BACK ISSUES   Back issues are available from the publisher at the current single issue rate.

MICROFORM   The journal is available on microfilm. For microfilm service, address inquiries to ProQuest Information and Learning, 300 North Zeeb Road, Ann Arbor, MI 48106-1346, USA. Bell and Howell Serials Customer Service Department: (800) 521-0600 × 2873.

ADVERTISING   For information and rates, please visit the journal's website at www.blackwellpublishing.com/MONO email: blackwellads@aidcvt.com, or contact Faith Elliott, Blackwell Advertising Representative, 50 Winter Sport Lane, PO Box 80, Williston, VT 05495. Phone: 800-866-1684 or Fax: 802-864-7749.

MAILING   Journal is mailed Standard Rate. Mailing to rest of world by Deutsche Post Global Mail. Canadian mail is sent by Canadian publications mail agreement number 40573520. Postmaster: Send all address changes to Monographs of the Societey for Research in Child Development, Blackwell Publishing Inc., Journals Subscription Department, 350 Main St., Malden, MA 02148-5018.

Sign up to receive Blackwell *Synergy* free e-mail alerts with complete *Monographs of the SRCD* tables of contents and quick links to article abstracts from the most current issue.   Simply go to www.blackwell-synergy.com, select the journal from the list of journals, and click on "Sign-up" for FREE email table of contents alerts.

CURRENT

Constraints on Conceptual Development: A Case Study of the Acquisition of Folkbiological and Folksociological Knowledge in Madagascar—*Rita Astuti, Gregg E. A. Solomon, and Susan Carey* (SERIAL NO. 277, 2004)

Origins and Early Development of Human Body Knowledge—*Virginia Slaughter and Michelle Heron in Collaboration with Linda Jenkins, and Elizabeth Tilse* (SERIAL NO. 276, 2004)

Mother-Child Conversations about Gender: Understanding the Acquisition of Essentialist Beliefs—*Susan A. Gelman, Marrianne Taylor, and Simone Nguyen* (SERIAL NO. 275, 2004)

The Development of Executive Function in Early Childhood—*Philip David Zelazo, Ulrich Müller, Douglas Frye, and Stuart Marcovitch* (SERIAL NO. 274, 2003)

Personal Persistence, Identity Development, and Suicide: A Study of Native and Non-native North American Adolescents—*Michael J. Chandler, Christopher E. Lalonde, Bryan W. Sokol, and Darcy Hallett* (SERIAL NO. 273, 2003)

Personality and Development in Childhood: A Person-Centered Approach—*Daniel Hart, Robert Atkins, and Suzanne Fegley* (SERIAL NO. 272, 2003)

How Children and Adolescents Evaluate Gender and Racial Exclusion—*Melanie Killen, Jennie Lee-Kim, Heidi McGlothlin, and Charles Stangor* (SERIAL NO. 271, 2002)

Child Emotional Security and Interparental Conflict—*Patrick T. Davies, Gordon T. Harold, Marcie C. Goeke-Morey, and E. Mark Cummings* (SERIAL NO. 270, 2002)

The Developmental Course of Gender Differentiation: Conceptualizing, Measuring and Evaluating Constructs and Pathways—*Lynn S. Liben and Rebecca S. Bigler* (SERIAL NO. 269, 2002)

The Development of Mental Processing: Efficiency, Working Memory, and Thinking—*Andreas Demetriou, Constantinos Christou, George Spanoudis, and Maria Platsidou* (SERIAL NO. 268, 2002)

The Intentionality Model and Language Acquisition: Engagement, Effort, and the Essential Tension in Development—*Lois Bloom and Erin Tinker* (SERIAL NO. 267, 2001)

Children with Disabilities: A Longitudinal Study of Child Development and Parent Well-being—*Penny Hauser-Cram, Marji Erickson Warfield, Jack P. Shonkoff, and Marty Wyngaarden Krauss* (SERIAL NO. 266, 2001)

Rhythms of Dialogue in Infancy: Coordinated Timing in Development—*Joseph Jaffe, Beatrice Beebe, Stanley Feldstein, Cynthia L. Crown, and Michael D. Jasnow* (SERIAL NO. 265, 2001)

Early Television Viewing and Adolescent Behavior: The Recontact Study—*Daniel R. Anderson, Aletha C. Huston, Kelly Schmitt, Deborah Linebarger, and John C. Wright* (SERIAL NO. 264, 2001)

Parameters of Remembering and Forgetting in the Transition from Infancy to Early Childhood—*P. J. Bauer, J. A. Wenner, P. L. Dropik, and S. S. Wewerka* (SERIAL NO. 263, 2000)

Breaking the Language Barrier: An Emergentist Coalition Model for the Origins of Word Learning—*George J. Hollich, Kathy Hirsh-Pasek, Roberta Michinick Golinkoff* (SERIAL NO. 262, 2000)

Across the Great Divide: Bridging the Gap Between Understanding of Toddlers' and Other Children's Thinking—*Zhe Chen and Robert Siegler* (SERIAL NO. 261, 2000)

Making the Most of Summer School: A Meta-Analytic and Narrative Review—*Harris Cooper, Kelly Charlton, Jeff C. Valentine, and Laura Muhlenbruck* (SERIAL NO. 260, 2000)

DATE DUE